DEMOCRACY
THE THRESHOLD
OF FREEDOM

By

HAROLD F. GOSNELL, Ph.D.

RESEARCH CONSULTANT, WASHINGTON, D. C.;
LECTURER, AMERICAN UNIVERSITY; FORMERLY
ASSOCIATE PROFESSOR OF POLITICAL SCIENCE,
UNIVERSITY OF CHICAGO

2799112

GREENWOOD PRESS, PUBLISHERS
WESTPORT, CONNECTICUT

Library of Congress Cataloging in Publication Data

Gosnell, Harold Foote, 1896-
   Democracy, the threshold of freedom.

   Reprint of the ed. published by Ronald Press
Co., New York.
   Includes bibliographical references and index.
   1. Suffrage. 2. Representative government and
representation. I. Title.
[JF831.G6 1977]   324   77-1256
ISBN 0-8371-9509-8

Originally published in 1948 by The Ronald Press Company,
New York

Reprinted in 1977 by Greenwood Press, Inc.

Library of Congress Catalog Card Number 77-1256

ISBN 0-8371-9509-8

Printed in the United States of America

PREFACE

THIS BOOK has grown out of many years of teaching, research, and active participation in government. In his courses on politics, elections, comparative government, and introductory political science the author has been unable to find the materials on suffrage and representative government that he needed. The present book has been written to fill this gap.

The first part of the book is on suffrage, which is regarded as the right of an individual to have his choices taken into account in the resolution of important decisions on issues of state. Most of the discussions of suffrage hitherto written have been purely descriptive and historical. Here the sociological implications of various extensions are considered. An attempt is made to evaluate the effectiveness of the suffrage in changing the position of newly enfranchised groups, and an analysis is made, in turn, of the results of the extension of the vote to special groups.

The thesis is here maintained that only when a group in a democratic country possesses suffrage can it guard its political position. The exact difference which suffrage makes in the status of a group is difficult to determine, since the group must achieve a position of some power before it can win the right to vote. An effort will be made to show that the ballot may be used as a means for advancing group interests.

Another proposition developed here is that suffrage is a beginning, a goal, an opportunity, the use of which depends upon the individuals concerned. Such persons must learn how to employ this right in order to secure a fair share of the benefits conferred by the state.

The second part of the book is concerned with the nature of representation and the operation of representative government. After setting forth some theoretical considerations, the evolution of representative institutions is discussed. In view of the prevalence of the representative principle in various societies, it is assumed that there are many different origins of representative assemblies. Consideration is also given to the effects of different devices of representation.

Some of the problems of representation are considered. What should be the relation of the legislator to his constituents? What should the voter expect of his representative? How does the legislature itself respond to political pressures, particularly those exerted by political parties? How may the voters exercise control directly over legislation? What are the tools the voter has with which to perform the tasks of democracy?

Some consideration is given to the relationship of democracy to different value patterns. How well does democracy work in comparison with other forms of government? Though standards for measuring the role of governmental institutions and practices are admittedly rough, nevertheless there are some data that may be examined. A government stands or falls by the wars won or lost, the riots avoided or running wild, the services rendered or not rendered, the acceptance or rejection of it by the mass of citizens.

The success of this or that governmental device is harder to ascertain than the success of a whole system. Within a democracy, what forms bring the best results? Here we have the record of votes cast, of votes not cast, of money spent, of money not spent, of orderly procedure or confusion, of services rendered and of services not rendered. The materials are imperfect, but they show something and they have not heretofore been systematically analyzed. The present book attempts to start this long-time job.

A quarter of a century ago Lord Bryce published a monumental work entitled *Modern Democracies*. He was a seasoned observer, and time has substantiated many of his conclusions. He ruled out in advance, however, any attempt to use scientific methods. Government to him was an art which could not be reduced to formulae.

The present book does not cover as wide an area as that covered by Bryce, but it assumes that government, or some aspects of it, may be made scientific. This is an assumption which Bryce was unwilling to make. In the social sciences the testing of significant hypotheses by quantitative or experimental methods is the nearest approach to the scientific method of the physical sciences. The science of politics is in the rudimentary stages. Insight and sound judgment are still all that are available on many points. The present book endeavors to marshall the best evidence at hand to test a number of hypotheses.

The author is greatly indebted to some of his former students at the University of Chicago. Without their aid the gaps would be far greater than they are. He is under special obligation to Alfred DeGrazia, Sebastian DeGrazia, Morris Cohen, Harold L. Elsten, and Margaret J. Schmidt. Specific mention of these persons will be made in the appropriate chapters. His former colleagues Charles E. Merriam, Quincy Wright, and Harold D. Lasswell have made many helpful suggestions. In addition he is indebted to V. O. Key, William Flory, Kenneth Hechler, and Ernest Mossner for reading parts of the manuscript.

For anything that is said in the book the author assumes full responsibility.

The Social Science Research Committee of the University of Chicago has been very generous in its support of this study. Its patience at the many delays is appreciated.

Different publishers have kindly granted permission to reprint brief extracts from different books which they have published.

HAROLD F. GOSNELL

Bethesda, Maryland
   October 6, 1947

CONTENTS

DEMOCRACY⌐

THE THRESHOLD OF FREEDOM

Chapter 1

CONSENT AND CONFORMANCE

"MAKE the World Safe for Democracy!" was a splendid war cry in 1917-1918. Lord Bryce's *Modern Democracies,* published in 1921, was somewhat nostalgic for the democracies of the nineteenth century but it was still hopeful for the democracies of the twentieth century. And then in 1922 there began a series of attacks on the democratic symbols. In the twenties and thirties these attacks were successful in Italy, Poland, Germany, Spain, and other countries. In 1938, Czechoslovakia, the last democratic island in eastern Europe, was swallowed up in the onward march of the German Nazi dictatorship. After this, other European democracies were overrun—Holland, Belgium, Norway, and—could it be!—La France. England was on the verge.

But democracy as an ideal and as a governmental device for achieving human goals did not die. On the Continent it lived on in Switzerland and in Sweden. Against what seemed to be overwhelming odds, the British saved their tiny island from the Nazi hordes. But the ideals of democracy also lived on in the hearts of the French, the Belgians, the Dutch, the Danes, the Norwegians, and the Czechs. It was a way of life that brutal repression, bribes, and terrorism could not blot out.

What has been the secret of the vitality of democratic ideals? It is necessary to go back to some of the historic statements of democratic objectives and see how these statements have affected the behavior of the peoples concerned. The American Declaration of Independence· of 1776 is such a document. Let us take the first sentence:

> We hold these truths to be self-evident, that all men are created equal,
> that they are endowed by their Creator with certain unalienable Rights,
> that among these are Life, Liberty and the pursuit of Happiness.

Although these words are vague they have nevertheless been inspiring and their meaning has been expanded many times to cover new situations. Does the phrase "all men" include women? Jefferson was far in advance of his age regarding the position of women, but there is no question that if he were to be here today he would be amazed at the advances made by women, and he might want to change the word to "persons" or say "men and women." Does the phrase "all men" include Negroes? Here again we can say that Jefferson was far in advance of his contemporaries, but if he were to be alive today even he would be taken aback by the many changes in the status of the Negro. The next key phrase is "created equal." Note that the word is "created." A literal interpretation would be that at birth persons tended to be equal. Babies are all about equally helpless, and have about equal chances of surviving the perils of infancy. Equal in what? Certainly not in physical strength, nor in mental alertness. Not in worldly goods, since some babies are born in luxury, and have everything that money can buy. But the words might mean equal in opportunity. In spite of their lack of definiteness, these words were used to bring about adult man and woman suffrage and to fight the battle of Negro rights.

Let us go on with the second sentence:

> That to secure these rights, Governments are instituted among Men, deriving their just powers from the consent of the governed.

The phrase "just powers from the consent of the governed" means what? In any society which is orderly all are among the "governed." This leaves out no one. In Jefferson's time suffrage was far from universal. It was limited by property and by religious restrictions. But the words set forth universal suffrage as a goal.

The third sentence reads:

> That whenever any Form of Government becomes destructive of these ends, it is the Right of the People to alter or to abolish it, and to institute new Government, laying its foundation on such principles and organizing its powers in such form, as to them shall seem most likely to effect their Safety and Happiness.

The meaning of this sentence is not clear since there is no indication as to how the right to alter or abolish a government may be exercised. Did the Germans have the right to abolish their Nazi government? They had a hard time trying to exercise this right. It took the ruin of their cities and the defeat of their armies to free them from the

Nazi yoke. These words, on the other hand, describe an ideal. Government should serve the welfare of the people or it should be abolished in one way or another, even by revolution if necessary. Such ideals of resistance kept up the spirit of the peoples of the occupied countries.

Foreign observers of American civilization have been impressed with the tremendous influence that the ideals expressed in the Declaration have upon American everyday life, vague as these ideals may be. American optimism, enterprise, sense of fair play, faith in its destiny, and high moral ideals may in part be attributed to the democratic creed. There are plenty of evidences that many Americans fail to live up to the democratic ideals, but this situation does not mean that they repudiate them as goals toward which they should strive. When a given group within the American culture is not given equality before the law and equal economic opportunities, the American conscience is disturbed. The groups which are falling short of the democratic creed feel guilty about their behavior and try to make amends by elaborate justifications. The groups which are discriminated against use the democratic symbols in their protests.

The French Declaration of the Rights of Man made by the National Assembly of France in August, 1789, is more explicit on some points than the American Declaration of Independence. It starts out with male babies. "Men are born and continue equal in respect of their rights." There is no mention of girl babies, and it took the French until 1945 to give the vote to women in any elections.

The Declaration continues: "The end of political society is the preservation of the natural and imprescriptible rights of men. These rights are liberty, property, security, and resistance to oppression." Here are two new concepts, "property" and "security." Does this mean that democracy and private property are to be associated together? Could we have democratic communism? What is meant by "security"? Security against one's neighbors, one's government, foreign powers?

There are, of course, many differences as to the meaning of such concepts as "liberty" and "equality" in the democratic creed. To some, liberty means freedom of economic enterprise, freedom from governmental restraints, while to others it means freedom from want attained by various sorts of positive government action. To one school freedom means the freedom of the labor contract and to another freedom means the protection of labor organization, collective bargaining, and the right to strike against the encroachments of an anti-labor capitalism.

In spite of these differences there are certain minimum objectives of the democratic process on which there is general agreement in the so-called democracies. Democratic equality involves equal treatment before the law, equality of economic opportunity, political equality in terms of universal suffrage, and social equality in terms of a mobile fluid society that refuses to recognize castes, religious creeds, and rigid class lines.

What is this democratic process which seems to have challenged the human spirit wherever its true meanings are grasped and there is some hope of applying its principles? "Democracy" relates to human behavior in a co-operative society. It is a system for making decisions regarding the power relations in society, a method for securing political obedience with the minimum of sacrifice of the individual's freedom. Its decisions are formal decisions, arrived at by rules which are accepted in advance. It is one of the available forms by which a society may organize itself and make formal decisions.

One of the essentials of democratic government is the procedure by which the consent of the governed is obtained. Unanimous consent as a governmental procedure for making decisions has been tried and found wanting. If a government cannot act until all members have agreed to a given course of action, stagnation results. The attempt to win the consent of all usually ends in inaction since a single group or a single individual can hold up the entire process. Where the voting process is free, votes are rarely unanimous. Consent under a democracy means partial consent. The convention of the majority rule has proved to be a useful one in ending deadlocks. It has been employed by the electorate, the legislature, administrative boards, courts, and other legally established bodies charged with definite government functions.

Governments purporting to have a measure of democracy which have tried to get along without the use of the majority rule have come to grief. The requirement for unanimity led the Holy Roman Empire, the Spanish Cortes in Aragon, the Hungarian diet, and the

Polish legislature to political disaster. On the other hand, the British House of Commons, based in part on the dogma of majority rule, survived many political storms.

Consent is almost always partial, but conformance must in theory be as complete as possible. Modern society is so interdependent that if conformance to laws and rules were not general, chaos would result.

Democracy differs from other forms of government in that conformance is obtained with the greatest possible amount of individual freedom. Majority rule means that more than half of the active electorate is in favor of a regime or a proposition. The winning of a majority is by peaceful means, by persuasion, by electioneering, by promises, by trickery sometimes, but not by wholesale threats or acts of violence. The conformance of the minority to a regime or a law is obtained by the minimum application of pressure under a democracy.

Governmental pressures may be exercised on the mind or on the body. Those brought to bear upon the mind are educational, ideological, or sentimental. Pressures on the body may be economic or physical.

Under a democracy the minimum of compulsion is brought to bear on the mind by the government. The controls over education are loose. Parents are permitted to send their children to schools of their own choosing within the limits of their financial means or their influence upon the public school system. Teachers are permitted to seek the truth and present it in their own way, provided the truths which they discover are not too distasteful to the parents and the community. Even when majorities are intolerant of the truth, as shown in the Scopes case trial on the teaching of evolution, held at Dayton, Tennessee, there is a loud minority which continues to fight for the truth. In the schools children are taught to obey laws and accept majority decisions.

Ideological pressures in a democracy are exercised by those who have access to press and radio. This access to the mass media is possessed by those who have funds or a genius for publicity or organization. Minorities are told by public speakers, the press, the radio, motion pictures that the democratic way is to conform until the majority can be changed. Anyone is free to try to change that majority by using any media or channel of communication that he can command, provided his arguments do not call for the use of violence. In practice the mass media are more accessible to some than to others, but in theory they are open to all. Democracy is here the threshold of freedom. It is up to the individual to expand and develop his powers over the mass media.

Sentimental pressures in a democracy may be exercised by anyone who knows how, provided that the sentiments aroused are not destructive of public order. A democratic government has its flag, its songs, its patriotic holidays, but any peaceful organization may also have its symbols that are calculated to arouse loyalty and affection for that organization.

As to the pressures exerted on man's physical body, a democratic government tries to minimize the economic rewards for conformance and the economic punishments for non-conformance. A democratic government uses fines, but very cautiously, and in accordance with an elaborate court procedure which provides many safeguards for the individual. A democratic government will give pecuniary rewards for conformance, but its powers to do so are limited. The wealthy voters are free to advocate that such rewards be kept to a minimum. A democratic government hesitates to use a rationing system for the distribution of goods because a pricing system gives the individual so much more freedom. Only in a war or famine crisis will a democratic regime turn to rationing. As soon as the crisis passes there is a reversion to the pricing system.

A democratic government is also loath to exercise physical pressure on the individual. Imprisonment, bodily punishment, and the death penalty are only imposed after careful court procedures have been followed which give the accused the maximum possible opportunity to protect himself.

In contrast to the democratic system, the pressures on the mind and the body are usually very harsh under a dictatorship. They have to be, since the individual's consent is not freely sought. The individual is highly regimented, ostensibly for the good of the state.

Under a dictatorship the schools are carefully controlled by the state. Private schools are not permitted to arrange their own curricula. Parents are greatly restricted in their right to criticize the public school system. Scholars are not free to seek the truth where they can find it.

Ideological pressures in a dictatorship are largely exercised by the state, which maintains a monopoly over the meeting house, the printing press, the radio, and the motion picture house. Private individuals are denied free access to the mass media, and if they try to circulate ideas of their own which are distasteful to the ruling clique they are liable to severe bodily punishments administered in an arbitrary fashion.

A dictatorship also tries to monopolize sentimental appeals. It is jealous of private organizations with their own rituals and symbols. It suppresses ruthlessly any that appear to be dangerous rivals. This applies to rival parties, social organizations, youth organizations, and even to churches.

In the economic field, dictatorship uses rewards and punishments without the formality of a legislative vote. Judicial procedures are used far less frequently in the determination of property relationships, particularly those involving the state. The property of anyone may be confiscated arbitrarily and given to the state or another individual. Since a dictatorship is likely to be a garrison state or crisis state, rationing is the rule rather than the exception. The pricing system is subordinated, particularly in international trade. The sphere of private enterprise becomes increasingly circumscribed.

So far as physical pressures are concerned, there is no limitation in a dictatorship upon their use by the government. Citizens may be thrown into concentration camps or may be executed without trial. Freedom of movement is far more limited, and all live in constant terror that they may be punished for failing to conform to one or another of the regulations or to the whims of this or that government officer. Conformance may be high, but the initiative of the individual is reduced to a minimum.

The dictatorships challenged the democratic way of life in the late thirties and the early forties. Not all the United Nations are democratic and there are sharp differences as to the meaning of the term. Great Britain, the British self-governing dominions, and the United States, however, are striving to achieve democracy as defined here. This form of government is a goal, not a landmark. In all the so-called democracies it is possible to point to spheres where the individual is not given all the freedom that he might have if the government and the people's understanding of it were more perfect.

There are many ways in which the United States falls short of being a democracy. In theory the majority rule means a majority of the population, but the Americans fall far short of this. In the presidential election of 1940, which brought out the largest vote in the history of the country up to that time, only 50,000,000 out of a population of 133,000,000 took part. Consent in the United States is partial indeed. Of course, the electorate does not include those under twenty-one years of age, some 46,000,000, and the aliens, some 4,000,000, but it also fails to include the adult Negroes in the South, some 6,000,000. Granting that these exclusions are democratic, the fact remains that Franklin D. Roosevelt with a vote of 27,000,000 did not win a majority of the potential vote of some 70,000,000.

In the United States, consent of the electorate is not always obtained by persuasion. In certain parts of the country, violence or threats of violence, trickery, fraud, bribery, and deceit are used to win a majority.[1] Fortunately, this is not true in most jurisdictions, but is nevertheless a blot on the American record and leaves the rest of the country to be criticized for tolerating such abuses.

Americans have not always been willing to abide by the majority rule. The Civil War of 1861-1864 was in part a battle to secure the acceptance of the majority principle. The Southern states which seceded to form the Confederacy were not willing to accept the decision which the voters made in 1860. They were clearly in the minority. It was the majority that they feared. Certainly a peaceful solution could have been obtained for the problems facing the South, one which would have been far less costly in human lives and goods, but the Southerners abandoned their political ideals in order to conserve what they thought were their best social and economic interests.

The securing of conformance by democratic methods requires a great deal of tolerance. In America the majority pressures on mind and body have been very severe at times. The Tennessee law against

---

[1] V. O. Key, *Politics, Parties, and Pressure Groups*, New York, 1942, p. 677; H. F. Gosnell, *Machine Politics*, Chicago, 1937, pp. 42-43, 85-90.

the teaching of evolution is a classic case of the intolerance of an American majority with respect to freedom of scholarship and teaching.[2] Ideological pressures are also severe. It is true that the President can be criticized and denounced even in wartime, but in World War II, Father Coughlin's *Social Justice* was barred from the mails by the Postmaster General on charges of violating the espionage act of 1917 in attacking the national war effort along lines closely paralleling Axis propaganda, and his broadcasts were discontinued.[3]

Sentimental pressures in the United States are also harsh from time to time. The conscientious objector had a hard time in World Wars I and II.

American states which bar peaceful parties from the ballot are denying freedom of candidacy.[4] Election regulations which eliminate frivolous candidacies are justified, but serious parties should be allowed to present their candidates.

The securing of conformance by harsh pressures and by violence is also not unknown in the United States. The AAA payments were a pretty heavy pressure on some of the American farmers.

During the Hoover administration, when the veterans wished to present their claims, the President called out the regular army, and evicted them forcefully from Anacostia Park.[5]

Democracy is yet to be achieved in the United States, but this country has gone farther along the road than some other countries. Since the British aristocracy is still strong, it might be said that America is more democratic in some ways than is Great Britain. This could not be said of the British self-governing dominions, with the possible exception of South Africa where there are racial restrictions more severe than in the American Southern states.

In 1945 the battle begun in 1914 to make the world safe for democracy was won on the military front. As the tumult and shouting died in Europe and Asia, the real battle for democracy began once again.

---

[2] P. Hibben, *The Peerless Leader: William Jennings Bryan,* New York, 1929. Chapter 30 discusses the Scopes case.

[3] *The New York Times,* May 5, 1942.

[4] Hugh A. Bone, "Small Political Parties Casualties of War?" *National Municipal Review,* Vol. 32 (November, 1943), pp. 524-528.

[5] B. M. Rich, *The Presidents and Civil Disorder,* Washington, D. C., 1942.

Chapter 2

THE BATTLE FOR SUFFRAGE*

FORMALLY defined, suffrage is the right or act of voting on some measure or candidate for office. In a democratic state, suffrage is the right of an individual to have his choice taken into account in the resolution of important decisions on issues of state. There must be recurrent occasions on which this right may be exercised, or the right becomes meaningless, for in the absence of a statutory scheduled election, the actual use of the vote may be indefinitely postponed.

To be effective, the vote must also be more than merely advisory. An advisory vote is not binding; policy-determining officials may or may not follow the decision reached at the polls. Many of the presidential preference primary elections in the United States are purely advisory. No special provision is included in these state laws to make sure that the delegates to the national nominating convention vote for the presidential candidate who wins the preference vote in the primary. As a result, the preference votes are frequently valueless, since the delegates do not feel that they must be bound by them. The delegates to the 1940 Republican National Convention ignored completely the voters' preferences and selected as a candidate a man who had not been considered at all in the primaries. The State of Illinois has a provision for an advisory, or public policy, referendum.[1] An affirmative or negative vote on such a measure has no legal effect, and its moral or advisory influence has frequently been negligible. Under a democracy as defined here, the right to vote must mean more than the right to express advisory opinions. The results of the election must have binding legal effects upon the officials or citizens concerned.

---

* Alfred DeGrazia assisted in the organization of this chapter.

[1] The Public Policy Act passed by the Illinois legislature in 1901 provides for the submission of any question of public policy upon the receipt of a petition signed by 10 per cent of the voters of the state. The function of the advisory vote might well be performed by a public opinion poll, which would result in considerable savings because only a small sample would be necessary.

Votes under a democratic system may decide a particular course of action, or they may merely determine which of a number of rival candidates for policy-making positions will be given the chance to put into operation programs which have been formulated in vague and ambiguous terms. Closely related to this problem is the question as to whether a representative should be the follower or the leader of his constituents. Obviously, a vote which has a definite legal effect is quite different from one which amounts to a carte blanche to a certain person or group of persons. However, the number of detailed questions which can be submitted to the electorate is limited and therefore the voting process must function in the realm of general mandates.

Under the democratic form of government, the election must involve a real choice. If there are neither rival candidates nor any effective opportunity to register a negative choice upon a proposition, then the ritual of balloting is not an election in a meaningful sense. For instance, in Italy during the period from 1925 to 1938 the voters were given a hand-picked list of candidates. They might accept or reject the entire list, but they were not permitted to substitute a list of their own. During this time the Secretary-General of the Fascist party contended in a speech that even the negative choice was not a real choice: "If the 12 million 'yes' votes should at once be transformed into 24,000,000 'no' votes, Mussolini would still remain the head of the government. If 24 million 'noes' were to be dropped into the urns, it would mean that Italy had turned into a lunatic asylum. All the more reason, therefore, why the wise ones would remain at their post of command." [2] In Germany, after Hitler's coming to power in 1933, huge numbers of voters were persuaded, cajoled, or coerced into voting in the so-called "elections" where the ballots could only be marked "ja". The vote had no power in this situation, since power implies an independent exercise of the will. [3]

[2] Gaetano Salvemini, "Totalitarian 'Elections' in Italy Today," *Social Research*, Vol. 4 (February, 1937).
[3] "On November 12, 1933, the voters were asked to approve of an all-Nazi list of candidates to the Reichstag. In the seven months since the previous election, all organized opposition had been eliminated, and the one-party state was now being climaxed by the election of an all-Nazi Reichstag. There were no opposition candidates; it was impossible to write in names of other persons (this would void the ballot); the voters could not even vote against the list, but could only refrain from marking it, and turn it in blank. The results gave the Hitler regime a 95.1

In the Southern States of the United States, the one-party system is approximated in the final elections. In South Carolina, for instance, only Democratic candidates appear in such elections, but in primary elections there is still freedom of candidacy. The one-party system in the Solid South has deprived the voters of that section of any real choice in presidential elections, and their electoral votes are almost always discounted in advance.

Another essential condition of the electoral process is that the result be determined by peaceful methods rather than by resort to violence. Elections become mere formalities when violent coercion is used to influence the participation of the electorate, the way in which the ballots are cast, or the compilation of returns.

In the Southern States of the United States immediately following the Civil War the electoral process was not free because of the presence of Federal troops at the polling places and in the executive offices. The removal of the Federal troops did not, however, remedy the situation; their role in controlling the electoral result was taken by the opposition, which used the Ku-Klux Klan and other squads of armed men to intimidate the newly enfranchised Negroes.

In the totalitarian countries, violence is used in an open and brazen fashion to get out the voters and control their behavior at the polls. It was clearly indicated in Nazi Germany before an election that whoever did not vote revealed himself as an enemy of the régime. Non-voters were paraded through the streets in disgrace. Open coercion and outright falsification of the election returns were employed in order to raise the percentage of popular approval.

But even in some countries calling themselves democratic we can find cases of the use of force to control the electoral process. Armed gangs have been used to control the ballot boxes on election day. Even troops or the police have been employed to conduct elections.[4] Meetings of the opposition have been broken up, and on election day workers of the opposing faction were not protected against violence.[5]

---

per cent majority on foreign policy and a 92.1 per cent majority on the Reichstag election. Thus the 18,000,000 opposition votes of March, 1933, elections were eradicated." *The New York Times*, November 12, 1933.

[4] H. F. Gosnell, *Grass Roots Politics*, Washington, D. C., 1942, Chapter VIII; Hartnett T. Kane, *Louisiana Hayride*, New York, 1941; Carleton Beals, *The Story of Huey P. Long*, Philadelphia, 1935.

[5] Dayton David McKean, *The Boss: The Hague Machine in Action*, Boston, 1940, pp. 142-144.

Not only must the election itself be conducted without coercion, but the results must be accepted peacefully. If an election precipitates a social upheaval or a civil war, it can hardly be said that the democratic process has been accepted. A survey of the history of elections shows that the limits of toleration of changes which may be brought about by voting vary with different nations. In the United States, the voters of the Southern States resorted to civil war rather than accept the verdict of the election of 1860 regarding the nature of the Union and the status of slavery. The issue was a basic one, but in some countries the use of violence to nullify the decision of the electorate may occur over relatively minor issues. The Brazilians, in the election of March 1, 1930, elected Dr. Julio Prestes president by a majority of 426,865. No great property interests were at stake in the campaign, and there was no class issue. All that was involved was the fate of the rival groups of politicians. Yet the Liberals refused to accept the dictum of the voters, and started an armed uprising which resulted in the surrender of the government of the Conservatives to the revolutionaries. Dr. Getulio Vargas was formally installed as temporary president, and he proceeded to entrench his clique firmly in power.

In order to place the institution of suffrage more adequately in its whole social context, it is necessary to consider the theories that have been advanced to explain and defend the various suffrage requirements, the conditions which have been associated with extensions of the suffrage, and the changes which have taken place in the status of the groups that have been enfranchised.

Theories

The theories regarding suffrage have been partially explanatory and partially normative, discussing both the origin and nature of suffrage and the ends which it is supposed to serve. Broadly speaking, these theories may be classified as individualistic, collectivist, or dualistic.[6]

The individualistic interpretation of the suffrage regards the right to vote as an innate natural right or as a private property right.

---

[6] Karl Braunias, *Das Parlamentarische Wahlrecht,* Berlin, 1932, Vol. 2, Chapter 1. See also W. J. Shepard, "Suffrage," *Encyclopaedia of the Social Sciences,* Vol. 14, pp. 447-450.

While the theory of suffrage as a natural right may be traced back to the classical writers of Greece and Rome, it gained effective consideration during the revolutions of the seventeenth and eighteenth centuries. According to the natural rights philosophy, suffrage was an abstract right arising out of the social contract and the doctrine of popular sovereignty. Curiously enough, this doctrine did not at first imply universal suffrage. The theories of John Locke regarding government by consent meant rather the right of revolution, which was justified when the government failed to respect the natural rights of the individual. Logically, it would seem that universal suffrage would also follow, and the radicals of the American and French revolutions so contended. Otis and Paine in America, and Condorcet in France, held that every individual had the right to take part in the formulation of law and in its administration. The moderates, however, took the view that suffrage was a product of positive law and could be limited to those who showed special fitness to exercise it. Evidences of such fitness were to be found in the ownership of land and in the holding of orthodox religious beliefs.

The extreme form of the natural rights theory of suffrage which came into general vogue in the United States after the third decade of the nineteenth century held that suffrage should be universal, at first for men and later for women, that all votes should be equal in weight, that the representatives should be the servants of the voters and subject to their recall, and that the individual voter was free to do what he pleased with his vote, that he might cast it or refrain from casting it.[7] This view implies a voluntaristic or anarchistic conception of man's political behavior. It predicates that membership in society should not coerce its members. When logically extended, this argument contends that if a man so desires he may refuse to participate in the group action, and the group will have no right to demand participation. If a very large number of people do not participate, then the foundations of popular government are undermined. Taking the extreme, if the election process is completely boycotted, the government cannot be democratic.

Even at the time of the French National Assembly there was criticism of the far-reaching implications of the natural rights philosophy

---

[7] A. Esmein, *Éléments de droit constitutionnel français et comparé*, 7th ed. by H. Nezard, Paris, 1921, Vol. 1, p. 399.

of suffrage. If suffrage was a universal, innate natural right, then the insane, women, children, and foreigners should also be permitted to vote. The radical defenders of the theory replied that even the insane and children had the right to vote, but that this right was passive for the duration of their political incapacity. During the nineteenth century the theory was frequently appealed to by disfranchised groups such as women, racial minorities, and those who failed to fulfill property requirements.

Another individualistic conception of suffrage is that it is an individual positive right similar to a property right. This theory is a residue of the feudal regime, since it conceives of the vote in terms of status, usually connected with the possession of land. In England, Chief Justice Holt, in the case of Ashby vs. White (1703) held that the election of knights belonged to freeholders of the counties, and that it was an original right vested in and inseparable from the freehold.[8] The moderates of the American Revolution did not regard this view as incompatible with the dogmas of natural law and rights. It was held by the radicals, however, to be contrary to the democratic doctrine of equality, since a property qualification for voting implied that those without property were unfit to vote. The chief defenders of the property qualification were the conservatives who felt that government should be aristocratic rather than democratic. Such men as Benjamin Constant in France, Edmund Burke in England, and Chancellor Kent in the United States thought that the government should be in the hands of the wealthy and the wellborn. The ownership of property was regarded as a rough measure of social worth. This is a concept which goes hand in hand with the concept of interest. To give the right to vote to those who have special private property interests at stake in the outcome of the vote assumes that those interests reflect worth, individual and social. These theories have been behind the various property, taxpaying, and financial requirements for voting.

In contrast to the individualistic theories of suffrage are the collectivist theories which view the franchise as a function to be performed in the interest of the community. As the German jurist, Georg Meyer, put it, "The voting privilege emanates from the legal

---

[8] Great Britain, *Court of St. James,* a report of all the cases determined by Sir John Holt from 1688 to 1710, or Ashby *vs.* White, *et al.,* Mich. 2 Ann.

system of the state. . . . In any system of suffrage, the welfare of the state is the only standard to be considered. . . . The question as to what kind of suffrage laws should exist in a state, is not a question of principle, but of political expediency." [9]

When the collectivist view is carried to an extreme, it is hard to distinguish it from the totalitarian view. The individual voter is a part of the organic whole of the state, and his act is only permitted by grace of the collective body. Those in control of the government at a given time may regard themselves as the arbiters as to what is the good of the state, and in consequence they may reduce the voters to a position of impotence. The totalitarian view of suffrage found in modern dictatorships has swept away all guarantees of individual rights and liberties and deprived the vote of any real power. According to the Soviet jurists, there is no individual right to vote. Suffrage is regulated according to the principles of revolutionary expediency. Special individual rights are not necessary, since the proletariat is sovereign.[10] In Nazi Germany it was claimed that everything was for the people, but nothing was done by or through the people. Only the "Fuehrer," to whom were attributed supernatural powers, was qualified to express the real or "objective" will of the state. It follows that the voters exercised no choices of their own.

A third theory of suffrage combines the individualistic and collectivist views in a kind of dualism. The adherents of this view claim that the individual must be considered in relation to the whole, and that the collective body must be viewed with reference to a subordinate but independent individual. Suffrage is an individual right, not a right over against individuals, but over against the community as a whole. The voter casts his ballot in the name of the state, for the state; the suffrage is at the same time an individual right and a social function. It is both a privilege and a duty. This view denies the totalitarian position that the "community will" should determine how the vote should be cast.[11]

---

[9] *Das Parlamentarische Wahlrecht,* Berlin, 1901, p. 6.
[10] Eugen Engel, *Das heutige Russland,* 1923, p. 150.
[11] This is the position most commonly held by political scientists. See L. Duguit, *Droit constitutionnel,* Paris, 1923; J. W. Garner, *Political Science and Government,* New York, 1928; Braunias, *op. cit.;* D. G. Ritchie, *Natural Rights,* London, 1916.

Conditions Associated with Suffrage Changes

The question of suffrage has been examined historically by several writers,[12] but less attention has been paid to its sociological implications. An historical view shows that there has been a general trend to place suffrage upon a broader and broader basis. From time to time this trend has been interrupted, and there are instances where it has been reversed. Minority groups have lost advances, and the modern dictatorship movements have deprived the ritual of casting ballots of nearly all its meaning. The fact remains, however, that over a long period of time the right to vote has been extended from smaller groups to larger groups.

The changes that have taken place in the suffrage may also be viewed sociologically. What social, political, economic, and other conditions have been associated with the extensions and retractions that have been made at different times and in different places? What generalizations can be made regarding the conditions which produce these changes?

Suffrage provisions are now to be found largely in the laws and constitutions of states. This was not always so, and limitations may still be imposed extralegally. In classical Greek and Roman times, the right to vote was on a traditional basis. Certain families, by custom, were entitled to declare their choices at recurrent elections. Aristotle saw in the family the basis of the state organization, and it was as members of families that men voted. Voting was a ritual that was accepted as naturally as the other rituals. "Not all of the inhabitants of Athens voted; but all the citizens voted just as they all took part in the worship on the Acropolis." [13] In modern states, with their expanded electorates, it is not practical to leave suffrage to tradition. It must be carefully defined by positive law, and legal safeguards must be thrown around its exercise. The development

---

[12] Charles Seymour and D. P. Frary, *How the World Votes: The Story of Democratic Development in Elections,* Springfield, Massachusetts, 1918, 2 volumes; A. Esmein, *op. cit.,* pp. 284-456; C. F. Bishop, *History of Elections in the American Colonies,* Columbia University Studies in History, Economics, and Public Law, No. 8, New York, 1893; K. H. Porter, *A History of Suffrage in the United States,* Chicago, 1918; A. E. McKinley, *The Suffrage Franchise in the Thirteen English Colonies in America,* University of Pennsylvania Publications, History Series, No. 2, Philadelphia, 1905.

[13] Seymour and Frary, *op. cit.,* Vol. 1, p. 2.

of the constitutional and statutory provisions regarding suffrage is a matter which concerns us.

Since a small group holding political power naturally resists any extensions of the franchise that may weaken that power, the pressure against suffrage extension is always considerable. This resistance may be overcome only when conditions are ripe, and when proper methods are employed by the group which seeks to be included in the electorate. So great has been the resistance in certain countries that the extensions have been made only after widespread social upheavals.

What conditions, then, are favorable or unfavorable to suffrage extensions? For purposes of convenience, the following conditions may be listed as favorable to enlarging the electorate: (1) social mobility, (2) economic independence, (3) war, (4) democratic modes of thought, and (5) organized agitation. The absence of these conditions tends to retard or to reverse suffrage extension.

Social Mobility

Although the concept of social mobility is a general and ambiguous one, it is very suggestive in trying to understand suffrage changes. In demanding the right to vote, a group must have ideas of social equality. In discussing representative government, John Stuart Mill said that the people must be willing to receive it.[14] They must not only be willing to receive it, but must aggressively demand it. The demand for equality springs from a consciousness of inequality and a belief in the feasibility of eradicating that inequality. The lower strata in a caste system may accept without question their position, but as they become aware of differences and of the possibility of changing, then they may demand more equal treatment. The desire to minimize this inequality crystalizes into a demand which is put into the framework of a system of morality. Mobility invites and fosters comparisons of status, and the difference between the right to vote and the lack of the right is conspicuous.

Mobility may mean vertical mobility (the movement of persons up and down in social status) or it may mean horizontal mobility (the movement of a culture trait or a person spatially on the same social plane.) The two types of mobility are closely related. Thus

---

[14] *Considerations on Representative Government,* New York, E. P. Dutton & Company, Inc. (Everyman's Library), 1905, Ch. I.

the feudal order is characterized by a low degree of social mobility as well as physical, and a pioneer community by the opposite characteristics. Between these extremes the Industrial Revolution introduced the property-less and shifting workers and the "middle classes" aspiring for power and wealth.

The concept of mobility affords a convenient framework for studying the relationship between economic, social, and suffrage changes. Sorokin points out that "mobility favors an increase of individualism followed by a vague cosmopolitanism and collectivism." [15] These characteristics are favorable to an extended franchise. The increase in individualism can rather simply be connected with the individualistic theories of the suffrage, the *Naturrecht* schools of Locke and Rousseau, while the vague cosmopolitanism fosters a consensus among the individuals of a unity and wholeness in society, rather than a rural village vision of life.

Mobility is closely related to the existence of independent employment, rapid communication, general education, or any of the other changes presaging a liberalized franchise. All these other things either cause mobility, foster mobility, or are produced by mobility — or react with mobility in all three ways. Thus the status society precludes much movement of persons either physically or culturally. This immobility prevents an exposure to new stimulation, and consequently lack of movement serves in turn to preserve the social order. No demand for equality can flourish under such circumstances.

Independence of Employment

Closely related to the concept of mobility is the concept of economic independence. Generally speaking, the greater the economic independence, the greater the chances are for political independence. Another way of putting it would be that universal suffrage does not seem out of place in a society where the average individual has considerable economic independence, whereas in a society where there are well-defined castes it is hard to get recognition for political equality. In the battle for suffrage, the achievement of economic independence tends to bring about increased grants of political rights.

---

[15] P. Sorokin, *Social Mobility*, New York, 1927, p. 143.

Under the feudal regime, the position of the serf, like that of the slave, was fixed by the rigors of custom. Under these conditions universal suffrage was anomalous and absurd. Serfdom and slavery are states of life, each aspect of which is coherently and rationally tied up with the other.

In modern industrial society, the relationship between economic and political equality is harder to discern. How independent is the industrial worker who may lose his job at the whim of his executive? What is the exact difference between the so-called "wage slave" of the industrial economy and the serf of feudalism? There is no gainsaying the fact, however, that the growth of industries and the dissolution of immobile medieval life have brought to the masses greater economic freedom. The modern wage earner may not be so independent as the medieval artisan, since the use of his skill depends upon large-scale organization and equipment. The industrial wage earner, however, is not tied to the soil; he is free to quit work, an important freedom when it takes the form of the strike; and he has other freedoms within the limits of modern industrial organization. The industrial wage earner has relatively greater economic independence, and he is in position to demand greater political rights than his ancestor could claim of the feudal or caste systems.

Economic independence furnishes a leverage which has been effectively used to compel dominant groups to share exercise of political power. It has been used by male workers, by women of all occupations, and by minority groups to achieve and safeguard the right to vote.

War

The story of suffrage is far from being an account of easy and smooth development of expediencies to fit the particular situation or gradual accretions of political experience which showed how much better for the democratic state a wide suffrage was. Along with other political institutions, the electoral procedures have had abrupt peaks of change, brought on at a particular moment by great social upheavals.

Wars abruptly bring about changes that would otherwise require many years of continual agitation. It is within the power of victorious groups to impose their ideology upon the form of government of a vanquished state. If the war has been fought in the name of symbols of democratic practices, the victors will attempt to extend these practices.

Not all wars, however, bring great changes immediately. Prior to the American Revolution, the regulation of suffrage had been within the control of the colonies. In the new state constitutions, no changes in suffrage requirements of far-reaching importance occurred.[16] The Revolution, on the other hand, brought independence from the mother country, with its limited suffrage, and so paved the way for later changes.

The American Civil War, however, brought immediate and drastic changes. Emancipation of the slaves came partly from abolitionist agitation, but more directly from the desire to strike a paralyzing blow at the Confederacy. Only with the greatest caution and the weighing of countless political elements did Lincoln finally decide on the move. Nor was there any thought in mind of prompt extension of suffrage rights to Negroes. In the wake of the war, though, Northern Congressmen struck in vengeance to give their party the advantage of the Negro vote, rationalizing the move in terms of the symbols in the name of which the North fought. There is final evidence that, at least until the Civil War, there was no general inclination in the North to extend the franchise to Negroes.[17]

In Europe during the nineteenth century, revolutions brought mass voting in their train. When Italians were fighting for national unity — and attacked from the north and from the south of the peninsula — plebiscites were held immediately in the liberated provinces to determine the majority will for independence. A people who had for centuries not voted at all, now voted themselves a nation on the ruins of petty despotisms.

The World War of 1914-1918 was followed by far-reaching changes in suffrage requirements. In the defeated nations, a short political revolution introduced democratic machinery. In Austria the Social Democrats formed Soldiers' and Workers' Councils which supported a Provisional National Council, and the latter, in turn, formed the new Austrian government based on suffrage for all classes. The Revolution of 1918 in Germany was followed by con-

---

[16] Porter, *op. cit.*, p. 11.
[17] Porter, *op. cit.*, p. 126.

stitutions which wiped out sectional differences in suffrage requirements, and eliminated the aristocratic compromises of the Prussian
type of suffrage.[18]   The electoral franchise was broadened to include
all male and female German citizens who were twenty years of age
or over, and the popularly elected assembly became potentially the
most important organ of government.

In the victorious nations there were also suffrage changes after
1918. The three principal parties of Belgium — the Catholic Party,
the Liberal Party, and the Labor Party — had united to form a government of national defense during the World War. This Ministry
of the Sacred Union secured the adoption of a law in 1919 which did
away with the plural vote, lowered the age requirement for voters
from twenty-five years to twenty-one, reduced the residence requirement from one year to six months, and gave a limited number of
women the right to vote in national elections. These reforms were
placed in the Constitution by an amendment of 1921.[19]

All the constitutions of Central Europe adopted after the signing
of the Versailles Treaty incorporated the principle of equal universal
suffrage. No special age or property qualification was to be necessary, and, with the exception of Yugoslavia, women were allowed to
vote under the same conditions as men.[20]   In Russia, the Bolshevists
went to the opposite extreme from the prewar view of suffrage, and
in their constitutions, until 1936, denied the right to vote to all persons who lived by private property or by "exploitation." [21]   In other
words, to the Soviets, property was a subversive element in the state
and not a criterion of personal worthiness. Outside the Soviet
Union moderation prevailed in accordance with leftist parliamen-
tarian ideals.

Apparently, then, the war greatly stepped up the process of de-
mocratizing the electorate. Not only in the belligerent countries but
also in the neutral states was this the case. The cause of women
suffrage in England was aided by the part women played in winning
the war, and by the repercussions of the democratic symbols used in
attacking the Central Powers. The same democratic effusion has-

---

[18] Harold F. Gosnell, *Why Europe Votes*, p. 76.
[19] *Ibid.*, p. 99.
[20] A. Headlam-Morley, *The New Democratic Constitutions of Europe*, London,
1928.
[21] A. Strong, *The New Soviet Constitution*, New York, 1937.

tened the enactment of the nineteenth amendment in the United
States.

Extension of the basis of power seems to be a means of uniting
dissentient domestic groups for external combat. In Germany, before defeat came in 1918, the Kaiser tried to unite all elements for
a final stand. He made concessions to the Social Democrats and
promised electoral reforms.

While the immediate effect of World War I was liberalizing so
far as suffrage was concerned, the aftermath of the war produced
economic crises which were unfavorable to the continued use of the
vote as a means of establishing and maintaining power relationships.
Italy, Poland, the Balkan states, the Baltic states, Germany, and
Spain, in the face of economic hardships and political disunity, one
after the other abandoned the practice of conducting elections to decide their affairs.

While it is still too soon to judge the effects of World War II
upon suffrage, it is worth noting that since 1945 woman suffrage has
been given an impetus in France and Italy, and a movement to abolish poll-tax requirements and to lower age requirements gained some
headway in the Southern States of the United States.

Modes of Thought

The various theories of the nature of suffrage were scrutinized
and criticized above, but their influence upon the granting of suffrage
rights was not discussed. A discussion of the effects of theories
upon the behavior of men would not wisely be included here. At
best, we can point out here the groups of symbols which have furnished ammunition for those who have battled on the issue of suffrage, as also the numerous individual arguments which have been
made on the subject. Long debates resound with fulminations and
sonorous quibbles over unintelligible points and inexplicable questions.

Doctrines and slogans of natural rights have been common in
most discussions involving the extension of suffrage. The extensions of suffrage which followed the American Revolution were
based upon the idea that every man has a natural right to participate
in the government. Abolitionists later saw no reason why, if white
men had such natural rights, black men should not also have them.

While the rights of women were not emphasized in the American and French revolutions, the natural rights philosophy nevertheless provided a favorable environment for equal suffrage. On the eve of the French Revolution, Condorcet forcibly announced his belief in equal political and educational opportunities for men and women. The National Assembly, however, rejected a proposed Declaration of the Rights of Women in 1789.

Since the Reformation, Western society has been increasingly materialistic in its valuations. The material standards set up for judging worthiness have made the state subservient likewise to pecuniary values, and as a consequence suffrage has historically been associated with wealth. The slogan of the American Revolution, "No taxation without representation," seemed securely founded on obvious truths, but its extension killed its usefulness to the landed property holders because the same slogan was used by the industrial bourgeoisie who protested real-property qualifications.[22] Finally it was possible to see that everyone contributed directly or indirectly to the state, and therefore deserved representation.[23]

Like the doctrine of natural rights, which was contradicted by slavery and feminine disabilities, the representation argument expired because all could use it equally well. Today such statements are used without their old force. More potent are arguments on behalf of the might of the state which may expediently deny or affirm the right to vote by virtue of the use to which it will be put for the state.

A growing emphasis upon positive law has gone hand in hand with the increasing materialistic content of modern culture. The influence of general legal changes upon suffrage almost inevitably causes the recitation of factors already discussed. The legalist's demand for consistency may appear to the sociologist to be merely a codification of what already exists in the attitudes and customs of the people. But it cannot be denied that there is an obligation on the lawmakers to develop uniformity of treatment of all persons.[24]

---

[22] Porter, op. cit., p. 29.

[23] J. S. Mill, op. cit., p. 281, recognized the function of direct taxes in making the poorer classes fully conscious of their burden in the government. He advocates a tax-paying qualification but this tends still to include everyone except those receiving relief.

[24] Elizabeth C. Stanton, et al., The History of Woman Suffrage, New York, 1881-1922, Vol. 4, Ch. 24 and passim. G. J. Bayles, Woman and the Law, New

The most easily recognizable and therefore most commonly known aspect of a state's machinery is its body of laws, and the presence of a liberal suffrage provision in one state creates a presumption in favor of its enactment in another state. There is more than coincidence in the granting of suffrage to women in Colorado in 1893, Idaho in 1896, and Utah in 1896, all of them neighboring states to the initiator of such a law, Wyoming (1890).

The judiciary tends to regard the suffrage not as an isolated problem but as a detail of the whole legal picture. Whereas woman could not so easily obtain suffrage rights apart from her whole legal status, she could obtain those rights once her advance pushed forward along the whole legal front. The analogy that confronts one at this point is very persuasive. John Stuart Mill stated during the period of the legal recognition of sex equality:

> No one now holds that women should be in personal servitude . . . It is allowed to unmarried, and wants but little of being conceded to married women, to hold property, and have pecuniary and business interests, in the same manner as men. It is considered suitable and proper that women should think, and write, and be teachers. As soon as these things are admitted, the political disqualification has no principle to rest on. . . .
>
> . . . There is something more than ordinarily irrational in the fact that when a woman can give all the guarantees required from a male elector, independent circumstances, the position of a house-holder and head of a family, payment of taxes, or whatever may be the conditions imposed, the very principle and system of a representation based on property is set aside, and an exceptionally personal disqualification is created for the mere purpose of excluding her. . . .[25]

A year before Mill's work was published, the New York legislature had enacted a law which changed most markedly the legal status of the American woman in New York. She could now engage in civil contracts and in her own business. She could control her own property and could be legal guardian to her children. Other states and other nations proceeded along the same lines of development. Where the legal status of women was generally conserved as of old,

York, 1901, gives a survey of the legal status of women in the United States at the end of the nineteenth century.

[25] *Considerations on Representative Government,* New York, E. P. Dutton & Company, Inc. (Everyman's Library), 1905, pp. 290-292, with the permission of the publisher.

as in those countries of preponderantly Roman Catholic religion, the women waited longer to obtain the right to vote.

The differences between the problem of woman suffrage and Negro suffrage in the United States are made apparent by the ease with which electoral rights were won. In the United States, suffrage came to the Negro like a bolt from the blue sky, confusing both friend and foe as to its meaning. The law did not fit the social system. It was a façade concealing a hollow interior so far as any real freedom for Negroes was concerned. Yet it cannot be said that the laws of themselves were of no use. By all those who regarded law as a command to be obeyed, apart from its other qualities, the new situation was accepted with some grace. And the new laws made possible the enforcement of suffrage rights by the use of machinery otherwise unusable. The very inertia of laws made for their acceptance in a spirit of resignation.

As Hamlet has put it, "There is nothing either good or bad, but thinking makes it so." Suffrage changes are closely linked with language behavior. The form of these changes, alterations of the existing laws, is in itself a manifestation of the linguistic basis of our civilization.

Organized Agitation

Rightly or wrongly, groups lacking the right of suffrage have felt that this right would put into their possession a weapon which they could wield to their own advantage. They have felt that they might protect themselves better from hostile sections of the population or even from a majority of the population, that they might satisfy their desires to direct the policies of the state, and that they would be able to obtain their share of the goods of life — and of the material and emotional satisfactions that can result from political action. To what extent these beliefs are substantiated in reality is the problem with which the next chapters will deal. Here we are concerned with the types of organized action taken by groups, and with the political maneuvers they have executed in seeking suffrage rights for themselves. Organized agitation may be classified according to the means employed, militant agitation using coercion whether physical or economic, and non-militant agitation using largely the methods of propaganda.

There has sometimes been profound disagreement between the militant and the non-militant suffrage groups. This is not the place to evaluate the philosophy of non-violence against the philosophy of violence, or the effectiveness of propaganda techniques as opposed to economic pressures. We are concerned with the use of these various methods to gain the suffrage.

Militant means have occasionally played an important part in obtaining the vote for certain groups. Huge demonstrations, strikes, boycotts, and riots have occasionally intimidated legislatures and monarchs into granting concessions. Monster mass meetings and threats of revolt played their part in forcing the British Reform Bill of 1832 through the House of Lords. Economic pressure by the large industrialists was also important in forcing the landed aristocrats to share political power. In Belgium, Russia, and Sweden, the device of the general strike was used in order to force the ruling classes to share the suffrage with the working classes. In the United States there is the famous Dorr armed rebellion in Rhode Island which sought to bring about suffrage changes. While the rebellion itself was a failure as a coup d'état, it nevertheless had some influence in bringing about a broadening of the franchise. The woman suffrage movement also had its militant as well as its non-militant agitators. In England and in the United States the militants used such devices as the hunger strike, heckling, demonstrations, and the like.

All organized suffrage movements, whether militant or not, found it necessary to use peaceful means of agitation. These involved for the most part the use of means of communication, the development of persuasive arguments, and the breaking down of hostile traditional attitudes. The platform, the periodical press, the occasional circular or book, the drama, the house-to-house canvass, the legislative lobby, the administrative lobby, and the political lobby were among the devices employed by successful suffrage movements.

Chapter 3

THE POOR MAN GETS THE VOTE

Property qualifications were firmly entrenched everywhere one hundred and fifty years ago, but now they have virtually fallen into disuse. Except for a few vestiges in the United States, and a property qualification for natives in the Union of South Africa, universal suffrage is the rule. All the influences discussed in the preceding chapter have been operating to bring about this change, but of particular importance were the factors of mobility and economic independence. It may be stated as a general principle that the more mobile the population of a given country, the faster were the suffrage changes.

The population of the United States, at least until very recent times, has been one of the most mobile in the world, and it was here that property qualifications were first abolished. Though seven of the American colonies had real property qualifications and the other six allowed the substitution of personal property for real estate, in the early state constitutions only five states retained the real estate qualifications. The new states generally incorporated no property qualifications whatsoever in their constitutions. By 1830, fourteen of the twenty-four states had adult manhood suffrage. By 1850 there existed in the United States adult manhood suffrage, including all but Negroes and a few foreigners.[1]

One of the striking characteristics of the American pioneer community was the absence of restrictions on movement of persons in space and on changes in the social status of individuals. If we examine the social origins of the presidents, we find that 48.3 per cent were classified as "upstarts" by Sorokin, meaning that they arose from low social strata, as compared with 23.1 per cent of the presidents of France and Germany.[2] The relation of this fact to suffrage

---

[1] K. H. Porter, *History of Suffrage in the United States,* Chicago, 1918.
[2] Pitrim Sorokin, *op. cit.,* p. 143.

conditions will be discussed later, but at the moment we are interested in showing how the pioneer environment was conducive to universal suffrage.

The leadership of the United States in broadening suffrage came in large part as the result of the free movement towards the West. The fact that there was abundant free land in the western territories made the limitation of suffrage in terms of property possession relatively meaningless when these lands became states.[3] Furthermore, the older states found a rising tide of protest against restrictions at home, in the face of freedom and equality in the hinterland. The disenfranchised could protest either by moving West or by agitating at home.[4]

There must also be listed the factors of social leveling, individualistic dogmas, free land, rapid movement, and the desire to attract new people, especially those with capital. A man was a man, and the land was new and needed to be turned.

Pioneer conditions are by no means exclusively equalitarian with respect to suffrage. It is to be expected that a small group in a hostile country will cohere closely and react with enmity against strange cultural groups. The American pioneers restricted the right of Indians to vote, and later the Negroes were barred.

Though property distinctions in the United States were less rigid than in Europe, and though there was less call for violent suffrage agitation, there was, nevertheless, the so-called "Dorr's Rebellion" of 1842 in Rhode Island. Acute dissatisfaction had accumulated against the provision in the Rhode Island Constitution which required real estate or rent qualifications for voting. It was apparent that little would be done by the propertied groups to change the situation, and the dissatisfied lower income elements banded together to establish their own state government. They elected Thomas W. Dorr as governor, and he then attempted to lead his followers to capture the state, declining the bid of concessions by the incumbent government. Before violence broke out, Dorr's army melted away

---

[3] For some time there was a close relationship between the ostensible requirements for enfranchisement in England and the American colonies. But these real property barriers formed a small hurdle in America, whereas they were often insurmountable walls in Britain.

[4] Frederick J. Turner, "Contributions of the West to American Democracy," *Atlantic Monthly* (January, 1903), pp. 83-96.

and he was captured. But the warning was heeded, and a Constitutional Convention embodied the substance of the protestant views.

After the Dorr rebellion there was no more violent *agitation* for adult manhood suffrage in the United States. Violence was used in the Reconstruction period following the Civil War to force an unwilling white population to accept adult male suffrage regardless of race, but this violence was not employed by the group enfranchised. When the Northern troops were withdrawn, violence was used to *prevent* the application of the principles of universal suffrage.

The middle of the twentieth century finds the United States with virtually universal adult suffrage. In some of the American states there are vestigial remains of the old property qualifications, but these are not important in relation to the total size of the electorate. Six Southern states have a poll tax requirement according to which a small tax from one to two dollars must be paid, and the receipt produced if a person wishes to vote.[5] In South Carolina and Alabama, a literacy test is waived for persons who possess property worth three hundred dollars. Nine American states have clauses in their constitutions which declare that a pauper may not vote. Four states have a prohibition against the participation of publicly supported persons in the balloting process. It is significant that most of these provisions are not recent ones, and that no attempt of consequence has been made to enforce them. In 1932 there was an abortive effort in Maine, under the old pauper law, to deprive persons on relief of the right to vote, but it was confined to two towns and was severely criticized.[6] The democratic belief in equal suffrage was too strong to revive this remnant of property voting.

In the older countries of Europe where there were no pioneer communities property qualifications were harder to uproot. Extensive economic changes were taking place, however, new concepts of value were arising, and at the beginning of the nineteenth century the vested rights of the landholders in the suffrage were challenged by the increasing economic power of those whose wealth depended upon commerce and industry. The *nouveaux riches* might purchase

---

[5] Emory Forbush, "The Poll Tax," *Editorial Research Reports*, Vol. 11, No. 1 (July, 1941); Library of Congress, *Current Ideas in State Legislatures: 1944-1945*, Washington, D. C., 1947.

[6] *The Literary Digest*, Vol. 114 (September, 1932), p. 6.

land holdings and acquire the right to vote, or they might agitate for political rights which were independent of land ownership.

As compared with the United States, universal adult suffrage was a long time in coming in Great Britain; there it required a bitter struggle. There were demonstrations and a threatened financial crisis before Parliament would pass the famous Reform Act of 1832, which, while doubling the size of the British electorate, only increased the ratio of those qualified to vote from 2 per cent to 4 per cent of the total population. Even this small advance had to be wrung from the House of Lords by a threat from William IV to create enough new peers to swamp the House. Because of the strength of the aristocratic tradition, the limited resources of the country, and the draining off of the more adventuresome elements to the colonies and dominions, British society has been much more immobile than American.

After 1832, suffrage in England was still defined in terms of the annual rental value of property either owned or leased. In the forties the Chartist movement arose with its demands for manhood suffrage, equal distribution of seats, the secret ballot, annual elections, and the payment of members. These Chartists used the methods of the strike, the riot, the demonstration, and the petition. Equalitarian influences from America were apparent in the movement.

The agitation of the forties did not bear fruit for twenty years, and then the Reform Act of 1867 which enfranchised the urban working classes was the result of a political maneuver on the part of Disraeli, the Conservative leader, who shrewdly observed that the poor man's vote might not be such a menace to the propertied interests as some of his colleagues thought. With this in mind, he boasted that he "caught the Whigs in bathing and stole their clothes." This reform increased the electorate by half a million, thus doubling the proportion of the total population qualified to vote. But it was still a low ratio, some 8 per cent of the total.

The Representation of the People Act of 1884 granted to the inhabitants of the counties the same voting rights that had been given to the cities in 1867. The size of the electorate was again doubled, the new ratio being 16 per cent of the total population. The Liberals, led by Gladstone, were responsible for this measure, and they put into effect at the same time the Chartist reform calling for a better system of apportioning the seats. Suffrage, however, was still defined in terms of property.

It was not until the Reform Acts of 1918 and 1928 that the property barriers were dropped. The passage of these acts was hastened by the universal conscription and mobilization measures of World War I, the growing power of British trade unions, and the decline of the influence of the large landed estates on British politics. It took such a major crisis as World War I to accomplish in England what the frontier had brought about in the United States.

On the Continent of Europe manhood suffrage was both slower and faster in coming than in England. In France it was more rapid, since manhood suffrage was introduced there by the Revolution of 1848. French constitutional history is not characterized by the gradualism of the British. Universal suffrage was foreshadowed by the French Revolution of 1789. The high property qualifications brought back by the regimes of 1814 and 1830 were points of attack for the dissatisfied elements, particularly in the urban centers where labor was beginning to organize and where radical economic doctrines were beginning to take root. In Germany, on the other hand, manhood suffrage was slower in coming than in Great Britain. Though it was introduced for elections of the Reichstag in 1871, the German states, particularly Prussia, employed the most rigid property qualifications on the Continent right up to the Revolution of 1918.

Just about the time that France was introducing manhood suffrage, Prussia adopted (1849) the famous "three-classes electoral law." While all male citizens twenty-five years of age were eligible as voters, the elections were open, indirect, and the value of an individual citizen's vote varied roughly with the amount of taxes he paid. The voters of each district were entered upon a list with their respective taxes, then divided into three classes such that each class accounted for one third of the total taxes paid by all the voters. Each class was entitled to elect one third of the delegates, who on their part chose the representatives to the Prussian Landtag. In other words, the voters in the highest tax-paying brackets who constituted some 6 per cent of the total electorate chose one third of the delegates, whereas the voters in the lower tax-paying group who made up three fourths of the electorate chose the same number.

While the agitation against this system was continuous from the time of its adoption, the law was not changed until disaster fell upon the King of Prussia's armies (the King of Prussia was also the German Kaiser), the King abdicated, and the German Revolution of 1918 had taken place.

The history of suffrage in Belgium is of interest because of the methods of agitation used by the advocates of universal suffrage. The constitution of 1830 contained graduated property qualifications, and the modifications made in 1848 provided for flat-rate property qualifications, under which about 2 per cent of the population could vote. It was not until 1893 that the suffrage was put upon a broad basis. In that year the trade-unionists, growing in numbers and in power, brought pressure to bear upon the government by a general strike. A compromise law was passed which provided for manhood suffrage with plural votes up to a total of three votes for the payment of taxes, the ownership of real estate, graduation from an institution of higher learning, or admission into the practice of a number of professions. Since this system placed the lower income groups at a great disadvantage, it was attacked vigorously by the Belgian Labor Party, which advocated manhood suffrage, "pure and simple," i.e., one vote for each individual voter. The party again tried the general strike in 1913, but it was not able to achieve its objective. The movement for the abolition of the property qualifications in Belgium gained a great impetus during World War I. The Labor Party was asked to join the Sacred Union for the defense of the country, and after the war the electoral law of 1919 did away with the plural vote.

In the Scandinavian countries, the history of suffrage followed a course somewhat similar to that of Belgium. As these countries became industrialized, as strong labor movements developed, as general literacy rose, and as it became apparent that national defense required the mobilization of all adult males, the demand for manhood suffrage became more and more insistent. The democratic wave which immediately followed the defeat of the Central Powers in 1918 swept away all the remaining obstacles.

The sweeping victories for adult suffrage in the years following 1918 proved to be empty in some cases because of the decline of parliamentarism in the twenties and thirties. In Russia, where the swing away from the property qualification was most pronounced — those with property, particularly industrial capitalists and the middlemen — were actually disfranchised; the one-party system virtually deprived the voters of any choice in political elections. Italian Fascism, the German Nazi regime, the Polish dictatorship, and other absolutist regimes made a mockery of universal suffrage. There is no question that the lower income groups were disillusioned with their experience with the vote. In Italy, Poland, Germany, and other countries of Europe, many voters in the lower income groups turned in despair to the new despotism. Instead of ushering in the millennium, universal suffrage sometimes brought fascism. But the dictatorial regimes established in Europe retained the shell of universal suffrage for propaganda purposes. In order to claim a full-throated "Ja", Hitler made no changes in the suffrage. It is unfortunate that the advocates of adult suffrage did not take a more realistic view of the device. If they had emphasized the need for organization, for education, and for leadership in the use of the ballot, the masses might not have been so disappointed in early attempts to achieve democratic equality.

The Poor Man Goes to the Polls

In the evaluation of the effectiveness of new franchise, the participation of the enfranchised groups is of importance. One argument which is always presented prior to the extension of the suffrage is that the groups to be included in the electorate do not desire the vote and will not exercise the right if it is given to them. This was the plea made by conservatives in the United States, Great Britain, Belgium, and Prussia, prior to the adoption of important suffrage reforms. What do the available records show about the electoral participation of the lower income groups?

Do the newly enfranchised lower income groups take advantage of the suffrage? It has been estimated that at the first election held under the American Constitution only 3 per cent of the population voted. This low ratio was due to the fact that one-half of the adult male citizens were disfranchised by the various property qualifications.[7] A half century later, when the United States was virtually

---

[7] E. M. Sait, *American Parties and Elections*, New York, 1939.

on an adult manhood suffrage basis except for the Negroes, the ratio had increased fivefold, since 15 per cent of the total population voted. Two American scholars estimated that in 1860 some 84 per cent of the eligible vote in the United States was cast at the presidential election which resulted in placing Abraham Lincoln in the White House.[8] This record was about as high as that achieved in England and other countries which had the limited suffrage. From this we may conclude that in the United States a large proportion of the lower income groups participated in elections. Later figures which give a breakdown by income show that there was a tendency for the lower income groups to neglect voting more than the higher income groups did, but the differences were not great and they were closely related to the issues of the day and the character of the political organizations.

The repeal of the poll tax provisions in three Southern states, Louisiana, Florida, and Georgia brought a marked increase in the size of the vote cast in the primary elections of those states. In Louisiana the poll tax requirement was abolished in 1934, and in the primaries that followed the vote was increased by more than one and a half times.[9] An equal or even greater increase in the size of the primary vote was brought about in Florida and Georgia by the repeal of the poll tax provisions.[10]

In Great Britain there were gradual extensions of the suffrage, as we have seen, in the nineteenth century. The most far-reaching extensions were those made in 1918 and 1928; these removed property and sex qualifications. In *Why Europe Votes,* the present writer made an analysis of the effect of these suffrage changes upon participation in voting.[11] The lowering of the suffrage requirements reduced the percentage of the total vote cast. From this it may be concluded that the lower income groups in Great Britain have not gone to the polls in such large numbers as have the upper income groups. The coming of woman suffrage at the same time as the abolition of the property qualifications, however, complicated the situation. There was undoubtedly considerable non-voting among

[8] Arthur M. Schlesinger and E. M. Eriksson, "The Vanishing Voter," *The New Republic,* Vol. 40 (October, 1924), pp. 162-167.
[9] H. F. Gosnell, *Grass Roots Politics,* Washington, D.C., 1942, p. 158.
[10] Emory Forbush, *op. cit.,* and *The New York Times,* June 30, 1946.
[11] Chapter 1.

women in the middle and upper income groups. Though there was
a difference of 9 per cent between the highest poll before 1918 and
the highest poll since, the peak of participation in the twenties
reached the level of participation in the nineties. British experience
then is substantially the same as American. The lower income
groups have evidenced some indifference, but have still come to the
polls in considerable numbers.

From the evidence available, it appears that participation in
elections increases with income level. The lower the general participation, the greater this class difference is. This difference in participation is always more marked in municipal elections than in
parliamentary.[12] A division by Tingsten of the voters in Basel,
Switzerland, in 1911, into three social classes based on occupation
shows that 77.5 per cent of electors in the first class participated,
71.1 per cent of the second class, and 66.8 per cent of the third class.
The same general results were found in the electoral statistics of
Zurich, Stockholm, Copenhagen, Saxony, and the Swedish second
chamber.[13] In America these results are corroborated by studies
made in the town of Delaware, Ohio, and in Pennsylvania.[14] Similar
conclusions have also been drawn for the American urban areas of
Greencastle, Indiana; Lansing, Michigan; San José, California; and
Chicago, Illinois.[15] Whatever the reasons may be, low economic
status is associated with low interest in voting.

One of the factors involved in the relatively low poll of the lower
income groups is the degree of organization. In general, the un-

---

[12] H. Tingsten, *Political Behavior*, London, 1937, p. 173.

[13] *Ibid.*, Chapter III, *passim*.

[14] Ben A. Arneson, "Non-voting in a Typical Ohio Community," *American Political Science Review*, Vol. 19 (1925), pp. 816-826; G. F. Dunkelberger and E. K. Rumberger, "Who Are the Voters?" *Journal of Educational Sociology*, Vol. 5 (November, 1931), pp. 159-161.

[15] In Greencastle, classified by dwelling as "Very Good," "Good," "Fair," and "Poor," the non-voters as percentages of each group numbered 9.2, 12.9, 14.9, and 20.0. The numbers used were small, being 216, 1132, 988, and 405.

In Lansing it was found that propertied and stable citizens were most interested in voting. Wayne Dennis, "Traits Associated with Registration and Voting," *Journal of Abnormal and Social Psychology*, Vol. 27, No. 3 (October, 1932), p. 270.

Re Chicago, see C. E. Merriam and H. F. Gosnell, *Non-Voting*, Chicago, University of Chicago Press, 1924. The authors say: "The better the quarters that a citizen lives in, the more apt he is to vote in presidential elections." See also H. F. Gosnell, *Machine Politics*, Chapter 5.

On Erie County, Ohio, see Paul Lazarsfeld, B. Berelson, and H. Gaudet, *The People's Choice*, New York, 1944, p. 43.

skilled workers have not been so well organized as the upper income groups. The skilled workers who belong to the trade unions are better voters. Take, for instance, the case of Viennese voters in the pre-Dollfuss period when there was an intense interest in politics among the working classes. Crucial issues were clearly drawn between labor and the interests of others, and the workers' parties got out the vote. The Viennese labor organizations were then among the most powerful in the world. Witness their bitter fight for their existence against tremendous odds. In the United States, a good illustration is to be found in the state of Pennsylvania, where, prior to the New Deal, indifference was widespread. In the late twenties the industrial workers of the state were largely unorganized. The New Deal brought a great increase in labor organization membership and at the same time in the popular vote.[16]

Party Affiliations of the New Voters

What were the effects upon party alignments of the extension of the franchise to the poor man? Was it to mean the rise of parties demanding a more equitable distribution of national income? Would the lower income groups be capable of producing leaders who would make their desires articulate?

In the United States the extension of the ballot to the lower income groups was not followed immediately by the rise of parties which were clearly divided on economic issues. As a matter of fact, it might be said that it took a hundred years to develop a major party program which was even roughly aimed at benefiting those who receive smaller incomes. Observers have stressed the classless character of the American party system and the extent to which party divisions cut across economic lines.[17] With the coming of the New Deal, however, it may be said that the voters of the different economic levels were presented with sharper alternatives.

The suffrage extensions of the early nineteenth century brought some vague gropings toward economic issues. The issue of the United States Bank raised by the Jacksonian Democrats tended to array the commercial and trading interests on one side, small shopkeepers and the agrarian interests on the other. The issue was not

[16] H. F. Gosnell, *Grass Roots Politics*, Washington, D.C., 1942, Chapter III.
[17] A. N. Holcombe, *Political Parties of Today*, New York, 1924.

clear cut, however, nor was it linked with any general program of economic betterment of the lower income groups. That a large proportion of the newly enfranchised voters were for General Jackson there can be little question.

Somewhat closer to an economic alignment were the party divisions of the Civil War period. The questions of free labor versus slave labor, and of homesteads versus large plantations, placed the small farmers in opposition to the big landed proprietors. As yet, though, the industrial workers had no political champions. Socialism, which had made its beginnings in Europe, did not take much of any root in the United States.

The thirty-year period following the Civil War did not furnish any party alignment which could be related to economic levels. There were minor party inflationist movements, but they made comparatively little headway. It was not until 1896 that economic issues between the major parties began to emerge again. William J. Bryan's stand on the income tax, as also his arguments against the gold standard, were aimed to attract the lower income group. That he received the votes of many in this group cannot be denied, but the Republicans managed to confuse the issue by appeals to the American traditions of personal achievement and business prosperity.

In 1912 both Theodore Roosevelt and Woodrow Wilson were edging their parties toward programs which would appeal to the lower income groups. Wilson's "New Freedom" was vague at first, but it took more definite form as his administration progressed. Direct appeals were made to organized labor, to the small businessman, to persons who would benefit by lower tariffs, and to debtor farmers.

Comparatively little direct evidence is available on the voting behavior of the different income groups in the United States prior to recent times. Where poor voters were concentrated in certain election areas, their group behavior could be reported on. In a few isolated places such as New York, Chicago, and Detroit, it was shown that the Democratic party was stronger in the twenties in the poorer working class districts than the Republican party. The picture was complicated by such influences as race, employer pressure, religion, and local leadership.

With the coming of the New Deal, economic cleavages were sharper, and the evidence regarding voting behavior was far more complete. Voters in the lowest income group showed a marked tendency to support President Franklin D. Roosevelt. The New Deal social security program, work relief program, and tax plans were attractive to the lower income groups. Figures of the Gallup public opinion polls, as elaborately analyzed by Wesley C. Clark, show that the Franklin D. Roosevelt administrations brought about a steadily increasing political cleavage between the upper and lower income groups until about 1940 when defense matters relegated some of the New Deal issues to the background and the relationship tended to level off.[18]

In England the changes in the composition of the political parties following each reform act passed in the nineteenth century were gradual, partly because the suffrage changes were gradual. The Reform Act of 1832 brought an end to Tory domination and inaugurated a period of Liberal party control. The Conservatives learned, however, how to win the support of a considerable number of the new voters, so the balance between the two major parties was restored. The Acts of 1867 and 1884 did not at first appear to change the party situation, but a closer examination shows that in the last third of the nineteenth century the Liberal party was leaning more and more upon the coal miners, the iron and steel workers, the textile workers and other trade unionists, the small farmers, the merchants who prospered under a free-trade situation, and the non-Church of England elements, whereas the Conservative party relied more and more upon the great landed estates, the propertied interests in the cities, the Empire traders, and the staunch supporters of the Church of England.[19] After the election of 1906, the Liberal party found it increasingly difficult to hold together the elements on which it had been based in the nineteenth century.

The Representation of the People Act of 1918 was followed by far-reaching changes in the composition of British political parties. Gone was the position of the Liberals as one of the major parties. In their place, as his Majesty's Opposition when the Conservative

---

[18] *Economic Aspects of a President's Popularity*, Philadelphia, 1943.
[19] E. Krehbiel, "Geographic Influences in British Elections," *The Geographic Review*, Vol. 2 (December, 1916), pp. 419-432.

party was in power, was the Labor party which took until 1945 to achieve a majority of its own. The Labor party drew its strength from the mining and industrial areas where the Liberal party was once strong, and it took time to attract the agricultural and the white collar workers. It was primarily a trade-union party and found it slow work to broaden its base. During this period the Liberal party declined rapidly, and as the middle of the century approached it was a mere shell of its former self. The Conservative party became the party of the upper and middle income groups. Because of its prestige, it was also able to attract many of the lower income elements as well.

Belgium experienced similar strengthening of the Labor party elements upon the elimination of plural voting in 1919. The political complexion of the Belgian Chamber of Representatives before and after the electoral reform of 1919 is shown in the following table [20]:

	1914	1919	1921
Catholics	99	73	80
Liberals	45	34	33
(Socialists)	40	70	68
Others	2	9	5

As in England, the Liberal party declined in strength with an extension of the suffrage, the extreme parties holding control of the state.

One of the dangers of the extended suffrage under given socio-economic conditions is the possibility of irreconcilable political parties which may be more inclined to depart from conciliatory "liberal" parliamentarism. The broadening of the franchise tends to produce parties based upon income differences and class issues. Dissimilarities in the political views of the high and low income groups account for this. Even in a rudimentary democracy such as that of Japan, the enactment of the Manhood Suffrage Law in 1926 signaled the birth of several proletarian parties, the Shakai Menshu-to (Fabian Socialist), the Rodo Nomin-to (Farmer-Labor Party), and others.[21]

---

[20] Thomas H. Reed, *Government and Politics of Belgium*, New York, 1924, p. 55.
[21] *Japan Year Book*, 1929, p. 84.

A most striking political change in representation followed the abolition of the three-class system of voting in Prussia after World War I. As might be expected from the previous cases, the greatest decline in representation occurred in the ranks of the Conservative party, which dropped from 46 per cent to 13 per cent of the total popular vote, while the greatest increase fell to the party at the opposite extreme, the Social Democratic party which increased its strength from 2 per cent to 42 per cent.

PERCENTAGE OF DISTRIBUTION OF POPULAR VOTES FOR PRUSSIAN POLITICAL PARTIES IN THE LANDTAG, 1913 AND 1919 [22]

Party	1913	1919
Conservatives	45.6	12.5
National Liberal	16.5	5.2
Democrats	9.0	16.2
Center	23.2	21.9
Social Democrats	2.3	42.1

The abolition of property qualifications has brought new political parties on the scene. Socialist, Labor, and Communist parties owe their origins to universal suffrage, and the same thing could be said of the parties of the small farmers such as the Swiss Peasants party, the Italian Popular party, and the Canadian Progressive party. The parties are no longer exclusive clubs for the rich and the wellborn. Though only a few of the new political parties based upon the lower income groups have been successful in winning majorities, all have made their influence felt upon the body politic. The programs of the mass parties are gradually being translated into legislation. Labor laws, social security measures, health and welfare legislation, and the measures regulating business have their origins partly rooted in devices for achieving democratic equality.

The Poor Man Runs for Office

What effect does the extension of suffrage to lower income groups have upon the composition of the ruling classes? Are the poor able to gain places in the seats of power for persons of their own class?

---

[22] H. Finer, *Theory and Practice of Modern Government*, New York, 1932, Vol. 1, p. 409.

In the United States, the extension of the suffrage to the lower income groups did not bring class parties, but it tended to abolish class distinctions as part of the unwritten qualifications for public office. The presidents of the United States prior to Andrew Jackson were of upper income group origin, and had enjoyed educational opportunities. Jackson, on the other hand, came from very poor parents, his formal education was extremely scanty, and his grammar and spelling were atrocious. Of humble origin and limited educational background also were Presidents Lincoln and Johnson.

The influence of universal suffrage upon the characteristics of officeholders may likewise be examined by studying changes in the City of New York. The New York State electorate in 1790 was limited to the large landholders, small freeholders, leaseholders, freemen, and electoral freeholders. Lawyers were also part of the dominant cultural and political group. Participation in New York City politics by the cultural leaders was the accepted pattern of conduct. Since only the esteemed classes could vote, the general level of prestige of politicians was high.

With the coming of universal manhood suffrage in New York, there began a large decline in the prestige of political office. The greater participation of the lower class elements in politics dismayed the old plutocrats who held office. The parvenus, however, were not so disdainful of connotations of commonalty, and their numbers increased among the elected officers of the state. The number of self-made politicians from the lower classes also multiplied.

The old plutocracy had, therefore, to reconcile their desire to dictate the laws with their disinclination to hold elective offices. Power without office meant machinations behind the scenes. In order to exercise power, the rich resorted to pressure-group activity, campaign contributions, and propaganda controls. With a partial stoppage of political energies and the decline in the number of offices which were acceptable as of prestige value, the old plutocracy shifted its energies to heightened social activity and to the cultivation of an elaborate "display" society. Ostentation rather than offices was the road to status.

Among the consequences of the broader franchise in the United States may be listed the evolution and perfection of party organization and electoral techniques — for New York's Tammany would never have developed from the 1790 electorate — the development of organized groups representing business, labor, and agricultural interests, the adoption of social and labor legislation covering such questions as the right to organize and the regulation of working conditions, the extension of universal free education, the withdrawal of many older aristocrats from political life, and the establishment of exclusive social cliques and clubs.[23]

Whereas a century and a half ago, prominent merchants and social "lions" led in the field of municipal politics, today the actual control of urban party organization is often in the hands of political bosses, few of whom sprang from socially recognized families. None of the parents of a selected group of prominent bosses were found on the social register of their particular city.[24]

The study of the relationship of suffrage changes in England to representation and legislation is most enlightening. An analysis of certain characteristics of the personnel of English cabinets from 1801 to 1946 shows the effects on representation to be gradual.[25] The sons of nobility constituted 78 per cent of the cabinet members during the period 1801 to 1831, 64 per cent in the period 1832 to 1866, 60 per cent from 1867 to 1884, and 58 per cent in the period 1885 to 1905.

The changes in English cabinet personnel from 1801 to 1946 may be summarized as follows:

(In Percentage Form)

	1801 1831	1832 1866	1867 1884	1885 1905	1906 1916	1917 1928	1929 1938	1946
Sons of the nobility...	78	64	60	58	49	29	23	10
Educated at one of the universities	78	78	76	83	80	59	69	50
Educated in a public school	62	55	59	66	50	52	52	10
In business or a profession	11	25	31	25	39	48	55	95

[23] Gabriel Almond, "Plutocracy and Politics in New York," University of Chicago, Ph.D. Thesis, 1938.
[24] H. Zink, City Bosses in the United States, Durham, 1930.
[25] Harold J. Laski, "The Personnel of the English Cabinet, 1801-1924," American Political Science Review, Vol. 22 (1928), pp. 10-24. Also additions by the author of this work.

The percentage of those cabinet officers having a university education, a mark of wealth, changed little after any of the suffrage changes prior to 1918. The same is true of the ratio of those educated at the so-called public schools, which are attended largely by the well-to-do. The percentage of those having an occupation outside of politics rose steadily except during the period from 1885 to 1905, during which the Conservatives held power most of the time. The changes were not great, since the struggle in England during most of the nineteenth century was not between capital and labor but between the large landed proprietors on the one hand and the industrialists and merchants on the other.[26]

The greatest change in the size of the British electorate occurred with the passage of the 1918 act, and this changed was accompanied by important changes in the characteristics of British cabinets. Whereas in the period 1906 to 1916, 49 per cent of the cabinet members were sons of the nobility, in the period 1929 to 1938 only 23 per cent of the cabinet members had such origins. Whereas in the first period, 80 per cent of the cabinet members were educated at a university, this was true of only 69 per cent in the second period. The percentages of those attending public schools were respectively 50 per cent and 52 per cent. There was an increase in the proportion of cabinet members who were in a business or a profession from 39 per cent to 55 per cent. Even more striking was the contrast after the Labor Party came to power in 1945.

It would thus appear that the lower classes were realizing their strength, and that the grant of suffrage caused fundamental shifts. Perhaps what is reflected is no shift in representation, but only a decline of one style of political personality in the face of active competition from new leader types sprung from new economic groups. That is, whereas in the early period, one background was most suitable for a cabinet officer, in a later period a different background was more desirable. How can we say the change came from the different classes of people voting and not from changes in general standards of fitness pervading all of the electorate? Furthermore,

[26] Furthermore, when only a few of the lower classes held the vote, there must have been less inclination for them to cohere closely. When great numbers were added, however, the amount of mutual support reinforced the bonds forming the lower class point of view, in accordance with the generalization derived from Tingsten, *op. cit.*, p. 21.

from these figures might be deduced only a parallel to the New York case, namely, that the decline of aristocrats in the cabinet occurred because a decline in the prestige of politics occurred. The social elite diverged now from the political elite. The most that can be affirmed is that with abundant substantiation from other sources these data can be accepted as showing a certain amount of change to be fundamentally associated with suffrage changes.

It is not to be expected that a change in suffrage requirements must bring a change in the social background of the ruling class which will entirely match the first change. Many leaders, especially in England, do not remain stationary in their views in the face of expanding opposition; they alter them to fit new situations.[27] As Siegfried said of England's elite, "Lack of resistance seems to be the distinctive trait of this social aristocracy. Year after year, month after month, they give way, wholesale and retail, as the French aristocrats did in the famous night of the fourth of August, 1789. One feels that because traditionally they are accustomed to govern, they insist willy-nilly on remaining at the head of affairs, although it may be only to carry out a policy that will ruin them. In order to continue to hold the reins, certain of their number agree to do whatever democracy asks of them. The façade will be preserved at any rate, since if a revolution ever takes place it will be carried out by lords and gentlemen." [28]

The abolition of the three-class system of voting in Prussia after World War I had a marked effect on the character of the representatives, as shown by the data gathered on the differences in personnel between the 1913 and 1919 parliaments in Prussia.[29] Particularly noticeable were the great decline in the number of agricultural proprietors in the Prussian Landtag, and the large increase in the num-

---

[27] "But to measure the effect of the enfranchisement of 1867 by the electoral gain of the Conservatives, or by the composition of the House of Commons before and after the introduction of the new suffrage, would obviously be illusive. There can be no doubt but that basic changes resulted from the enormous increase in the electorate; these changes were retarded by the unequal distribution of seats, by the complexities of registration, as well as by corrupt electioneering, and were by no means complete until after 1885. But, even before the third Reform Act, they began to affect radically the relation of constituency to candidate, the attitude of members, and consequently the character of legislation." Seymour, *op. cit.*

[28] Andre Siegfried, *England's Crisis,* translated from the French by H. H. and Doris Hemming, Harcourt, Brace & Co., Inc., New York, 1931, p. 188.

[29] See Table in Appendix.

ber of private, party, and union officials. Also striking was the increase in the percentage of professional men who were elected to the Prussian Landtag in 1919. The percentage of teachers in the Landtag rose from 5.4 to 15.5.

In this, as in the English case, we have proof of much change coterminous with the extension of suffrage. It is obvious that Socialist sentiment in Prussia had been effectively dammed up by the system of suffrage before the war. The Junkers had been in office by the grace of the three-class system, and not by the grace of the masses of peasants and workers.

The fears of the conservatives regarding universal suffrage have not been realized in the form anticipated. No cataclysmic revolutionary economic changes have been brought about by popular majorities. In England, the Labor party with a program based upon the inevitability of gradualism took half a century to capture a majority in the House of Commons. In Sweden, the Social Democratic party has come close to a majority, but it is not a revolutionary but a revisionist party. In the United States, labor and Socialist parties have made comparatively little headway. The New Deal program moved in the direction of social reform within the framework of the capitalistic system. The question may be raised as to why the lower income groups have been so slow in making demands.

So long as there is great disparity in incomes, equal suffrage will not mean equal political power. The rich will have greater control over the means of mass communication — the press, the radio, the motion pictures. They will also be in better position to finance the political organizations. This will enable them to pay for canvassers, to rent meeting halls, to buy literature, to obtain publicity talent, and to secure the other assistance that is necessary to advertise candidates and win elections.

To run as a candidate is an expensive business; a poor man cannot afford to do it unassisted. He must have friends who will raise the money for him. The poor must be well organized if their voice is to be heard. Their organizations must be financed by themselves if they wish to be independent, and their leaders must be willing to spend money for political purposes. In addition, the members must be willing to sacrifice time and effort in attending meetings, seeing their neighbors, addressing, mailing, and delivering literature, and in the other innumerable tasks that are necessary for political success. In some countries the trade-unions do this, but in others the trade-unions are non-political.

There are groups of low-paid workers that are very difficult to organize. Farm laborers, domestic service workers, and store clerks are among these. Citizens in these occupational groups are not likely to be well organized politically. They are not likely to have a press which represents their views. Their access to other means of mass communication is also likely to be limited.

When the poor man acquired the ballot, it did not mean that he automatically obtained power to vote himself a larger share of the national income. If such was his desire, he found it was necessary to discover others who agreed with him, not only on the general aim but also on how it might be accomplished. The winning of the right to vote was only the beginning of a long struggle for equality of economic opportunity.

Chapter 4

WOMEN GO TO THE POLLS

THE DISFRANCHISEMENT of women until comparatively recent times has been the product of the legal, religious, social, and economic disabilities imposed upon them. Before the struggle for the ballot could be won, women had to secure greater recognition in the home, in the church, in the courts of law, in the schools, in the professions, and in the workshops. As women increased their mobility, their economic independence, and their literacy, they came closer to achieving political rights. It is hard to realize now how submerged women were one hundred and fifty years ago. At that time their property rights, their control over marital status, their freedom of assembly, and their professional opportunities were rigidly circumscribed.

Before the Industrial Revolution, the patriarchal organization of the family and the burden of home duties left women practically no time or opportunity for political agitation. With the coming of the capitalistic economy, the women of the wealthy bourgeoisie acquired property which they wished to protect, and leisure time which they could use to secure that protection. On the other hand, the women of the working classes were often forced to seek employment in the factories. Women industrial workers became potential trade-unionists, and it was natural that the socialist agitators should take up the cause of equal rights for women.

Women suffrage was first adopted in countries which were predominantly Protestant and bourgeois. The growth of coeducation, the demand for a single standard of sexual morals, a liberal economic tradition, the feminist agitation of the great literary leaders, the increasing use of women in business offices, and the gradual elimination of legal disabilities were among the conditions which favored the granting of equal political rights to women. Women were employed more and more as teachers and as stenographers and clerical

workers. Women secured the right to vote in states where they had
secured emancipation along other lines.

While the rights of women were not emphasized in the American
and French Revolutions, it was soon clear that the natural rights
philosophy provided a favorable atmosphere for the beginning of
feministic agitation. The bourgeoisie invoked the doctrine of natural rights in their own struggle for political power against the landed
aristocrats. On the eve of the French Revolution (1788), Condorcet came out strongly for equal political and educational opportunities for men and women.[1] The National Assembly, however,
rejected a proposed Declaration of the Rights of Women in 1789.
While Thomas Jefferson was opposed to political activity on the part
of women in the United States, Thomas Paine was not. Through
the efforts of a Quaker preacher, the state of New Jersey placed in its
revolutionary constitution of 1776 the provision which conferred the
suffrage upon "all inhabitants of full age who are worth fifty
pounds." When a number of women took advantage of this provision, the legislature excluded them (1807) by limiting the suffrage
to white male citizens. In this period women gained no permanent
political rights, but the question of their status in a democratic
and liberal regime had definitely been raised.

Equal suffrage for men and women as a permanent institution
began in the United States when the state of Kentucky gave school
suffrage to widows in 1838. Shortly after the Revolution, co-
educational schools had been established by the Society of Friends
in several American states. When the newer frontier communities
began to establish public schools, these were often made coeduca-
tional for reasons of economy. In days when men were needed for
the strenuous activities of farming, hunting, and trading, women
teachers gradually began to outnumber men teachers in the elemen-
tary schools. It was therefore natural that women should be given
a voice in the control of the schools. The state of Kansas, another
frontier state, gave all women the franchise in school matters in
1861, and other states followed gradually until by 1919 over half
the states in the Union permitted women to vote in school elections.

---

[1] "Essai sur la Constitution et les fonctions des assemblées provinciales,"
Œuvres, edited by Arago, Vol. 8, p. 141. See also *Œuvres,* Vol. 9, pp. 14-20, and
Vol. 10, p. 119.

The newly settled West was ahead of other regions in eliminating sex restrictions on the suffrage. Even though most of the woman suffrage crusaders were found in the Eastern part of the United States, nevertheless the first general woman suffrage victory came in the Territory of Wyoming in 1869. This action was variously regarded as provoked by the desire to attract much-needed women settlers, as a publicity scheme for Wyoming, and as a recognition of the role women played in settling the Wild West.

Gradually the adjoining states removed the provisions which disfranchised persons on account of sex. In the nineties the Populist movement aided the suffragists to win victories in Colorado (1893), Idaho (1896), and Utah (1896). The Progressive revolt of 1912 broke the hold of the old line party machines in some of the Western states, so that by 1915 the population of the suffrage states was 17 per cent of the total population of the United States.

Mention must also be made here of the influence leisure has upon the demand for the right to vote. Admittedly, many voters may as well have no leisure for all the time they spend thinking and working on matters of state. The long nights of the peasants' winters certainly give ample leisure, but little of it is consumed politically. Nevertheless the possession of regularized leisure does bring to its owner a connotation of genteel status which has been monopolized by a few rich during most of history.

Bourgeois women, among the beneficiaries of the new leisure, have been most numerous in seeking the franchise. Even though economic and social conditions may have been favorable, nowhere has equal suffrage for men and women been achieved where there was not a militant movement working for that end.[2] The famous Seneca Falls Convention of 1848, called by Elizabeth Cady Stanton, Lucretia Mott, and a number of other women, most of them Quakers, was the beginning of organized action on the part of American women.[3] This convention resulted from the refusal of a London abolitionist meeting to admit women delegates. While such a gath-

---

[2] Jacob Frieze, *A Concise History of the Efforts to Obtain an Extension of Suffrage in Rhode Island,* Providence, 1842 (3rd edition, 1912) ; Mrs. F. H. McDougall, *Might and Right by a Rhode Islander,* Providence, 1844.

[3] Carrie C. Catt and Nettie R. Shuler, *Woman Suffrage and Politics,* New York, Chas. Scribner's Sons, 1923; Elizabeth Stanton *et al., The History of Woman Suffrage,* New York, 1881-1922, 6 vols.

ering excited ridicule from many quarters, it secured the support of men like William Lloyd Garrison, Wendell Phillips, William Henry Channing, John Greenleaf Whittier, and Ralph Waldo Emerson. In the beginning women's rights were tied to abolitionism, since women were considered by many as legal slaves.

Later on, a national organization was effected under the same leadership. Though abused as "unsexed," "ludicrous," and "wicked," and regarded as neurotic eccentrics by many of the formers of public opinion, outstanding women persisted in their efforts, bolstered in their fight by the sympathy of many men.

When the post-Civil War amendments to the Constitution were being drafted, and the currents of radicalism were flowing swiftly on the national scene, women tried by conventions, mass meetings, and petitions to arouse Congress to the justice of their claims. But in the Fourteenth Amendment, Congress specified "male" inhabitants as the basis for limiting the representation of any state in the Federal government, and the Supreme Court decided that a Mrs. Virginia Minor could not use the first section of the Fourteenth Amendment to justify her voting at an election, inasmuch as suffrage is not a necessary incident to citizenship.[4]

As they turned their attention and energies to the states, the women at first found the same difficulty. Notwithstanding the agitation of Eastern crusaders at their convention, the Kansans voted down a referendum on woman suffrage in 1894. Well-organized efforts failed likewise in the New York Constitutional Convention of 1915, largely opposed by the big corporations and the liquor interests.

The National Woman Suffrage Association (1869) and the American Woman Suffrage Society (1869) coalesced in 1890 into the National American Women's Suffrage Association and carried on remarkably well-organized and persistent work. With the publication of a weekly magazine, and a membership of 200,000 before World War I, this organization was well equipped to conduct an extensive and influential campaign all over the nation. Every form of publicity, demonstration, political pressure, and buttonholing of individuals was resorted to on an immense scale. Assiduous application finally won over the Tammany organization, and with it the

---

[4] Minor vs. Happersett, 21 Wall. 162 (1874).

Empire State in 1917. The tactics thus far employed relied upon slow and steady pressure to prove that women deserved the vote. Some could not wait for evolution to run its course, however, and in 1912 Alice Paul, the Washington lobbyist for the N.A.W.S.A., and Mrs. August Belmont, split from the non-militant American woman suffragists, and with their followers founded the Congressional Union, later known as the National Woman's Party. This group applied on a smaller scale the notorious and embarrassing tactics of the English suffragettes, namely, mass meetings, picketing, and, *when in prison,* hunger strikes.

In Great Britain the woman suffrage movement was dominated until the twentieth century by such persons as Dame Millicent Fawcett, who was prominent in the National Union of Women's Suffrage Societies, an organization uniting various non-militant groups. On the question of tactics she wrote, "Let us prove ourselves worthy of citizenship, whether our claim is recognized or not." [5]

About 1905 the Women's Social and Political Union, a new organization under the leadership of Mrs. Emmeline Pankhurst, together with some Laborites, began to employ militant tactics. Practical experience in politics had convinced Mrs. Pankhurst and her "suffragettes" that eternal vigilance and a willingness to face danger and bear suffering were the roads to democracy. Heckling of opponents, mass demonstrations, and hunger strikes were employed to shock and stimulate the public mind. Only when World War I broke out were these tactics abandoned.

Miss Breckinridge has summarized the movement of woman suffrage in the United States from the beginning to its final culmination:

> The ratification of the Nineteenth Amendment to the United States Constitution in 1920, after fifty-six campaigns for the ratification of

---

[5] E. C. Stanton *et al., History of Woman Suffrage,* Vol. 6 (1922). Ch. 51 by Millicent G. Fawcett.

"In 1913 the N.U.W.S.S. organized the greatest public demonstration it had ever made. We called it the Pilgrimage. It meant processions of nonmilitant suffragists, wearing their badges and carrying banners, marching towards London along eight of the great trunk roads. These eight processions, many of them lasting several weeks, stopped at towns and villages on their way, held meetings, distributed literature, and collected funds. It was all a tremendous and unprecedented success, well organized, and well done throughout. The Pilgrimage made a very great impression and was favorably commented on in the organs of the press which had never helped us before."

amendments to state constitutions, nearly five hundred organized efforts with legislatures, two hundred twenty-seven appearances at state party conventions, thirty appeals before national political conventions, and nineteen campaigns with successive Congresses, meant the admission of women in all the states to the right to vote, and the closing of one era in the movement toward equality of sexes.[6]

So it would seem the militant tactics worked, but they were abetted by years of preparation and local organization, and by the fact that the leaders both here and in England were women of high character.

In Britain, in a struggle which bore strong resemblances to the American experience, all women over thirty years of age were granted equal suffrage with men in the Representation of the People Act of 1918. Ten years later the anomalous age requirement was removed, and the suffrage provisions for men and women made exactly the same.

On the continent of Europe the spread of woman suffrage paralleled that in English-speaking countries. The first trials were made in the Scandinavian countries where coeducation, advocates of women's freedom, such as Ibsen, and leading feminists like Camilla Collet and Ellen Key paved the way. In Finland, women taxpayers were permitted to vote in local rural elections in 1863; in 1906 women were given full suffrage rights. Norway gradually extended the suffrage to women after the turn of the century, removing the last barrier to equal voting rights in 1913. Denmark followed, lagging a few years behind Norway. In other parts of Europe the agitation for women's rights was carried on by bourgeois feminists and by trade-unionists. The German Social Democratic Party came out for woman suffrage at its famous congress in Erfurt in 1891, following the stand taken on this issue by its leader, August Bebel. It took the crises in government created by World War I, and postwar revolutions, however, to overcome the prejudices against women's participation in politics. The Russian Revolution of November, 1917, produced a constitution which proclaimed complete equality of the sexes. The German Constitution of Weimar, like the constitutions of Austria, Czechoslovakia, and Poland, extended full

---

[6] In President's Research Committee on Social Trends, *Recent Social Trends*, New York; McGraw-Hill Book Co., Inc., 1933, Vol. 1, p. 737.

suffrage rights to women. Since 1920 the franchise has been granted to women in Sweden, Spain, Brazil, Uruguay, Turkey, and a number of other countries.

Of the democratic countries, Switzerland still holds out against the tide of woman suffrage. Prior to World War II, the French Senate, the more conservative body, persistently rejected woman suffrage provisions passed by the Chamber of Deputies. After liberation in 1944, women received the vote in France.

The Fascist movements in Europe meant, in general, a setback for feminists. In Italy the trial of municipal woman suffrage was not made in the twenties because all local selfgovernment was abolished by Mussolini. After the downfall of Fascism, woman suffrage was introduced. In Germany the rights and privileges which women had achieved during the republican regime were swept away by the Nazis. Governmental changes in Turkey, however, resulted in strenuous attempts to improve the status of women.

The Participation of Women in Elections

In all countries where woman suffrage has been proposed, a common argument against its introduction has been the claim that women in general do not desire the vote and would not use it. The first trial of woman suffrage might be expected to show a smaller response on the part of women than of men who had been accustomed to participating in politics for centuries. Timidity and uncertainty stayed the votes of many women.

In a few American states the number of registered voters has been reported by sex, and these figures can be used to show the trend of women's participation in elections.[7] Shortly after the introduction of partial woman suffrage in Illinois (1914), the women who registered in the city of Chicago constituted 32 per cent of the total number of persons on the registration books.[8] Scattered figures show that in the first trial of woman suffrage in the country as a whole, the percentage of registered female voters varied from 18 per cent in Louisiana to 45.5 per cent in Indiana.[9]

---

[7] Colorado was one of the first suffrage states, and it has been estimated that 42 per cent of the registered voters in this state were women in 1906. See Helen Sumner, *Equal Suffrage*, New York, 1909, pp. 100 ff.

[8] Chicago Board of Election Commissioners.

[9] See Table I in the Appendix.

It is significant, however, that there has been a slow but steady increase in the proportion of women voters since 1920. The greatest relative increase in the proportion of women voters was found in Louisiana, but in Vermont the official figures show the number of women registered is practically equal to the number of men registered.[10] By 1928, in parts of California, women registered in the same proportion as men. Another way to approach this same subject is to ascertain the percentage of the estimated number of potential women voters that registered over a period of time. Whereas only 49 per cent of the adult female citizens in Chicago registered for the presidential election of 1920, ten years later 57 per cent registered for the state and congressional elections.[11] Though the increases in the number of women voters have not been marked in some parts of the United States, the general trend towards sex equality in participation is unmistakable.

A number of isolated studies made in widely scattered parts of the United States show some of the influences which have been operating to retard the fullest exercise of the suffrage by women.[12] Foreign-born women have not registered in as large proportions as native women; women in the lower income groups have been more indifferent to politics than those in the higher income groups. Lack of education is also keeping some women from voting. As compared with men, women who have no interest in politics are less likely to vote.[13]

In the United States, primary elections are frequently more important than general elections. Consequently the participation of women in primary elections indicates something about their role in politics. A well-known American journalist has said, "The undeniable fact is that in every city in the country, and in every state, women suffrage has increased the power of the political machines and the political bosses, particularly in the primaries, where all nomi-

---

10 In Louisiana the increase was from 18 per cent in 1920 to 40 per cent in 1938. For Vermont figures see the *Vermont Legislative Directory*, 1945, p. 295.

11 Estimates based upon the Census figures.

12 C. E. Merriam and H. F. Gosnell, *op. cit.;* H. F. Gosnell, *Getting Out the Vote*, Chicago, 1927; B. Arneson, "Non-voting in a Typical Ohio Community," *American Political Science Review*, Vol. 19, pp. 816-825; R. Martin, "Municipal Electorate," *Southwestern Social Science Quarterly*, Vol. 14 (December, 1933), pp. 193-237.

13 P. F. Lazarsfeld, B. Berelson, and H. Gaudet, *The People's Choice*, New York, 1944, p. 48.

nations are made." [14]   He arrived at this conclusion on the ground that the women failed to vote as heavily as the men in primary elections. When the vote is low, the machine has an easier time controlling the result.[15]   In Chicago the ratio of women who actually voted in the primary was 3.6 per cent less than the ratio of women registered in 1920, and fourteen years later it was 2.6 per cent less.[16]   Thus it appears that the initial hesitancy has practically been overcome. In such western states as California and Arizona, the women have shown just about the same interest in primary elections as the men. Such a generalization as the journalist's cited above, is not, therefore, well substantiated.

Until 1944, men outnumbered women as registered voters in all parts of the United States except in a few isolated areas which were found in the outlying parts of metropolitan regions or in small college towns.[17]   In certain European countries, however, women have outnumbered men on the lists of registered voters from the beginning of full equal suffrage. In Great Britain and Sweden women constitute 52 per cent or more of the enrolled voters. One of the highest ratios was found in Esthonia, where 56 per cent of the registered voters were women.[18]   The British women voters did not outnumber the men voters until after the Act of 1928 which removed the higher age requirement for women. What interest have the women voters shown in the exercise of the franchise in those countries where they outnumbered the men? Some European countries have kept separate records of the votes of men and women so that it is possible to answer this question with more precision than in the United States. In a few exceptional cases, the percentage of

---

14 F. Kent, *The Great Game of Politics,* New York, 1924, p. 168.

15 There is some evidence to support the view that a small minority of women are more hesitant at first about declaring their party affiliations than are men. In the state of Pennsylvania in 1924, some 12 per cent of the women did not indicate their party registration, whereas only 5 per cent of the men failed to do this. Eight years later, however, the proportion of women who failed to take this initial step as primary voters dropped to 4 per cent, and that of men to 3 per cent. See *Pennsylvania Manual,* 1925-1926.

16 Records of the Board of Election Commissioners of the City of Chicago.

17 In Palo Alto, California, the women registered voters outnumber the men. In seven areas of Chicago (with an aggregate number of registered voters of 54,747), in 1930, the percentage of women registered exceeded 50 per cent of the total. Women were credited in 1944 with casting 50.3 per cent of the vote. *The Washington Post,* September 12, 1946. See also George Gallup, *The Gallup Political Almanac for 1946,* Princeton, 1946.

18 K. Braunias, *Das Parlamentarische Wahlrecht,* Berlin, 1932, Vol. 2, p. 105.

women voting has been higher than that of men. Thus, in Finland, in 1919, when prohibition was an issue; in Czechoslovakia and Belgium, where women apparently feared the penalties for non-voting as much as, or more, than men did; and in Linz, Austria, in 1927 and 1930, women equaled or surpassed the voting records of men.[19] In most countries and at most elections, however, the proportion of eligible men voting has exceeded that of eligible women. The disparity was greatest in the Soviet Union (38.8 per cent more of the eligible men than of the eligible women were registered) and least in Austria (3 per cent). There has been a rapid advance, however, in the interest Russian women have shown at the polls. In 1926, 43 per cent of the women eligible voted in the elections to the city soviets, and 28 per cent in the elections to the village soviets. The corresponding figures for the years 1934 and 1935 were 90 per cent and 80 per cent.[20] This enormous increase was in part the product of a concerted drive to increase the participation of women in the affairs of the Soviet Union. The response was great because the new generation of Russian women has been conditioned to doctrines of sex equality. On the average, from 6 per cent to 12 per cent fewer women than men go to the polls. During the Weimar republican régime in Germany, a number of detailed studies were made which showed that women's participation in elections was less than men's in every age group.[21]

Experience has shown that fears of the anti-suffragists that women would not make use of the vote were unfounded. While there were at first and still are a few more female than male non-voters, the disparity is not great and has been continually lessening. In those countries still using the democratic process, there has been a slow but steady tendency toward equalization between the sexes.

If we seek further discriminations within the feminine group itself, we find that married women participate more frequently in elections

[19] Hartwig, "Das Frauenwahlrecht in der Statistik," *Allgemeine Statistische Archiv,* Vol. 21 (1931), pp. 167-182.
[20] N. K. Krupskaya, *Soviet Woman: A Citizen With Equal Rights,* Moscow, 1937, p. 21.
[21] Tingsten, *op. cit.;* W. L. Woytinsky, *Die Welt in Zahlen,* Vol. 7 (1928), p. 106; A. Zurcher, *The Experiment with Democracy in Central Europe,* New York, 1933, p. 68; Hartwig, *op. cit.;* M. Bernhard, "Die Frauen in Politischen Leben," *Zeitschrift für Politik,* Vol. 19 (1929), pp. 142-147; R. H. Wells, *German Cities,* Princeton, 1930, p. 71; and H. F. Gosnell, *Why Europe Votes,* Chicago, 1930, pp. 93-96, 178-179, and 156-157.

than do unmarried women.[22] Widows and divorced women are midway in their interest in voting. Differences are due partly to the younger ages of unmarried persons. Unoccupied women vote more frequently than employed women, and it is an open question whether leisure, work at home, or youth influence participation of women.

Husband and wife have a tendency to behave in the same manner — either they vote together or not at all. The husband may vote and the wife abstain frequently, but the wife rarely votes without her husband's doing likewise.[23] This indicates an expected dependent relationship on the part of the wife.

Women as Party Organizers

The basic conditions of harmony, and the identity of interests between women and their menfolk, combine to prevent any permanent organization of women to combat male political groups. So far as concerns political aspirations, a woman usually has more interests in common with males of her own social status than she has in common with women of different social strata. As a consequence, women have ventured into masculine parties and have worked towards diverting party activities according to their ends.

Long before women were given the franchise they were used as canvassers by the men-controlled political organizations. In countries with a strong labor movement, women trade-union organizers were used for political work. Conservative parties employed with especial effectiveness women whose social prestige had persuasive results politically. The advent of woman suffrage greatly intensified the political activity of women in the party organizations as canvassers, speakers, delegates to party conventions, members of party committees, and candidates. Political parties began to hold special conventions for women, to issue women's publications, and to give women places in the regular party hierarchies.

In the American states which first adopted woman suffrage, women were soon taking a very active part in the canvassing of votes. Fifteen years after the adoption of equal suffrage in Colorado, it was reported that "Where the size of the community

---

[22] Tingsten, *op. cit.*, pp. 175-177.
[23] B. Berelson and P. F. Lazarsfeld, "Women: A Major Problem for the P. A. C.," *Public Opinion Quarterly*, Vol. 9 (1945), pp. 79-82.

justifies canvassing in any systematic way, women are employed in somewhat larger numbers than men."[24] The passage of the National Woman Suffrage Amendment multiplied the number of women canvassers several thousandfold. Women were slow in assuming party responsibilities in the South; but in the metropolitan communities of the North many were given positions as precinct captains. In such cities as Philadelphia and Chicago, where there were strong party organizations, women gradually worked their way up as local party executives. One Democratic ward leader in Chicago boasted in the thirties that one fourth of his precinct captains were women![25] On the other hand, women have had a difficult time in securing recognition in the political clubs of New York City, where prejudice against women politicians still seems to be strong.[26] An outstanding success of women as canvassers has been achieved in Cincinnati, where the women furnished the backbone of the volunteer organization which inaugurated and supported the city-manager form of government. As one observer has put it, "The experiment in Cincinnati is unique because there has been developed something in the nature of an independent municipal political party having no selfish purpose. The women will work for such an independent political party ... and will devote to it large amounts of time between elections when men cannot be induced to do much of anything. They will persist; they will secure support; they will get out the vote."[27]

Above the lowly precinct executive stand the city, county, state, and national party committees. Except where the party rules or the state law requires equal representation of men and women on the party committees, women have made little progress in securing positions as higher party executives. By 1906 the state conventions of both the major parties in Colorado provided that the state central committee should be composed of an equal number of men and women. A few of the county central committees followed the example of the state conventions. This so-called fifty-fifty plan of

[24] Sumner, *op. cit.,* p. 64.
[25] A study of local party leaders in Philadelphia discovered one "Rosie Popovits," regarding whom her ward leader said, "She is the best man on the ward committee." See J. T. Salter, *Boss Rule,* New York, 1935, p. 193.
[26] R. V. Peel, *The Political Clubs of New York City,* New York, 1935, pp. 127, 248.
[27] C. P. Taft, *City Management: The Cincinnati Experiment,* New York, Rinehart & Company, Inc., 1933, pp. 235-236.

representation was adopted by the Democratic National Committee in 1920 and by the Republican Committee in 1924. The experience of some of the women on these committees has been disappointing. As one woman member of a national committee put it:

> I have seen many women develop to a point where they could defeat men at their own tactics . . . But the result has not been that intended by the proponents of the measure. For in many cases, as soon as women used their knowledge to their own advantage against some men on the committees, they found themselves replaced by women who did not have such knowledge.
>
> For the fifty-fifty law merely makes places for women on these committees. The individual women can retain their places only if they can win a following to put them there . . . As men are already powerful and have their following, it is easier for them to elect women they want than for women to organize a following of their own.[28]

In spite of the difficulties which they had to overcome, some American women have risen to positions of power and leadership in their parties. One measure of the influence of women in the political parties is the number chosen as delegates to the national nominating conventions. On four occasions, nearly one fifth of the delegates to the Democratic National Convention have been women. Since 1920, from 7 per cent to 12 per cent of the delegates have been women at the Republican National Conventions, and since 1916 women have served on the important convention committees in both parties.[29] In 1928, at the Republican convention, Mrs. Willebrandt

---

[28] Emily Newell Blair, "Women in the Political Parties," *Annals of the American Academy of Political and Social Science,* Vol. 143 (May, 1929), pp. 222-223.

[29] S. Breckinridge, "Activities of Women Outside the Home," *Recent Social Trends,* Vol. 1, p. 741, compiled the following figures regarding women delegates from the National Democratic and Republican Convention Proceedings for the various years. M. J. Fisher and B. Whitehead, "Women and National Party Organization," *American Political Science Review,* Vol. 38 (October, 1944), p. 896, brought them down to date.

Year	Republicans		Democrats	
	Delegates	Alternates	Delegates	Alternates
1912	2	..	2	1
1916	5	9	11	11
1920	27	129	93	206
1924	120	277	199	310
1928	70	264	152	263
1932	88	305	208	270
1936	61	222	252	333
1940	78	231	208	347
1944	99	264	174	332

presided over the committee on credentials and presented the argument for the majority report on the floor of the convention. Another woman, Mrs. McCormick, took a vigorous part in the convention fight against Herbert Hoover.

In the democratic countries of Europe, women have for some time played an important role in the party organizations. The British Conservative Party enlisted the aid of women in electioneering, long before the days of woman suffrage, through an organization known as the Primrose League. Since this League was not an integral part of the party organization, the Conservatives formed separate local associations, or sections, for women after 1918. In the thirties the chief agent of the British Conservative Party was a woman. The Liberal and Labour party managers likewise established special women's organizations. While the Labour Party utilized to advantage the women trade-union organizers and women socialist agitators, the other parties exploited the social prestige of titled women. Now, besides having special women conferences, publications, and social functions, all the parties encourage women to attend the regular party conferences.[30] The political parties in the other European countries which experimented with woman suffrage used similar methods in organizing the women.

The position of women in the party hierarchy of countries which have the one-party system has varied from place to place. The Nazi party in Germany declared that no woman was eligible to join the party.[31] On the other hand, the Communists in the Soviet Union have encouraged women to become full-fledged party members. In 1927 it was found that 12.8 per cent of the members of the party in the Soviet Union were women, some of whom had been elected members of the Communist Party Central Committee.[32] Kemal Atatürk, in Turkey, likewise welcomed women as members of his National Party.

On the basis of obvious facts we can conclude that women have not organized among themselves to compete in the political field; but certain evidence points to the conclusion that women affiliate

---

[30] J. Gaus, *Great Britain: A Study of Civic Loyalty,* Chicago, 1929, pp. 254-258; H. F. Gosnell, *Why Europe Votes,* Chicago, 1930, pp. 28, 29.

[31] Alice Hamilton, "Women's Place in Germany," *Survey Graphic,* Vol. 23 (January, 1934), pp. 26-29.

[32] W. H. Chamberlain, *Soviet Union* (Rev. ed.), Boston, 1931, p. 65.

with certain political viewpoints more generally than with others. Baseless forebodings about the political behavior of women are numerous and contradictory. Women have been accused of radicalism and of conservatism, of reformism and of indifference, of insurgency, emotionalism, and idealism.[33] Many of the theories are generalizations from specific instances. We are interested, however, in concrete data which are broad enough to be generalized.

Party Affiliations of Women

In the United States, separate records for men's and women's votes have been kept only in the state of Illinois, and in that state just for the period from 1913 to 1920. These records show that in the presidential election of 1916, the proportion of women voters supporting Hughes was almost the same as the proportion of men voters supporting Hughes. In other words, about one half of the men voters were Republican, and the same held for the women voters. A slightly larger proportion of the women voters than of the men voters, however, supported Wilson, the Democratic candidate. One interpretation of this would be that the women were attracted by the Democratic slogan, "He kept us out of war." In contrast with some fears expressed, the men were more inclined to vote for Debs, the Socialist candidate, than were the women. The election of 1920 was a landslide for Warren G. Harding, the "dark horse" nominee of the Republican convention. It was found that in all parts of the state women more than men were consistently in

[33] J. K. Bluntschli, the German-Swiss jurist, contended that if women voted they would either duplicate present voting alignments or they would tend to strengthen the clerical parties. *Politik,* Book X, Chapter ii.

Antisuffragists in the United States were afraid that the emotionalism of women might unsettle the American system of government, that their idealism might lead to impractical governmental experiments, and that the radicalism of some of them would be dangerous to the existing economic order. See C. E. Merriam, *American Political Ideas,* New York, 1920, pp. 94, 95.

And in Frank Kent, *Political Behavior,* New York, 1928: "So long as they (women) lack the economic independence of the male, they will lack political independence — not all of them, of course, but always the great majority." P. 288.

"Just her bent for education, her aptitude for the long process of reform, her fresh interest in government for government's sake, her freedom from economic or party entanglements — these characteristics of the new electorate may bring into political life the very stimulus that, at the moment, it needs to turn it forward towards new successes by which to justify democracy. . . ." See Marguerite M. Wells, "Some Effects of Woman Suffrage," *Annals of the American Academy of Political and Social Science,* Vol. 142 (May, 1929), pp. 215, 216.

favor of Harding.[34] Harding's campaign photographs pictured him as a handsome man, while the stories about Cox's family life may have alienated some women.

After 1920, Illinois no longer kept separate records of how men and women voted. A study of voting behavior in Chicago, made by the present writer, using certain statistical devices, seemed to indicate, however, that from 1928 to 1940 there was still a decided tendency for the women to favor Republican candiates.[35] One reason for this was the fact that a larger proportion of the women registered in the higher rental areas, where the Republican Party was usually strong. The Republicanism of the women in Chicago and other parts of Illinois was in part the product of the failure of the party workers in the Democratic strongholds to get out their full quota of women voters. While the Illinois figures show some slight differentiation between the national party preferences of men and women voters, in the main they confirm the view that voting in general does not follow sex lines.

In state and local elections in Illinois, the women voters have from time to time shown distinctive tendencies. At some elections women voters in Chicago have been numerous in those precincts where a relatively large number of split tickets were cast. A study of the 1915 mayoralty election led one statistician to conclude that there was a sex difference in the election concerned. William Hale Thompson, the Republican candidate, was opposed by some of the reform elements because of his past connections with spoils politicians. It was found that on the average, throughout the city, men and women voted for Thompson to approximately the same extent, but judging by the precincts, the women tended to vote in blocks to a greater extent than did men. If the precinct was a "Thompson precinct," the majority given to Thompson by the women was greater than that given by the men, and if it was an "anti-Thompson precinct," the majority against Thompson given by the women was greater than that given by the men.[36] In other elections where

---

[34] M. Willey and S. Rice, "A Sex Cleavage in the Presidential Election of 1920," *Journal of the American Statistical Association,* 1924, pp. 519 ff.

[35] H. F. Gosnell, *Machine Politics: Chicago Model,* Chicago, 1937.

[36] One precinct in particular is a notable exception. There existed in this precinct a very strong anti-Thompson women's organization, with the result that though 77 per cent of the men voted for Thompson, only 12 per cent of the women did so. See T. L. Kelley, *Statistical Method,* New York, 1924, pp. 184-185.

"Thompsonism" was an issue, there was also evidence of sex differences. In the Republican primary of 1920 there was a marked tendency for the women to oppose the Thompson candidate for governor more strongly than the men.[37]

Party registration by sex has been kept in a few states for varying lengths of time. These figures do not show how the men and women vote in final elections, but they raise certain presumptions. In Pennsylvania, the percentage of women registering with the Republican Party was slightly less than that of the men in 1924. In the thirties a political upheaval occurred in the state and the registration of Democrats greatly increased. The women lagged slightly behind the men in changing their party allegiance.[38]

The voting tendencies of women may also be studied in jurisdictions which have combined woman suffrage with popular lawmaking. In some American states these experiments have been going on side by side for some years. On the basis of certain calculations regarding voting in Portland, Oregon, after seven years' experience with woman suffrage it was concluded that the women voters, in comparison with the men voters, were more opposed to the eight-hour day for women; to a single tax; to extending certain forms of government; and that they were more in favor of prohibition and of making minor changes in governmental procedure.[39] Another study based upon the separate election returns for men and women available in Chicago prior to 1921 showed that the women tended to vote in about the same way as the men, except that they were more favorable to prohibition measures and to propositions which involved the protection of public health.[40] Native white women of native parentage showed much more independence in voting on measures and more interest in the recommendations of civic agencies than did women of foreign parentage. Ten years later an analysis based

---

[37] Sixty-six per cent of the men and only 53.5 per cent of the women voted for Len Small, the Thompson candidate for governor in the Republican primary. (Figures from the records of the Board of Election Commissioners of the City of Chicago.)

[38] See Appendix.

[39] W. F. Ogburn and I. Gotra, "How Women Vote: A Study of an Election in Portland, Oregon," *Political Science Quarterly*, Vol. 34 (September, 1919), pp. 413, 433.

[40] C. O. Gardner, *The Referendum in Chicago*, University of Pennsylvania, Philadelphia, 1920, p. 26. See also D. M. Maynard, "The Referendum in Chicago," University of Chicago, Ph.D. Thesis, 1927.

upon correlation techniques indicated that the women voters in Chicago were still considerably "dryer" than the men, and that they were more inclined to vote against bond issues condemned by civic agencies.[41]

In most European countries which have tried woman suffrage it is impossible to determine whether sex produces differential voting behavior. Great Britain has never kept separate returns of the votes of men and women. A number of persons, however, have made inferences regarding the effect of the feminine vote in recent British elections, and *Mass-Observation* has made some surveys which are relevant.[42] The general consensus seems to be that the women voters in Great Britain have not altered the results of any general election. In some constituencies, it has been claimed, the new women voters supported the British Labour Party in large numbers, while in others they supported the Conservative Party. *Mass-Observation* found that 86 per cent of Worktown wives admitted that they always voted for the same candidates as their husbands. In 1938, however, women were more pro-Chamberlain than men, wanting peace at any price. A London survey showed that 67 per cent of the men were indignant at the potential "betrayal" of the Czechs, as compared with 22 per cent of the women.[43] This was a striking difference which may have had its influence upon British appeasement policies. Party voting in England has, in general, followed occupational, religious, and sectional lines rather than sex lines, except where moral, religious, or peace questions are involved.

During the Weimar Republican regime in Germany, sample figures were collected at a few elections which gave the votes for the different parties by sex.[44] Each of the samples indicated that the women strongly favored the Catholic Center Party and disliked the

---

[41] Gosnell, *Machine Politics: Chicago Model,* Chicago, 1937.

[42] J. A. R. Marriott, "The Answer of Demos," *Fortnightly Review* (July, 1929), p. 12; A. Hopkinson, "The Election," *Contemporary Review* (July, 1929), p. 12; R. L. Mott, "Retrospect on the British Election," *Southwestern Political and Social Science Quarterly,* Vol. 11 (December, 1930), pp. 260-277; M. A. Hamilton, "Women in Politics," *Political Quarterly,* Vol. 3 (April, 1932), pp. 266 ff.; B. A. Gould, "Women's Part in the New Campaign," *Labour Magazine,* Vol. 10 (January, 1932), pp. 393-395; *Mass Observation,* "The Non-voter," *New Statesman and Nation,* Vol. 16 (December, 1938), pp. 956, 957.

[43] Charles Madge and Tom Harrisson, *Britain by Mass Observation,* London, 1939, Chapter 11. American poll-takers have criticized the methods used by Mass Observation.

[44] Woytinsky, *op. cit.,* p. 43; Finer, *op. cit.,* p. 413.

parties of the extremes, particularly the Communist Party. At first the women were lukewarm in their attitudes toward the Nazi Party, as compared with the men, but in the election of 1933 they supported the Nazi ticket more strongly than did the men.[45] In Cologne about 14 per cent more of the women than of the men consistently supported the Center Party. The 1930 election results show that in Frankfurt-am-Main, Regensburg, and Thuringia, the women voters favored the parties of the right and middle and avoided the parties of the left. It is probable that in 1933 the so-called national coalition (Nazi and German national party) owed its majority to the strong support of the women voters.

Before 1932 considerable significance was attached to the fact that women supported the moderate and conciliatory parties in great numbers. As Tingsten has put it, "The precarious position of the democratic regime in Germany, particularly after the successes of the National Socialists and Communists in the election of 1930, to a certain extent was camouflaged by women suffrage."[46] The women might support a democracy at the ballot boxes, but they stopped short of the barricades.

German women also showed more conservative tendencies in voting on measures than did the men. The men's vote alone on the confiscation of the Princes' property in 1926 would have carried the measure, but the women stayed away in larger numbers than the men, and thereby defeated it, since abstention from voting was practically the same as negative voting.[47]

Spain was the first of the Latin countries in Europe to experiment with woman suffrage, and its experience has undoubtedly proved discouraging to anticlerical elements in other Latin countries. After the victory of the Republican-Socialist coalition in 1931, a progressive constitution was adopted which included woman suffrage. In 1933, when the women voted for the first time, the parties of the Right and Right Center won important gains.[48] The leaders of the revolution discovered that more Spanish women were against them than for them.

---

[45] Tingsten, *op. cit.*, pp. 37-65.
[46] *Ibid.*, p. 47.
[47] Gosnell, "The German Referendum on the Princes' Property," *American Political Science Review*, Vol. 21 (1937), pp. 119-123.
[48] F. E. Manuel, *The Politics of Modern Spain*, New York, 1938, p. 126.

Excellent material compiled by Tingsten all points in the same direction towards the generalization that women behave more conservatively at the polls than men.[49] The best evidence one could have on this question would be the proportion of women as against men supporting a particular political party of known views regarding the existing social structure. This evidence we have in several significant cases.

In analyzing the data for our purposes, it is convenient and clear to devise an index which in one figure represents an answer to the question as to whether women support a particular party. This index Tingsten forms from other figures by the following procedure. He finds the percentage of men voting for a party at a given election; he does the same for women. Then the "sex index" is the percentage of the male percentage which the female percentage amounts to. Therefore a high sex index (*viz.*, over 100) for a certain party means that the women favored that same party to a greater extent than the men did; a low sex index (*viz.*, under 100) means the opposite; a sex index of precisely 100 shows no difference in support among the sexes.

Elections to the German Reichstag from 1924 to 1930 give direct evidence of women favoring the conservative parties rather than the parties of radical change. The German parties participating may be reduced to three groups: the Socialist parties,[50] the Anti-Socialists,[51] and the bourgeois parties. In every case the sex indexes substantiate the hypothesis.

	May 4, 1924	Dec. 7, 1924	May 28, 1928	Sept. 14, 1930
Socialist	82.9	82.9	88.3	88.5
Anti-Socialist	112.4	113.4	113.2	112.5
Bourgeois ..	112.4	115.9	115.6	126.6

Furthermore, we see the same thing occurring when we place the presidential candidates in the elections of 1925 and 1932 in their order according to their political beliefs. Thus, we may place in

---

[49] The following materials are derived from Tingsten, *op. cit.*, pp. 40 ff.
[50] Social Democrats, smaller Socialist parties, and Communists.
[51] Includes National Socialists with fluctuating sex index of 85.3 (1924), 70.8 (1928), and 87.9 (1930). In 1933 the sex index for the Nazis was as high as 113.8 in some cities.

Extreme, Middle, and Rightist groups the following candidates, and see how the sex index increases with conservatism.

Election of			
March 29, 1925...........Extreme		Thalmann	77.6
		Von Ludendorff	73.2
	Middle	Hellpach	92.9
		Held	95.7
		Braun	97.3
	Right	Jarres	108.9
		Marx	109.0
March 13, 1932...........Extreme		Hitler	93.6
		Thalmann	71.1
	Middle	Hindenburg	116.7
		(Catholic, bourgeois, Social Democratic)	
	Right	Duesterberg	101.5

Again in Austria in 1927, the sex index of the Socialists was 88.8, while that of the other parties was 109.3; in 1930 the respective indexes were 90.7 and 107.3. If the composition of the Nationalrat (legislature) were reordered on the basis of what manhood suffrage alone would produce, it would compare with the actual final composition as follows:

1927	Actual Result	Manhood Suffrage Only
Landbund	9	11
Social Democrats	71	76
Unity List	85	78
1930		
Heimatblock	8	10
Nationale Wirtschaftsblock und Landbund..	19	19
Social Democrats	72	78
Unity List	66	58

Distaste for the Marxist parties was so strong among women in Germany that when the shift of women voters occurred it was much more to the side of the National Socialists. In general, then, the leftist groups in capitalistic countries have been politically astute in attempting to block the extension of suffrage rights to women.

In the Soviet Union, women have not shown the same distaste for Marxist doctrines. Since 1917, religious and bourgeois ideas have been ridiculed by the Soviet authorities. The new women voters in Soviet Russia have supported the Communist party. This is a part of the new cultural pattern which the leaders of the party have been trying to construct.

In the United States the parties are tinged innocuously enough so that probably fewer women are determined in their voting behavior by convictions for or against radicalism. The Harding-Cox election study of Illinois, cited previously, bears a bit of evidence for this view. Whereas the difference between the Republican sex index (99.4) and the Democratic sex index (101.4) was insignificant, the sex index for the Socialist party was 58.3, for the Socialist Labor party, 69.2, and for the Prohibition party, 246.7.

In general it can be said that the political divisions of men and women voters have been strikingly similar. In bourgeois countries, where women have chosen different party affiliations, they have favored conservative and ecclesiastical movements. Radical innovations in government and revolutionary decisions on public policy cannot be expected as yet from the women voters. The chief differences between men and women are on peace and moral issues.

Women as Elective Office Holders

Women do not have to vote in blocs in order that women be elected to office. But the obstacles placed before women in politics often make their success difficult. Forces which for long prevented the enfranchisement of women now attempt to keep them from office. A free voter has the right to discriminate against women at the ballot boxes.

In the United States, women began to make their appearance in elective school offices even before they could vote. Later, in the jurisdictions where they obtained the school suffrage, many more were selected as school officers. After complete enfranchisement in the state of Colorado, women captured the office of state superintendent of public instruction in 1894 and have held it continuously since that date.[52]   Colorado women also ran successfully for elective positions on local school boards and municipal councils.

Like other groups which are gradually winning the battle for political rights, women have found it easier to capture legislative positions than to win important administrative posts. Many women served as state legislators before one was finally chosen as a governor.[53] In Colorado the introduction of equal suffrage enabled a number of women to serve as state representatives in the nineties.[54] After the passage of the Nineteenth Amendment women began to run for legislative positions in all parts of the United States. School teachers, widows of legislators, lawyers, doctors, and homemakers were among the women candidates. Thirty-four sat in the state legislative sessions of 1921.[55] Twenty-five years later there were 230 women serving as lawmakers in the states.[56] The highest proportions were attained in Arizona, New Jersey, New Mexico, and Utah, but the greatest numbers were found in Connecticut and New Hampshire, in each of whose large legislative assemblies there were nearly twenty women.

American women who have served in the state lawmaking bodies have on the whole been well qualified. Miss Sumner found that the early Colorado women legislators "averaged above the men members as a whole in intelligence, but none of them could be classed with the most able of the men.[57] Over 80 per cent of the early

---

[52] Sumner, *op. cit.*, p. 131, and Secretary of State of Colorado, *Abstract of Votes Cast.*

[53] In Texas in 1924 and 1928, and in Wyoming in 1924.

[54] Sumner, *op. cit.*, p. 130.

[55] Breckinridge, *op. cit.*, p. 323. Figures compiled by the League of Women Voters and by American Legislator's Association differ slightly from these.

[56] *The Washington Post*, September 12, 1946.

[57] Sumner, *op cit.*, p. 130. Miss Sumner stated baldly that "a man of very doubtful honesty may be nominated and elected, but not a woman." P. 92. Along the same line A. Laurence Lewis said: "Since the extension of the franchise to women, political parties have learned the inadvisability of nominating for public offices drunkards, notorious libertines, gamblers, retail liquor dealers, and men who engaged in similar discredited occupations." *Outlook*, Vol. 91 (April 3, 1909), p. 782.

This pious hope has not been borne out by subsequent events. In one of the Far Western states an adventuress was elected as a state representative from a tenderloin district of an urban community. This woman could not be beaten in her own district, and she boasted about her ability to blackmail certain legislators and state administrative officers. (Manuscript Document). The election of an adventuress to the state legislature in a Middle Western state was also brought to the attention of the author. While it is well known that sirens have played a role in politics down through the ages, it was not expected by the suffragists that they would turn up in legislatures.

women legislators had had college or university training.[58] An investigation made after ten years of experience with equal suffrage in the nation as a whole found that "nearly two thirds of the women elected since 1920 have been identified with women's organizations in their communities and states," and "that over three fourths of them showed a special interest in that which is generally called women's legislation." [59] A fair proportion of the women lawmakers had enjoyed previous experience in public affairs.

Women have also been successful in winning important state-wide elective positions in a number of commonwealths. Only in Oklahoma are women still fighting for the constitutional right to run for governor, lieutenant governor, secretary of state, state auditor, attorney general, state treasurer, superintendent of public instruction, and state examiner.[60] In one state or another women have been elected to all these positions, excepting attorney general. Of the two women who have been elected to gubernatorial office, Mrs. Nellie Tayloe Ross of Wyoming (1924) and Mrs. Miriam Ferguson of Texas (1924 and 1932), both may be said to have "inherited" their places. Mrs. Ross was nominated by a Democratic convention to fill out the unexpired term of her husband who died in office, and Mrs. Ferguson was selected to fill the place of her husband, a former anti-suffragist, who was disqualified because he had been convicted of misappropriation of state funds during his administration as governor. Mrs. Ferguson's re-election was bitterly contested and she won by a very narrow margin. The women elected to executive posts have in general rendered acceptable service. In New York state, however, a woman secretary of state was convicted of misappropriation of funds.

Twenty-six years after the passage of the woman suffrage amendment there were ten women members of the House of Representa-

---

58 Dorothy A. Moncure, "Women in Political Life," *Current History,* Vol. 29 (January, 1929), p. 641.
59 Breckinridge, *op. cit.,* pp. 330, 331.
60 State election Board, *Directory of the State of Oklahoma,* 1935, p. 135. State Question No. 211, as shown by the records of the Secretary of State: "To amend Section 3, Article 6, of the Constitution of Oklahoma so that women, as well as men, shall be eligible to the office of Governor, Lieutenant Governor, Secretary of State, State Auditor, Attorney General, State Treasurer, Superintendent of Public Instruction, and State Examiner and Inspector." Vote: Yes, 114,968; No, 154,669.

tives (2.3 per cent) and no woman member of the Senate.[61] The one former woman Senator who served any length of time was from the state of Arkansas, which first elected her in 1932 to fill the vacancy caused by the death of her husband. She was re-elected for the full term largely through the efforts of the late Senator Huey P. Long, who campaigned vigorously on her behalf. Of the women members of the House, two have served 12 consecutive terms and are now reaping some of the benefits of the seniority rules. One of these, Mrs. Mary T. Norton, was chairman of the important Labor Committee. A close observer of Washington affairs has said regarding the Congresswomen:[62] "Even though the women don't talk much, they have an excellent record of attendance and miss few roll calls. . . . No members work harder than they do on their committee assignments, and more and more of them are being placed on important committees. They are conscientious and willing to work, facts which their masculine colleagues appreciate and make use of."

In certain European countries women have been more successful in winning positions in the national lawmaking body than they have in the United States. The device of proportional representation has sometimes made it easier for women to win legislative positions. Nearly 8 per cent of the members of the Finnish Parliament of 1929 were women; and this ratio was approximated by the Danzig, Austrian, Dutch, and German parliaments of 1930. Until recently the ratio of women members in the lower houses of the British and Swedish parliaments has been about the same as that found in the American House of Representatives. In Great Britain, the single-member-district system has made it hard for women to secure seats in the House of Commons. In the Swedish lower house 6 per cent are now women.[63]

In Russia the newly emancipated women have made remarkable progress in achieving leadership in spite of a lack of tradition and

---

[61] *Congressional Directory*, 79th Congress, 1st Session, Washington, 1945.

[62] Alice Roosevelt Longworth, "What Are Women Up To?", *Ladies Home Journal*, Vol. 51 (March, 1934), p. 9.

[63] In the House of Commons from 1931 to 1935 there was no woman member from the Labour Party. In the elections of 1935, one woman Labour candidate was returned, although thirty-three women candidates fought under Labour Party auspices. *Report of the 36th Annual Conference of the Labour Party*, Edinburgh, 1936, p. 5. In 1947 there were 24 women in the House of Commons out of 640 members, or about 3.8 per cent. Alice Fraser, "You Are Losing Ground," *Mc Calls*, August, 1947, p. 2.

experience. In the Soviet Parliament in 1945 there were one hundred and eighty-nine women Deputies out of eleven hundred and forty-three, and one third of the local deputies were women.[64]

Appointive Positions Secured

Women were appointed to important public positions before they could vote and run for elective offices. Their success in winning elections for their own candidates, however, has extended their opportunities in the public service. In governmental employment, as in private employment, women have had to fight for equal pay for equal work, and for chances to advance to higher posts. Lack of experience, lack of confidence, and a hostile attitude on the part of men have been among the obstacles which they have had to overcome.[65]

As women gained the suffrage in different American states, their numbers increased gradually in the public services. In Colorado, equal suffrage in the nineties brought "women employment in somewhat greater numbers as clerks and stenographers in public offices, and the equalizing in most public positions of their salaries with those of men doing the same work." [66] In other states women were appointed as factory inspectors, as members of state boards of education, as charity commissioners, as health commissioners, as librarians, and as other state officers or employees long before 1920. After that date, women strengthened their hold upon clerical, social service, and library positions, and they won, in addition, the headships of some important state departments. In North Carolina there was a woman commissioner of public welfare in 1921; in Pennsylvania, a woman occupied a similar post in 1923; and in New York, a woman was made chairman of the State Industrial Board in 1926.

One of the by-products of woman suffrage in the United States has been the appearance of women precinct election officials in all parts of the country. In some communities women have displaced men entirely as election officials. There is no question that the

---

[64] Embassy of the Union of Soviet Socialist Republics, *Information Bulletin,* March 7, 1946.

[65] For an account of growth of positions available to women in the British public service, existing disabilities, and future prospects see *Women Servants of the State* by Hilda Martindale, London, 1938.

[66] Sumner, *op. cit.,* p. 178.

presence of women on precinct election boards has improved the atmosphere of polling places and increased the efficiency of election administration. Women election officials are far less likely to be involved in election frauds than men. At any rate, the records of the Cook County Court, of Illinois, show that for the twelve-year period from 1922 to 1934 there were 256 men and only 44 women convicted of violating the election laws, although the women outnumbered the men as judges and clerks of election.[67] The honest and efficient service rendered by women as precinct election officials has led to the appointment of women election commissioners in some jurisdictions.

Women were first employed by the American Federal government some seventy-five years ago when they obtained a few clerical positions. After 1883 the Civil Service Act opened a number of opportunities to them in spite of the fact that many of the examinations were given to male applicants only. Just prior to the coming of woman suffrage, the newly established Women's Bureau made a report which led to the liberalizing of the civil service examination rules so far as women were concerned. Since 1920 women have continued to struggle against discrimination in the Federal service. The Federal Reclassification Act of 1923 marked some distinct steps forward in the direction of equal pay for equal service.[68] In 1945, over one third (38 per cent) of all Federal employees, and over one half of those in the District of Columbia (60 per cent) were women.[69]

In addition to the positions secured under the civil service rules, women have been placed in positions of responsibility by presidential appointment. In the years immediately preceding their enfranchisement, they held such positions as chief of the Children's Bureau, member of the Industrial Commission, member of the United States Employees' Compensation Commission, assistant attorney general, chief of the Women's Bureau, judge of the Juvenile Court, commissioner of the District of Columbia, and Civil Service Commis-

---

[67] Compiled from the records of the Board of Election Commissioners of Chicago, and from H. M. Robertson (Editor), *Partial Record of the Conduct of Elections in Chicago and Cook County, December, 1922 to June, 1934*, pp. 47-80.

[68] Breckinridge, *op. cit.*, p. 727.

[69] Monthly Report of Employment, Executive Branch of the Federal Government, July, 1945. (Prepared by Statistical Division of the United States Civil Service Commission.)

sioner. After securing the vote, women were appointed to a number of additional posts in the Federal government, including such offices as assistant district attorney, municipal judge for the District of Columbia, consular agent, collector of customs, collector of internal revenue, trade commissioner, division head in the State Department, judge of the Customs Court, member of the Board of Tax Appeals, judge of the Circuit Court of Appeals, ambassador, member of the Social Security Board, and member of the cabinet. During the first decade of woman suffrage the proportion of women postmasters increased from a little more than one tenth to nearly a fifth.

The adoption of woman suffrage did not bring about all the changes hoped for by its advocates. It failed to purify politics, to bring equal rights, and to achieve equal opportunities for men and women. But it did raise the level of politics, bring women a little closer to the ideal of equal rights, and open many new opportunities to women. As women achieve equality in education, their influence on politics will be felt more and more. When one considers the legal and economic position of women a hundred years ago, no one can deny that political agitation and participation has accomplished astounding results.

Chapter 5

THE BALLOT AND DIVERGENT NATIONAL ORIGINS

THE DOCTRINE of democratic equality implies that each of the inhabitants of a given territory should possess an equal opportunity to choose the rulers over that territory upon fulfilling the usual requirements of age and residence. A closer examination of this thesis reveals a number of borderline questions. Suppose there are important differences among the inhabitants as to culture and national origins. Will each of the different groups have the same voice in political affairs? If the rule of the majority is followed, it might involve the persecution of nationalistic minorities. A majority composed of a given group which was bound together by ties of common language, history, and social background might be intolerant of minorities which had different language habits and social customs. The inhabitants of a given territory may be of divergent national origins because of conquest or because of voluntary migration. Each of these situations presents some special problems.

A conquered minority whose culture pattern differs from that of the conquering majority may present a serious problem of political assimilation. Thus the partition of Poland at the end of the eighteenth century did not destroy Polish nationalism. The Poles in Germany, in Austria-Hungary, and in Russia constituted an indigestible mass. What role should such an element have in the democratic process? It happened that none of these countries was democratic in the fullest sense of the term. It is clear, however, that an irreconcilable minority can interfere with the successful operation of a democratic political system or of any other. The British discovered this in their attempts to govern Ireland; the solution of the problem was Irish independence.

The democratic principle of equality implies the right of self-determination of national boundaries. This principle is extremely

78

hard to apply under certain circumstances. When peoples of different national origin have been well intermingled, a majority decision by means of a plebiscite does not solve the problem of self-determination. The minorities may be dissatisfied with the result of the plebiscite and keep up agitation for a change. But these are questions of international law and politics, and are not directly related to the suffrage provisions within a given state.

When differences in national origins are the result of voluntary migration, the problems of equal participation are internal ones and therefore directly related to the suffrage. Here the question is: How soon shall the foreign-born be admitted into the political process?

Modern times are characterized by high mobility of population. People do not so generally spend their entire lives in a single locality. This is especially true of the industrial democracies. As a consequence, large numbers of immigrants constitute a problem in many democracies. Shall they be granted, immediately upon entering the country, the right to vote provided they fulfill all other requirements? No democratic nation now believes so. The reasons for a delay are more than merely the reasons behind residence requirements, although there are similarities. For citizenship requirements are expected to limit the electorate to persons possessing common fundamental values.

There are three general ways in which citizenship may be acquired in modern states: by birth within the territory of a state, by birth of parents who are citizens of a state, and by naturalization. In a discussion of how the privilege of voting may be gained, the first two methods of acquiring citizenship do not concern us. On the other hand, the requirements for naturalization are also in effect requirements for the exercise of the suffrage. The extent of human migration in modern times makes the question of acquired citizenship an important one. What are the characteristics of aliens that may unfit them to act as voters? What period of probation must they go through before they are admitted into the full rights of citizenship?

Since citizenship involves the status of an individual with reference to a particular state, it is a matter to be determined by the law of that state. While naturalization laws vary widely in details, most of them contain certain essentials in one form or other. The foreign-born person must reside for a given period of years, usually five, in the country in which he seeks citizenship. He must produce witnesses as to his good moral character, and he must take an oath of allegiance to his new fatherland. In France before 1940 the period of residence was only three years, and in special cases only one, but in Belgium it was ten years.[1]

The minimum residence period for naturalization in the United States is five years and three months. Prior to the passage of the comprehensive Naturalization Act of 1906, which centralized administration in the Federal Bureau of Naturalization and Immigration, naturalization was left for the most part to the states, and many grave abuses arose. It is likely that many persons naturalized before 1906 did not fulfill even the minimum residence qualification. Gavit has collected figures which show the great increase of naturalization around election time during this period.[2] For the past forty years, however, naturalization has been carefully regulated, and on the average it takes a person about ten years to complete the process. This means that the foreign-born voters have time to learn the English language and something about American political institutions.

In the United States, 36 per cent of both the foreign-born males and females were aliens in 1940, but a much larger proportion of non-naturalized males than of non-naturalized females had their first papers.[3] Ever since the passage of the Cable Act in 1922, the ratio of foreign-born women naturalized has tended to fall lower than that of foreign-born men. It is clear that a majority of the aliens who have taken no steps to become citizens are women who must now take out their own papers even though they marry citizens.

A further analysis of the census figures shows that non-naturalization is most prevalent among immigrants from certain European countries. Two thirds or more of the Irish, Swedish, Norwegian, and German immigrants were naturalized, as compared with one half of Polish, Italian, and Hungarian. These figures have been

---

[1] R. W. Flournoy and M. O. Hudson, *A Collection of Nationality Laws of Various Countries as Contained in Constitutions, Statutes, and Treaties,* New York, 1929, p. 31.

[2] J. P. Gavit, *Citizens by Choice,* New York, 1922.

[3] Of the adult male aliens, approximately 38 per cent are declarants. Of the adult female aliens, only 18 per cent are declarants. For original figures, see Seventeenth Census of United States, 1940, Vol. III, *Characteristics of Population by Age,* Part I.

interpreted by some uncritical persons as giving evidence of a causal relationship between birth in southeastern Europe and non-naturalization. The naturalization figures, however, show that the variations are largely the result of the fact of longer residence in this country. A relatively small proportion of Polish and Italian immigrants were naturalized in 1940 because these groups have been in the country for a shorter time than most other immigrants. On the other hand, it is likely that the restriction of immigration that followed World War I was in part the result of the antipathies expressed toward the immigrants from southeastern Europe.

The requirement of citizenship for voting in the United States has disfranchised a large number of adult persons, particularly women of Polish, Russian, and Italian birth. Some years ago the present writer made a study of naturalization and non-naturalization in the city of Chicago.[4] Since the adult foreign-born persons in the city constituted 5.6 per cent of the total adult foreign-born persons in the United States, the findings of the Chicago study show something about the processes which are going on. A comparison of the characteristics of the group of naturalized and non-naturalized adults in Chicago brought out the fact that newness to the country, extreme youth, bachelorhood, lack of family cares and responsibilities, lack of schooling, and lack of knowledge regarding American political institutions were all variables more or less closely related to non-naturalization. These influences may be regarded as important in the political process, particularly ignorance of the English language and ignorance of American political methods.

In general, the survey showed that ignorance was the greatest single cause of non-naturalization. Most of the non-declarants were ignorant of political affairs, the English language, or the provisions of the naturalization laws. In some cases this ignorance is excusable, as it was associated with short residence in this country. In other cases it was due to neglect. While there are some aliens who feel that the requirements for naturalization are too difficult, there are others who will not forswear allegiance to their old country. Yet

---

[4] H. F. Gosnell, "Non-naturalization: A Study in Political Assimilation," *American Journal of Sociology*, Vol. 33 (May, 1928), pp. 930-939; "Characteristics of Non-naturalization," *ibid.*, Vol. 34 (March, 1929), pp. 847-855. Unpublished materials in the possession of the writer.

in the main, the non-declarants represent a group that is gradually being diminished by time.

The naturalization process keeps some persons from becoming voters because they fail to fulfill all the requirements. The application of the rules laid down in the naturalization law is of importance because it indicates what kind of persons are kept from becoming voters. In the United States, admission of an alien to citizenship is regarded as a judicial matter, although in some European countries it is made an administrative matter. Each American case is decided according to its merits. The courts apply the principles to the individual aliens coming before them. The Bureau of Naturalization represents the executive arm of the government before the Courts which act on these cases, partly as prosecutors of those who seek to avoid the law and partly as counselor for those who are legally entitled and eager to proceed according to the law.

An examination of a select group of foreign-born persons in Chicago showed that ignorance of the English language, timidity, and inertia were the chief reasons for failing to complete the naturalization process. The records of the naturalization office also indicated that misconduct, including false statements, and offenses involving moral turpitude, defective witnesses, and unwillingness to accept naturalization in the army were also grounds for turning down applications for citizenship. The courts canceled naturalization certificates of persons not attached to the principles of the Constitution.[5]

An examination of the characteristics of the non-naturalized indicates clearly that there are fairly valid grounds for excluding this element from the electorate. At one time, on the other hand, there were as many as seventeen states in the American Union which permitted persons who had taken out first papers to vote. This liberal suffrage provision was adopted in order to attract foreign-born persons to sparsely settled states in the Middle West. It had the definite effect of slowing up the naturalization process in those states.[6] As the western states became more populous, and as the character of the immigrants began to change in the United States, one commonwealth after another abandoned the liberal provisions regarding alien

---

[5] L. Gettys, *The Law of Citizenship in the United States,* Chicago, 1934.
[6] Gavit, *op. cit.,* p. 217.

voting. A person could take out first papers as soon as he established residence in the United States, and there was no assurance whatever that he would complete the naturalization process. The first World War greatly hastened the abandonment of alien suffrage. During the twenties and thirties there was fear of foreign radicalism and other so-called undesirable elements. As a result, at the present time not one of the American states retains the alien suffrage provision.

The military exigencies in the position of other countries have not permitted them to allow such lenient provisions regarding foreign-born persons. Except in the Soviet Union, it is likely that citizenship will remain the qualification of participation in political affairs.

A frontier state that desires to attract foreigners and foreign capital to its territory may waive the citizenship requirements for voting. The American frontier has vanished, but Argentina and Chile allow foreigners to vote under certain conditions. In Chile, aliens of five years' residence may vote in local elections. In the unusual Australian case, British subjects are entitled to vote although they may have only recently entered the country, provided they fulfill the residence requirements.

Participation in Elections

American immigrants never agitated for the suffrage as a group. The frontier states which wanted to increase their population offered the ballot as an inducement for foreigners to settle within their borders. While political conditions may have spurred some Europeans to migrate to the United States, it is probable that economic and social considerations were paramount. The immigrants who sought new opportunities had to weigh in the balance the sentimental attachments they had to the country of their birth. Under the modern state system, patriotism is instilled at an early stage of the individual's development. The shift from one national loyalty to another is a wrenching process. Participation in the political life of the new fatherland may not come naturally to some. This is especially true of the foreign-born women who were conditioned to an inactive political role in their native lands.

Before the electorate was enlarged to include women, the available evidence indicates that the participation of the foreign-born in

American elections was just as high as that of the natives.[7] It was natural that the men who had gone to the trouble to complete the naturalization process would take advantage of one of their newly acquired privileges. After the adoption of woman suffrage, the voting record of the foreign-born was slightly lower than that of the natives, largely because of the indifference of many foreign-born women. The Polish, Italian, and other newer immigrant women had the lowest records of the foreign-born women. On the other hand, the Czech women in one part of a metropolitan center showed more interest in voting than did the native white women.

Party Affiliations and National Origins

The political affiliations of persons of different national origins are closely linked with the constitutional history of the countries concerned. In Great Britain, until the formation of the Irish Free State in 1921, the Irish Nationalist Party was a thorn in the flesh of the body politic. In the German Empire from 1870 to 1918, there was a Polish party which represented the nationalistic ambitions of the people living in the areas that were once part of an independent Poland, and in Austria-Hungary, prior to the revolution of 1918, there were Polish, Czech, Hungarian, German, and Serbian political parties. After the Versailles treaty, Germany no longer had the province of Posen, and as a result there was no Polish party. The situation in the states carved out of Austria-Hungary was not so simple. In Czechoslovakia there were Czech, Slovak, and German political parties which persisted right up until the conquest of the country by Germany.

In general it might be said that, where a people living in a given area which has fairly clearly defined boundaries have once enjoyed political independence, they are not likely to be quickly assimilated into the political system of a conquering neighbor. If the conqueror permits freedom of association and allows the conquered to participate in the political process, then the conqueror must expect a nationalistic party. Unless the conquered peoples are moved bodily from the soil, the nationalistic parties are likely to persist. The Fascist

[7] H. F. Gosnell, *Getting Out the Vote*, Chicago, 1927, p. 115; B. A. Arneson, "Non-Voting in a Typical Ohio Community," *American Political Science Review*, Vol. 19 (1925), pp. 816-825.

method for solving problems arising out of differences in national origins was forced mass migrations accompanied by wholesale executions and starvation. The assumptions of democracy call for plebiscites, full compensation for all voluntary removals, and toleration of minorities left behind.

The United States is a new country, and the immigrants who came from different countries were scattered widely. At the time when the Constitution was put into effect, the American people were largely of English Protestant stock. During the next century and a quarter, immigrants of other origins flocked to America. It was inevitable that they would have an impact upon the political institutions, but they never furnished the basis for nationalistic parties. The immigrant heritages were usually stripped away, and the immigrant found it natural to join one of the pre-existing American political parties. These immigrants had an effect upon the composition of the major parties, but they brought about no fundamental change in the system itself. As a group they showed no one single political tendency. They divided among the various parties on the basis of economic, religious, and social considerations.

Thomas Jefferson was the first political leader to make a calculated bid for the ballots of the foreign-born. In his campaign for the presidency in 1800, he attracted the Irish immigrants because of his opposition to the Alien and Sedition Act, his plea for religious toleration, and his obvious sympathy for the lower income groups.

This early affiliation of the Irish with the Democratic Party proved to be a lasting union and one of considerable importance to the party. The Irish were predominantly Catholic and also intensely nationalistic. This meant that they soon became a cohesive force in American politics, a bloc of voters which could be attracted by the party which on domestic issues did not interfere with the parochial schools, and which in its foreign relations lent a sympathetic ear to the demands of the Irish nationalists. Throughout the first hundred and fifty years of the American republic, the Democratic Party was the political grouping which fulfilled these conditions.

After the Irish, the Germans were the next immigrant group to throng to America in large numbers. The German immigrants were less united in their religious beliefs and their political aspirations than were the Irish. Almost two thirds of the German immigrants were Lutherans, one third were Catholics, and there was a sprinkling of freethinkers, including some who had a Marxian antireligious background. Politically, the German immigrants were disunited; they included conservatives, liberals, clericals, and socialists. Out of such diversity no central political tendency developed among the German-American elements. The German Catholics tended to join the Democratic Party for the same reasons that the Irish joined it. In the fifties the German farmers in the Middle West joined the newly formed Republican Party since they were interested in homesteads and opposed to the extension of slavery. After the Civil War they continued to support the Republican Party although they were opposed to the corruption of the Grant administration and were not in sympathy with the dry stand taken by some Republican candidates.

In the twentieth century the Democratic presidents took positions in international politics which tended to strengthen the Republicanism of the German-American elements. Both Woodrow Wilson and Franklin Delano Roosevelt opposed German aggression in Europe and led the country in wars against Germany. The German aliens became enemy aliens, and their position in the United States was made most uncomfortable. In the election of 1920 the German-Americans registered their displeasure at the Wilson peace policies by voting for Harding, the Republican candidate. Similarly, in 1940 and 1942 some of the German-American elements were dissatisfied with the foreign policy of the Roosevelt administration and voted for Republican candidates.

After the peak of the German immigration, the southern and eastern European immigrants were the most numerous. Of Italian or Slavic origin, these new groups settled in the cities rather than on the farms, and their politics, like that of the Irish, tended to be Democratic. Their attachment to the Catholic Church, their national aspirations, and their need for the kind of guidance which the local Democratic machines were willing to furnish, reinforced their attachment to the Democratic Party. There were many influences, however, which attracted a considerable number of the Polish and Italian immigrants to the Republican Party. In areas where trade-unionism was backward and pressures from the employer were strong, the workers might be forced to support Republican candidates. During the twenties, in cities where the Republican party machines were strong, as in Chicago, Philadelphia, Pittsburgh, and Detroit, the Italians were attracted by the special privileges which they could enjoy by being on the winning side — jobs, protection as bootleggers, rewards on election day, and recognition on the party ticket.

The thirties brought fundamental changes in the political situation. Hard times, a reaction against the prohibition laws, a feeling of disappointment in the non-action policies of President Hoover, and a new political personality swept the Republicans from power in most of their old strongholds, including Pennsylvania.[8] Under President Franklin D. Roosevelt the trade-unions were built up to a point they had never before achieved in American history. Against this tide the Republicanism of the Italian and Polish immigrants afforded little opposition. An illuminating study made in Detroit revealed that the foreign-born voters showed a constantly increasing tendency to vote Democratic during the thirties.[9] The difference between the politics of the native and foreign-born elements was ever increasing until after Pearl Harbor, when the German- and Italian-Americans showed signs of disaffection.[10] Voters of foreign origin tended to support President Roosevelt and the New Deal because of the attitude of this regime on labor questions, on religious minorities, on relief policies, and on social questions. A combination of trade-unionism, liberal relief policies, Catholicism, and in the case of the Poles, interventionism, cemented the foreign-born to the Democratic Party.

Recognition of the Foreign-Born in Politics

Since all whites in the United States can trace their origin to European white stocks, there were no insuperable obstacles to the rapid political assimilation of the foreign-born. The rate of Americanization depended upon such factors as language habits, religious beliefs, economic status, and occupational skills. In general, the less time consumed by the immigrant group in making a language adjustment, the closer its religious beliefs were to those prevailing in the

---

[8] H. F. Gosnell, *Grass Roots Politics,* Washington, D. C., 1942, Ch. 3.
[9] Edward H. Litchfield, *Voting Behavior in a Metropolitan Area,* Ann Arbor, 1941.
[10] L. H. Bean, F. Mosteller, and F. Williams, "Nationalities and 1944," *Public Opinion Quarterly,* Vol. 8 (1944), pp. 368-375.

community, and the higher its economic status, the more rapid was its political assimilation and subsequent political recognition. This situation gave advantages to the English, the Irish, the Scandinavians, and the Germans. It retarded the recognition of the Italians, the Russians, and the Poles. These latter groups, however, found that they could overcome the initial disadvantages. English could be learned, the United States had become less Protestant by the very process of immigration, and there were economic opportunities for the energetic, regardless of national origins.

A few examples will illustrate the process. The Irish immigrants achieved recognition at an early stage in American history. The first governors of several States were Irish Americans, and the success of the Irish in municipal politics was outstanding.[11] The fact that most of the Irish Americans were Roman Catholics was a retarding factor in their recognition in the politics of some states. With the lapse of time, however, this characteristic became an asset, particularly in the largest cities. In 1928 for the first time in American history an Irish Catholic was nominated for President by one of the major parties. If Governor Alfred E. Smith had been nominated in 1932 instead, there is little question that he would have been elected. It may thus be said that there is no bar to the Irish achieving the highest political honors in the United States.

Since the German and Scandinavian immigrants were largely Protestant, thrifty, skilled, and relatively literate, they were soon on an even footing in politics with the English stocks. Of German origin were such outstanding political leaders as Gustav Koerner and Carl Schurz. German Americans have achieved the highest posts in municipal, state, and national politics, and they have enjoyed the reputation of being in the forefront in civic reforms. The Scandinavian Americans can also point to members of their group who have been governors, senators, or representatives. Such names as Lenroot, Lindbergh, Olson, and Stassen are familiar in American politics.

The Italian and Slavic immigrants have found the achievement of political recognition a slower process than have the older immigrant groups. Though language difficulties, greater illiteracy, a peas-

---

[11] F. J. Brown and J. S. Roucek (Editors), *Our Racial and National Minorities,* New York, 1937.

ant background, and greater religious differences have contributed to the retardation of full participation in the political life of America, these hindrances are gradually being overcome in municipal and state politics and in some parts of national affairs. Mayor La-Guardia of New York was of Italian origin, Mayor Cermak of Chicago of Czech origin, and Judge Jarecki of Cook County, Illinois, of Polish origin. These men and others in Congress have shown that birth in eastern or southern Europe cannot prevent a man from succeeding in American politics.

Unlike race or sex, foreign white ancestry is not an insurmountable obstacle to the highest positions in American politics. There have been no presidents of Italian or Polish origins, but who can say what will happen in the United States during the next fifty or seventy-five years? In some of the South American countries, foreign ancestry is sometimes an asset in politics. This is now true of the larger North American cities which have become the new or industrial frontier.

Democratic doctrines call for recognition of the equality of man regardless of his nationalistic origins or cultural beginnings. Most of the so-called democracies have created certain barriers in the way of the participation and recognition of the foreign-born in politics. Time can overcome most of these barriers where there are not marked physical differences.

Chapter 6

THE NEGRO VOTES

In countries with a democratic form of government, but in which there are widespread beliefs regarding so-called "racial" differences, the logical application of the democratic principle of equality presents many difficulties. The existence of such beliefs arising out of physical and social differences is contrary to the principles of democracy. To say that one "race" is superior to another is to contradict the democratic ideology. In other words, if one group, which may be easily distinguishable by color of skin or by other physical characteristics, regards itself as "superior," it is difficult to solve questions involving race relations by the ritual of voting. The idea of "one man, one vote" regardless of his color or ancestry is repugnant to a cultural group which regards an outgroup as inferior.

No attempt will be made here to expound the causes of racial intolerance.[1] What can be done is to show how beliefs in racial differences made a complete extension of equal suffrage rights throughout the whole population a difficult and delicate problem. Those factors in racial prejudice which prompt the dominant group to restrict the voting ritual to its own members will bear examination.

One of the essential conditions of successful democratic government is the existence of a will upon the part of the citizens to accept decisions arrived at by electoral and representative processes. If there is a field of human affairs which is held to be beyond the power of the regularly constituted governmental authorities, then it is difficult to apply the democratic machinery. In South Africa, the southern States of the United States, and in Australia, the dogma of white supremacy is something which cannot be challenged suddenly by the ordinary legislative processes without social upheaval. In

---

[1] A most exhaustive work on the subject is G. Myrdal, *An American Dilemma: The Negro and Democracy,* New York, 1944, 2 vols.

other words, there is no will to accept a democratic decision which threatens the beliefs in the superiority of the white people.

The question as to the erasure of racial distinctions in the suffrage strikes immediately at deep-seated taboos. The vote as a token of equality between races is rejected by the dominant group. Economic differences, variations as to national origins, and sex differences may be overlooked in extending the suffrage, but racial differences are not so easily brushed aside. With reference to property qualifications, it might be said that the popular mind looks upon them as "quantitative" in character. A man may not have property today, but he may have tomorrow. There are all gradations of property, and it is easy to say with Thomas Paine, "When a broodmare shall fortunately produce a foal or a mule, that, by being worth the sum in question, shall convey to the owner the right of voting . . . in whom does the origin of such a right exist? Is it in the man or in the mule?" [2] Thus the property qualification can be made to look ridiculous. On the other hand, the apologists for the supremacy of one race over another are quite serious about the alleged inferiority of the less fortunately placed racial group. Some of these apologists go so far as to claim that the less privileged group is subhuman.[3]

When a primitive culture group is easily distinguished by color of skin and other characteristics from a culture group with a more advanced technology, racial discriminations are likely to arise. One of the forms of discrimination is exclusion from participation in political life. When Negroes first came in contact with white groups, they found themselves at a disadvantage because of their more primitive culture patterns. The white groups in many places have persisted in exploiting this situation regardless of democratic pronouncements and vast changes in the educational status of the Negroes.

If the white population faces overwhelming numbers of Negroes, the color line is likely to be more strictly drawn. Thus, in the Union of South Africa, where the white population is a small minority, no

---

[2] *Selections from the Writings of Thomas Paine* (National Home Library), Washington, D. C., 1935, p. 171.

[3] W. O. Brown, "Rationalization of Race Prejudice," *The International Journal of Ethics* (April, 1933), pp. 299-301; L. C. Copeland, "The Negro as a Contrast Conception," in Edgar T. Thompson (editor), *Race Relations and the Race Problem*, 1939, pp. 152-179; and Myrdal, *op. cit.*, pp. 103, 104.

attempt is made to conceal the bitter race prejudices of the English and the Dutch against the natives. Only a small and diminishing group appears on behalf of native suffrage. Before the Union was formed in 1909, the Cape of Good Hope had been attacking the problem of the colored races with greater tolerance and tact than the nearby provinces. One of the reasons for this was the larger proportion of white people living in this province than in the others. In the provinces with heavy native populations, the Transvaal and the Orange Free State, the franchise was confined solely to whites. The Union of South Africa Act imposed qualifications of literacy, property, and residence upon any black or colored person who wished to vote in Cape Province.

In spite of the stringent exclusion, there was considerable agitation against those few colored persons who did vote, and the result was the Representation of Natives Act of 1936. This created a separate native franchise, an advisory Native Representative Council, an elected white senator from each of the four provinces, and, in Cape Province, three white representatives to the House of Assembly and two to the Provincial Council, all to give voice to native wishes. This act left the influence of the Cape natives greater than that of the natives in the other provinces, but it was not regarded as a net gain. There was still a bar to the election of Negro legislators.

The aggravation of the anti-native sentiment in South Africa may be traced to the increase in the number of poor whites, *bywoners,* the granting of the franchise to this group in 1931, and the increasing organization of native protest groups. The economic lot of the poor whites was a hard one, but instead of turning to economic reforms they sought refuge in race intolerance. Where there are beliefs in racial differences, those farthest down in the economic scale are likely to hold them most tightly.[4] As one commentator put it, "South African political circles, therefore, are in fact predominantly concerned about the Native Problem, not as a fundamental issue of economics and land, but rather because in the old Cape Colony something fewer than fifteen thousand blacks still have votes to balance about 900,000 Europeans."[5]

---

[4] Myrdal, *op. cit.,* pp. 67-75.
[5] W. M. Macmillan in *The Spectator,* Vol. 150 (May, 1933), p. 150.

In the United States the conflict between the democratic ideology and the dogma of white supremacy has existed down to the present. In this country all noticeable mixtures of white and colored strains are regarded as colored. In his battle to achieve suffrage rights, the American Negro has handicaps that did not confront the foreign-born groups. He started farther down as a slave.

According to the Constitution of the United States, a Negro slave was counted as three fifths of a person for purposes of apportioning representatives in Congress among the various states. In other words, a slave was regarded as a being that was not quite a man. Standing between the slaves and free white persons were the free Negroes, who were "free" but did not have the full rights of citizenship. Before the Civil War, all Negroes were deprived of any voice in elections, except for a scattered number of free Negroes in the New England States.[6] All the northern states outside of New England barred even free Negroes from participating in elections by the insertion of the word "white" in the qualifications for voting.

During the slave period, the political influence of the Negroes was at a low ebb, but it was not absent. The white planter class lived in fear that some of the Negroes might become revolutionary on the model of those in the West Indies. The history of the successful, ruthless, violent revolutions in Santo Domingo and Haiti struck terror into the hearts of the Southerners. These misgivings were greatly heightened by Negro insurrections in the United States, particularly the one threatened by Denmark Vesey in 1822, and the one initiated by Nat Turner in 1831. The memory of the killing of fifty-four white persons by Turner and his followers became part of the tradition of the South, and so strengthened the view that the Negro must be kept in his place.

The repression which followed the insurrections did not prevent some slaves from escaping to the northern states and becoming abolitionist and suffragist orators. Notable among these was the mulatto, Frederick Douglass, who escaped from Maryland when he was twenty-one years of age and became an agent for a Massachusetts

---

[6] E. Olbrich, *The Development of Sentiment on Negro Suffrage to 1860,* Madison, 1912; C. P. Patterson, *The Negro in Tennessee;* G. Y. Stephenson, *Race Distinctions in American Law,* New York, 1910; K. H. Porter, *History of Suffrage in the United States,* Chicago, 1918.

Antislavery Society.[7] He attracted the attention of William Lloyd Garrison and other abolitionists because of his abilities as a speaker. Despite many difficulties, he spoke in various parts of the United States and in England.

Even though Douglass and other Negroes were active on behalf of the cause of emancipation and enfranchisement, it cannot be said that the Negroes won freedom and the suffrage by their own efforts. Emancipation was a military measure designed to win the war, and the suffrage amendment was a political device by means of which the newly formed Republican Party hoped to win elections.

It was immediately clear that the exercise of the suffrage by a group which had been deprived of educational opportunities, which enjoyed no economic independence, and which had not developed the necessary organization to protect its position in the democratic state, could not be sustained without outside support. When the Federal troops withdrew from the South in 1877, it was not long before the whites, who had formerly occupied the dominant economic, social, and political position in the region, asserted themselves. The new Negro voters were deprived of the franchise in spite of the Fifteenth Amendment to the United States Constitution which stated: "The right of citizens of the United States to vote shall not be denied or abridged by the United States or by any State on account of race, color, or previous condition of servitude."

The southern whites regarded Negro suffrage as an intolerable punishment for losing the war. Their dismay at what happened is illustrated by the following extract which is typical of contemporary accounts: "The maddest, most unscrupulous and infamous revolution in history has snatched the power from the hands of the race which settled the country—and transferred it to its former slaves, an ignorant and feeble race." [8]

The experience with Negro suffrage in the southern American States during the Reconstruction Period may be viewed as a testing ground for certain democratic devices. In the literature on the Reconstruction Period, a great mass of material has been collected

---

[7] F. Douglass, *Life and Times of Frederick Douglass*, Hartford, 1882, p. 216; B. T. Washington, *Frederick Douglass*, Philadelphia, 1907.

[8] *Charleston News*, June 12 and 15, 1868, cited by F. B. Simkins and R. H. Woody, *South Carolina During Reconstruction*, Chapel Hill, 1932, p. 110.

to show that the trial of democracy under the unfavorable conditions prevailing in the South after the Civil War was not a success, materially or psychologically. Volumes of evidence have been accumulated to demonstrate the corruption and inefficiency of the governments founded on Negro suffrage.[9] On the other hand, some scholars have observed that the disfranchisement which followed Reconstruction was contrary to the tenets of American democracy.[10]

Southern scholars have begun to take a newer view of the period.[11] The Negroes were never in a majority, and those who were elected to public office were for the most part educated in the North. The carpetbaggers were agents of the Federal Government who were trying to help the South to its feet, and the scalawags were mainly poor whites who saw a chance to effect something of a revolution against the wealthy aristocrats. Graft and inefficiency were present, but these failings were not confined to the South during this period.

Once the pressure of the Federal troops was gone, the Southern whites employed the harsh political methods that are used by a dominant culture group to subordinate a group that is regarded as inferior. Force in the form of tar and feathers, whipping, other forms of torture, and killing, was applied vigorously. In addition, all types of fraud were employed: gerrymandering, inadequate voting facilities, dilatory tactics, withholding of returns, fraudulent election counts, ballot box stuffing, padded lists, and discriminatory enforcement of the election regulations. Social pressure, such as business ostracism, unofficial banishment, and segregation, was used to keep the Negroes from the polls. Finally, bribery in all its forms was employed. Colored voters were paid to stay at home, or, where a poll tax receipt was necessary in order to vote, these receipts were used as admission fees to circuses and other entertainments. With their lack of organization, leadership, education, and economic independence, the Negroes could not withstand these pressures. They were eliminated as effective elements in the electoral process of the Southern States.

---

[9] C. G. Bowers, *The Tragic Era*, Cambridge, 1929; R. L. Norton, *The Negro in Virginia Politics 1865-1902*, Charlottesville, 1919; F. A. Bancroft, *A Sketch of the Negro in Politics*, New York, 1885.
[10] Myrdal, *op. cit.*, pp. 441-445.
[11] Simkins and Woody, *op. cit.*

Beginning with the nineties, the Southern States attempted to legalize the disfranchisement of the Negro voters. Various constitutional devices were adopted to make it difficult or impossible for colored persons to register and qualify as voters. Literacy tests, poll tax qualifications, technical requirements for registration, disfranchisement of all persons convicted of petty crimes, and unusual residential requirements were among the legal devices employed. The constitutional experts of the South also tried to avoid the disfranchisement of illiterate whites by the so-called "grandfather clause" which extended the vote to persons whose ancestors voted before the Civil War. While this particular device was frowned upon by the courts when it was brought up for review,[12] the other devices were held to be legal. The appeal made by the Negroes for protection under the Constitutional guarantees of the Thirteenth, Fourteenth, and Fifteenth Amendments yielded them small comfort.[13] Theoretically, the Federal Government could have passed laws to guarantee the vote to the Negro, but the North decided that it would let the South run its own affairs. In the absence of a Federal "force law," suffrage was a matter which each Southern State could decide for itself.

Perhaps the most effective method used by the Southern States to disfranchise the Negro was the device of the white primary. The Civil War left the former Confederate States so bitter at the Republican Party that only Democratic candidates could make any headway. In a one-party State, the power to nominate is equivalent to the power to elect. In any one of the States in the deep South, the Democratic primary became the real occasion for choosing those who would be in power. By confining the Democratic primaries to white voters, the Negro could be effectively deprived of any choice in political affairs. The State of Texas became so bold as to mention the word "white" in its primary laws. These laws were brought before the United States Supreme Court, and there they were declared unconstitutional.[14] For a while the courts permitted the Texas

---

[12] Guinn vs. United States, 238 U. S., 536 (March, 1927).

[13] Regarding the interpretation of the Ku-Klux Klan Act, see United States vs. Harris, 106 U. S., 629 (1883). On the Fourteenth Amendment see Civil Rights Cases, 109 U. S., 3 (1883).

[14] Nixon vs. Herndon, 273 U. S., 536 (1927); Nixon vs. Condon, 286 U. S., 73 (1932).

Democrats to limit their primaries to whites by party rule, but even this expedient was declared unconstitutional in 1944.[15] This did not mean, however, that Negroes generally were permitted to participate in Democratic primaries. The Southern States might still use the various devices that were employed to prevent the registration and voting of Negroes in general elections.

The disfranchisement of a racial minority in the Southern States furnished valuable material regarding the effects of exclusion from the electoral process. It is difficult to say whether disfranchisement is the result of the Negroes' inferior social and economic status, or whether the Negroes lack social prestige and economic resources because of disfranchisement. The Negro cannot vote because of his social status which "unfits" him for voting, but he cannot improve his status because he does not possess the vote. This is the principle of the vicious circle which is of fundamental importance in understanding the position of the Negro. There can be no question that the Negroes in the South are not in position to claim the full benefits from the State services to which they are entitled by reason of the amount of taxes they pay and the general position they have in the social order. Not only have the Negroes received a smaller share of the public funds, whether for education or for such improvements as sewerage, streets, lights, and paving, but they have also suffered a social humiliation in Jim Crow public carriers and general segregation. Their weak political position has also been in part responsible for their inability to protect themselves against certain types of violence such as race rioting and lynching.[16]

As John Stuart Mill pointed out, a group that wants to vote must be willing and able to do what is necessary to keep the vote.[17] In the latter half of the nineteenth century, the American Negroes were not able to hold the voting rights which had been extended to them. But the situation was not a static one. The disfranchising constitutions placed great emphasis upon literacy tests and the understanding clauses. As Negro education advanced, these provisions presented

---

[15] Smith *vs.* Allwright, 321 U. S., 649 (1944).

[16] The National Association for the Advancement of Colored People, *Thirty Years of Lynching in the United States: 1889-1918,* 1919; Frank Shay, *Judge Lynch,* New York, 1938; Walter White, *Rope and Faggot,* New York, 1929; Arthur Raper, *The Tragedy of Lynching,* Chapel Hill, 1933.

[17] *Representative Government,* London, 1865.

fewer and fewer obstacles in the struggle for suffrage. It became more and more difficult for the white registrars to turn down college-trained Negroes everywhere. There were persistent educated Negroes who rose above obstacles, who appealed to the courts, who threatened an economic boycott, and who voted.[18]

The American Negroes have not lacked in courage and determination to stand up for their rights of citizenship in the face of threats of violence. In the thirties and forties of the twentieth century, the old devices of the nineteenth century did not work. In the city of Miami, Florida, Negroes participated in a 1939 local election in spite of attempts on the part of certain white citizens to intimidate them by reviving the white-hooded disguises and symbols of the Reconstruction days. Prominent among the Negro leaders who led this defiance of the old Ku-Klux Klan tactics were two young men who were willing to risk physical violence to stand up for their rights. This was a skirmish in a long battle for freedom. The results may not have been far reaching, but they represented some gains in political recognition and self-confidence for the group.

The disfranchisement of the Negroes has not been accomplished without unfortunate consequences upon the South itself. So overpowering has been the issue of "white supremacy" that other questions have been pushed to the background. The white Southerners do not dare to split on political, social, and economic questions for fear that the different white factions might appeal to the Negro vote. Disfranchisement has thus become a bogeyman to plague the Solid South. It has undermined respect for law, order, and public morals, and it has perpetuated the one-party system which has deprived the South of its share in the national nominating process, since no presidential candidate is likely to be selected from a section whose vote is counted in advance. It has also lowered the economic level of the South, since no group can be depressed without depressing the whole region.

Since the passage of the Constitutional Amendments following the Civil War, the right of the Negroes to vote in the Northern States of the American Union has never been questioned.

The Northern Negroes constitute a control group for their

---

[18] Myrdal, *op. cit.,* Chapter 22.

brothers in the South and therefore what they do with the suffrage is a matter of great interest. The Negro suffrage question is a dynamic one in American politics. Its solution may not be in sight, but the situation will not remain stationary.

Brazil

When compared with the United States and South Africa, the suffrage situation in Brazil presents many striking contrasts. Most observers agree that there is no attempt to deprive the Negro of the right to vote in Brazil. As a matter of fact, there is little racial antagonism, although there are social barriers that prevent miscegenation between upper-strata whites and lower-strata Negroes. There have never been laws discriminating against Negroes since their emancipation was granted before the Republic was founded.

In Brazil there has never been a life-and-death struggle over a racial question, and there exists little race prejudice of the type that is found in the United States and the Union of South Africa. Racial barriers to the exercise of the suffrage have been lacking, but in practice the mere requirement of residence tends to disfranchise many colored persons in the lower income groups who are in the transient class.

General Considerations Regarding the Battle for Negro Suffrage

Democratic principles are not applied in the case of so-called racial groups where the relations between the races take on the aspects of a caste system. The disfranchisement of Negroes is thus a function of the social order. What are some of the characteristics of this order?

Independence of occupation is a factor which is important in the case of the American Negroes who were slaves before they attained citizenship, and who, as tenant farmers in the Southern States, have yet to achieve real freedom from the soil. In the case of the natives of South Africa, this is not true since they were more independent economically before the whites came and upset their culture patterns.

Both mobility and lack of mobility have been of effect in enforcing racial discriminations in the electoral process. Where a culture group is closely attached to a given community, and where its freedom of movement is impeded either by custom or by law, it is not likely to participate in the democratic process. In Brazil and other parts of South America, the nonparticipation of the Negroes and Indians is related to these conditions. On the other hand, the American Negroes who have the wanderlust and who fail to establish residence in any one place for any length of time effectively disfranchise themselves.

The degree of urbanization is a related factor. While Thomas Jefferson viewed the process of urbanization with apprehension so far as the future of democracy was concerned, it is in the cities that nationalistic and racial barriers to political equality have been overcome. Urban life gives greater economic independence, more educational opportunities, and more cultural contacts for submerged groups. It was in the cities that Negroes of the United States first began to win back the right to vote. It is in the cities that those forums, fraternal clubs, and discussion groups are found which furnish the basis for group life and group demands.

The relative strength of the divergent racial groups is also a consideration of importance. Where the disadvantaged group is a tiny minority, then it may be treated with tolerance by the ruling majority. This is the situation in the Northern States of the American Union where the Negroes are less than 10 per cent of the total population; there they are allowed to vote freely. Where the disadvantaged group approaches or exceeds a majority, however, then it is likely to be held in restraint, as in the Union of South Africa and the Southern American States.

According to the democratic ideal, all persons, regardless of color or other distinguishing characteristics, should have equal suffrage rights. In Brazil, race prejudice is practically nonexistent. Brazil may be less democratic than the United States and the Union of South Africa in some respects, but not in her treatment of citizens of varying physical characteristics.

As in the case of other suffrage disabilities, so in the case of disfranchisement on account of a belief in race, the question may be raised as to what difference the ballot makes. When American Negroes who have been deprived of the vote move to a section where they are permitted to vote, do they show an interest in participating in elections? What are the voting alignments of a submerged group which finally wins the ballot? What does such a racial group accomplish by participation in politics? Is there any tendency for the dominant cultural group to assert its supremacy when the unpopular cultural group acquires some political power and influence? Does a group which is making a transition from a disadvantaged position make use of democratic devices to advance its own interests?

Participation in Elections

The Negroes and the Indians in Brazil are not disfranchised in the Brazilian Constitution, but in practice not a very large proportion of them vote. The economic and social position of the Negroes is such that they do not pay much attention to voting. Their eyes have not been opened to the possibilities of political action.

In the United States the Negroes have advanced so rapidly in literacy and economic resources during the past eighty years that they are well aware of the advantages of political methods.

Election returns in the United States are not kept by racial groups, but the concentration of Negro population in certain areas makes it possible to estimate the proportion of Negro voters and to study their general voting behavior. In the Northern States, Negroes live for the most part in the large cities, where they have been segregated, not as a matter of law but as a matter of fact. Hostile white communities and high-priced housing have constituted the barriers to the general spread of Negro residence in metropolitan centers.

The available election returns and a number of isolated surveys indicate that in general the Northern American Negro shows as much or only slightly less interest in voting than do the whites.[19] The participation is higher in the metropolitan centers than in the smaller towns where the number of Negroes is so small that it fails to furnish the basis for much community life.[20] There are also

---

[19] In a survey made in Chicago in 1924, the author found the ratio of adult Negro citizens voting lower than that for adult white citizens. See his *Getting Out the Vote*, Chicago, 1927. An analysis of the census materials for 1920 and 1930, however, showed that the ratio of adult citizens voting was about the same for Negroes and whites. In fact, it was higher for the Negroes in 1930 than for the whites. If a liberal allowance is made for mobility, the Negro voting ratio looks even better. See his *Negro Politicians*, Chicago, 1935, p. 374.

[20] James K. Pollock, *Voting Behavior: A Case Study*, Ann Arbor, 1939, p. 28; B. A. Arneson, "Non-voting in a Typical Ohio Community," *American Political Science Review*, Vol. 19 (1925), pp. 816-825.

variations as between the larger cities. Thus it appears that the percentage of estimated eligible Negro voters registered is higher in Chicago than in Detroit.[21] In Chicago, the Negro community is older, political organization has progressed farther, Negro leadership has been more aggressive, and the party machines have been more ruthless in their methods. Considering the group's lack of political experience and educational opportunities, the showing is remarkable. It is clear that the Negroes are not as apathetic about voting as they have been pictured by some. So far as presidential elections are concerned, the participation of Negro voters is almost as high as that of any other group. On the other hand, the voting record of the Negroes is inferior to that of the whites in other elections and in proposition voting, particularly when the issues at stake have no direct bearing upon the status of Negroes. In Republican primary elections in the twenties, in those cities where the Negroes were in a strategic position, there was little difference between the voting records of the whites and the Negroes.

Party Affiliations of Negro Voters

A corollary of the dogma of white supremacy is that, if the allegedly inferior race is given the vote, it will not know how to use it and will lapse into either anarchy or some form of absolutism. Lord Bryce did not think that the "backward races" were capable of self-government, and he stated that "it would be folly to set up fullblown democracy" in Central and South America, in Russia, and in China.[22] While Lord Bryce did not state his premises clearly, it is apparent that he believed in the British aristocracy, the "white man's burden" — a euphemistic way of describing the existence of "advanced" and "backward" races. There is a vast difference between the assumptions of the British statesman and those of the Swedish economist, Gunnar Myrdal, who has written with great scientific insight upon the political, social, and economic implications of the race problem. Bryce talks about the dogma of human equality, but he does not refer to the dogma of white supremacy. He does not find

---

[21] On Detroit see E. H. Litchfield, *Voting Behavior in a Metropolitan Area,* Ann Arbor, 1941, p. 13.
[22] James Bryce, *op. cit.,* Vol. 2, Ch. 71.

democracy a success in Mexico, India, the Southern States of the American Union, China, or South Africa.

Lord Bryce does not consider whether "races" are advanced or backward because of innate characteristics or because of differences in the environment. Among his possible expedients for dealing with "backward" peoples, he does not list education. The omission is significant. On the other hand, one of Myrdal's primary concerns is the trend toward equalization because of the improvement of the educational opportunities of the disadvantaged groups.

A Frenchman, Francis Delaisi, writing before Hitler came to power, built a whole theory of dictatorship on the backwardness of the peoples of the outer fringe of Europe, the southern Italians, the Spanish, the Turks, and the Russians.[23] His theory was not racial, but economic and social. Lord Bryce would add the "racial" element. Delaisi's theories were exploded by the rise of the Nazi dictatorship in Germany. Here was a dictatorship in an advanced country. In a negative fashion, Hitler's triumph was also a refutation of the racists. Here was an advanced people reverting to a primitive form of government. Cultural backwardness or the color of the skin are not crucial factors in the establishment of despotic governments.

In the United States of America it is possible to watch the process of Negro enfranchisement and gradual participation in politics because in the South the Negroes do not vote as a rule, whereas in the North they do. It has been said by some that the Negro is too politically incompetent to do anything but sell his vote to the highest bidder.

Since their freedom was granted by a Republican President and protected for a time by a Republican Congress, the Negroes from the beginning flocked to the Republican banner. During the Reconstruction Period, the South was Republican. When the Negroes were deprived of the vote following the withdrawal of the Federal troops, the South went Democratic.

In the North, where the Negroes retained the function of voting, they retained also their Republican affiliations until the presidential election of 1936, except in the border states and in New York City.

---

[23] *Les Deux Europes*, Paris, 1929.

The apologists for Negro disfranchisement in the South made the charge that the Negro vote in the cities of the North was controlled by the corrupt political machines. It was alleged that the Negroes, whether they voted Democratic, as in Memphis and New York City, or Republican, as in Philadelphia and Chicago, were cogs in party machines.[24] In any case, the Negro vote was said to be a controlled one. Intimidation, tricks, and favors determined how it would be cast.

In national elections the Negroes were overwhelmingly Republican until the presidential election of 1936. There were variations in the popularity among Negroes of different Republican candidates, but these were not great. Warren G. Harding was the most favored during the twenties, and Herbert Hoover the least favored. The decline in the Republican vote among Negroes during the twenties was the product of the growing "lily white" Republican movement in the South, which had its repercussions in the North. Hoover's success in breaking up the Solid South in his contest against Alfred E. Smith in 1928 encouraged the Republican leaders to disparage the Negro vote, and as a result the Negro political leaders in the North were apathetic regarding Hoover. Probably more than two thirds of the rank and file of the Negro voters, however, were loyal to the party of Lincoln, the emancipator, in the Hoover elections.

While the 1932 presidential election marked an upheaval in the political attitudes of the whites, there was far less change in the affiliations of the Negro voters. Franklin D. Roosevelt was an uncertain quantity in this election so far as the Negroes were concerned, and the vice-presidential candidate, John Garner, of Texas, was regarded by Negro voters as objectionable. Doubts as to Roosevelt's health raised the question as to whether a Southerner might be in the White House. Four years later the Negro vote began to shift strongly to the Democratic party. The New Deal policies had brought tangible results to the Negroes as well as to the whites, the President and Mrs. Roosevelt had displayed friendly attitudes toward Negroes, and the Democratic machines in the Northern cities had begun to exert the same pressures on the Negroes to support their candidates that they had exerted for many years on the foreign-born

---

[24] Gosnell, *Negro Politicians;* Bunche, *op. cit.*

voters. The ratio of the Negro vote in Chicago which went Democratic in national elections rose from 23 per cent in 1932 to 65 per cent in 1944.[25] In other words, the Democratic percentage more than doubled. This was a larger relative increase than Myrdal found in Baltimore, Detroit, Kansas City (Kansas), New Haven, Pittsburgh, or Wilmington, where there was only a 40 per cent or 50 per cent increase.[26] One of the reasons for this differential was the strength of the Negro Republican organization in Chicago in 1932. The power of this organization was not broken until the implications of the New Deal were clear to the electorate and the local Democratic machine had become well entrenched. As the Republicans were swept from local offices, the Democrats gained control of the police, the schools, municipal public works, and all other local services. This meant that the Negro municipal employees, gambling interests, and others who were dependent upon the local government were compelled to join the Democratic ranks.[27]

Once the spell of Republicanism was broken, the behavior of the voters tended to resemble that of the white voters. The New Deal attracted the younger voters in the lower income brackets, particularly those who belonged to labor unions. The Democratic Party now had a program for the disadvantaged groups, which clearly included the Negroes. In the South the Negro farmers were encouraged to participate in the Agricultural Adjustment Administration programs and to vote in the AAA referenda. While the AAA programs did some actual damage to the economic position of the Negro, the Farm Security Administration plans were designed to improve the lot of all low income farm groups.

The Negro voters in the Northern part of the United States are concentrated in the states having large metropolitan centers, i.e., New York, Pennsylvania, Ohio, Michigan, Illinois, and Missouri. In presidential elections these are key States, since in them the balance between the two major parties has tended to be a close one in recent years. This means that the Negro voters are in position, if properly

---

[25] H. F. Gosnell, "The Negro Vote in Northern Cities," *National Municipal Review*, Vol. 30 (May, 1941) and St. Claire Drake and H. Cayton, *Black Metropolis*, New York, 1945, p. 360.

[26] Myrdal, *op. cit.*, p. 496.

[27] Gosnell, *Negro Politicians*, p. 134, and Ralph J. Bunche, "The Negro in the Political Life of the United States," *Journal of Negro Education*, Vol. 10 (July, 1941), pp. 567-584.

led, to wield considerable influence upon both the major parties. A candidate who had the reputation for being unfriendly to Negroes might lose the crucial margin of victory in these strategic States.

Recognition of Negroes in Politics

The Negroes may gain the right to vote, but if they do not have the opportunity to choose representatives from their own group they may find their voting rights meaningless. This is the situation in the South African Union where the natives are permitted to vote for white representatives only. A group that is to be truly represented must have freedom of choice as to candidates.[28] It must also develop its own political leaders, who should be able to discover, interpret, and advance the interests of the group.

In the United States the development of Negro political leaders has been a slow and laborious process. During the Reconstruction Period it was the free Negroes, largely college trained in the North before the Civil War, who early assumed positions of leadership. Many of the Negro Congressmen from the Southern States were of this description.[29] The last of these, C. H. White, from North Carolina, a graduate of Howard University, delivered his valedictory address on January 29, 1901. It was twenty-eight years before another Negro was to serve in the United States Congress. In 1928 Oscar De Priest, a Chicago real estate operator who was born in Alabama, was elected as a Republican from the First Congressional District in Illinois, located in Chicago. When the tide turned against the Republicans in the thirties, Congressman De Priest was replaced by a Negro Democrat. Although the Negro vote is estimated to be between one and a half and two millions,[30] there are only two Negro representatives in the national legislature. The Southern States having a Negro population of 25 per cent or more have the same total vote, and fifty-two members of the House of Representatives and fourteen members of the Senate. In national politics, the Negroes have a long way to go.

In State and local politics the Negroes have secured a measure of recognition, but they are still greatly under-represented. Negro

---

[28] See Chapter 8 below.
[29] W. F. Nowlin, *The Negro in American National Politics*, Boston, 1931.
[30] Bunche, *op. cit.*, p. 580.

legislators have been chosen in nine States, and in the metropolitan centers Negroes have been chosen as members of city councils, county boards, and municipal court systems.[31] The single-member-district plan favors the selection of a Negro representative when the Negro population is concentrated in a given legislative district, but often enough the districts will be so gerrymandered as to prevent such representation. The single-transferable-vote plan (proportional representation) has also enabled the Negroes to choose a representative of their own group when their votes were large enough and well enough organized to make up a quota.[32] Only occasionally has a Negro been chosen from the entire electorate of a city by the ordinary plurality system. A county commissioner from Cook County, Illinois, located in Chicago, was one of the exceptions to the rule that Negroes were chosen to elective office only from constituencies which were overwhelmingly Negro in composition.

The opportunity to run for elective office is an important aspect of universal suffrage, but it is one which can be taken advantage of only by the few. It is in the appointive field that the more numerous and more permanent positions in the public service are to be found. A disadvantaged group which is seeking political rights will find that appointive positions contain more solid recognition in the long run. Beginning with the first administration of President Grant, a number of Federal appointive positions were opened to Negroes. The great abolitionist, Frederick Douglass, shrewdly preferred a Federal appointment to an elective position in a reconstructed State government. He was successively commissioner to Santo Domingo, minister to Haiti, marshal and recorder of deeds for the District of Columbia. The collapse of the reconstructed governments in the Southern States did not affect his status. In addition to a secure position for himself, he acted in an advisory capacity for a number of administrations.

During the dark days following disfranchisement in the Southern States, Negro political leaders hastened to rebuild their shattered prestige by securing Federal appointments. A number of them held

[31] Myrdal, *op. cit.*, p. 501.
[32] H. F. Gosnell, "Proportional Representation: Its Operation in Cincinnati," *Public Affairs,* Vol. 2 (March, 1939), pp. 133-135, and "Motives for Voting as Shown by the Cincinnati P.R. Election of 1929," *National Municipal Review,* Vol. 19 (July, 1930), pp. 471-476.

such positions as register of the Treasury, consular agent, collector of internal revenue for a given city, collector of a port, collector of customs, or postmaster of a city. While the policy of different national administrations varied as to what positions would be filled by Negroes, all presidents, Republican and Democratic alike, continued the precedent set by President Grant of appointing some Negroes to important Federal posts.

The differences between the two major parties as to the amount of recognition to be given to the Negroes in the matter of Federal appointments have tended to diminish. Beginning with President Taft's administration in 1909, the Republican Party began to be less and less liberal in its distribution of important posts to Negroes. The inroads made into the Solid South in 1920 and 1928 encouraged the Republican leaders to try to build up a "lily white" constituency in that section. On the other hand, with the inauguration of the New Deal under President Franklin D. Roosevelt, new opportunities in the public service were opened to Negroes. President Roosevelt took the view that in working out a program to aid the underprivileged groups he could not neglect a minority as large as the Negro group. While he had a difficult situation to handle because of the attitude of the Democratic Party leaders from the South, nevertheless his administrators tried to reduce or eliminate discrimination in carrying out the various programs. A Division of Negro Affairs, or a Race Relations Office, was created for one after another of the emergency agencies established during the Roosevelt administration. Especially in those agencies concerned with agriculture, relief, public works, housing, and education, was attention paid to the question of race relations. Advances were also made in the regular government departments. Negroes were not given Federal jobs in proportion to their numbers, but the Democratic Party had demonstrated that it could be more liberal in its recognition of Negroes than recent Republican administrations had been. During World War II many advances in private employment were secured for Negroes through the Fair Employment Practices Committee of the Federal Government.

The position of the Negroes with reference to the suffrage in the United States cannot be considered apart from their social and economic position. During the Reconstruction Period they were deprived of the right to vote because they lacked economic power, social prestige, and political education. Once the Negroes were disfranchised in these regions, it became clear that they would be deprived of social and economic opportunities on that account. Where they could not defend themselves by means of the ballot, they received the smallest share of the public funds, whether devoted to education, police and fire protection, water supply, road building, recreation, or health services. In the North, where the Negroes were permitted to vote, they received a larger share of the benefits of state action. While in the North there were still discriminatory practices, race riots, and severe competition for jobs and places to live, the ballot was available as a weapon which could be used to prevent the worst abuses. There the Negroes found the police less brutal, the courts fairer, educational opportunities greater, recreation facilities more adequate, health services superior, and public works facilities more evenly distributed than in the South, where they were virtually deprived of the suffrage. In the United States the relationship between the vote and a share in the public services is even closer than in some of the European democracies where the administrative officials are freer from political pressures.

The benefits which Negroes can derive from the use of the ballot depend upon the size of the vote which they can muster, the way in which they use it, the extent to which they are able to develop leaders who can guide the group wisely, and the extent to which the rank and file can be educated to follow such leadership. There are many pitfalls on the way to political power. Indifference, shortsightedness, fear of white violence or ostracism, lack of confidence, lack of integrity in the face of bribes or favors, and ignorance are all obstacles which stand in the way of the Negro's making the best of suffrage.

Chapter 7

NEGLECTED FRINGES OF THE SUFFRAGE

THE DEMOCRATIC doctrine of consent cannot be pushed to its logical extremity without creating absurdities. A government to be democratic does not have to have the consent of every living human being under it. It would be ridiculous to try to obtain the consent of infants, insane persons, and persons incarcerated for major crimes. In order to protect local self-government from outsiders who might be herded in by unscrupulous politicians, various governments have devised residence requirements for voters. In addition, some democratic states have felt that in modern times the written word is such an important medium of communication that it is reasonable to require voters to be able to read. All of these special qualifications for voting have been justified on the ground that they are safeguards of the democratic process.

In applying these qualifications, there are marginal cases where it could be argued that persons are unjustly deprived of the right to vote, contrary to democratic ideology. The consent of a child under one year of age would be meaningless, but what about the consent of a man twenty years of age in a state which requires voters to be twenty-one years old? Should the soldier fighting for his country be deprived of the vote because he fails to fulfill residence requirements? Should the war worker who has removed to a new location lose his vote on that account? Should the person who has been deprived of educational opportunities be also deprived of the vote and of the chance to try to improve the educational opportunities of his children? Should a person be deprived of the vote because he happens to live on one side of a street, while those who live on the opposite side vote? These and other marginal questions are of great importance to those affected. For purposes of convenience, they may be grouped under three main headings: age, residential, and educational qualifications

Age Qualifications

The age requirement is probably the oldest of all requirements for participation in political affairs. In primitive societies, the rudimentary beginnings of government were based upon age groupings. While exact ages were not usually employed, three main groups were clearly recognizable — preadolescents, adolescents, and married persons or elders. It was generally agreed that preadolescents should not have any share in managing the political affairs of the group. One of the first forms of government was gerontocracy, which is still found among Bantu peoples of the British East African protectorate and among some of the primitive tribes of Australia.[1] The Bantus have an "elder" organization which consists of the following grades: unweaned babes, babes able to walk, uncircumcised boys, circumcised boys, warriors, married men with children; next grade, executioners and military staff, arbitrators of disputes; highest grade, (oldest) with sacerdotal duties.

The bridge between the primitive gerontocracies and the modern democracies has a long span, but the impress of age groupings has been lasting. There is no present-day democracy which does not exclude preadolescents and give special powers and privileges to those of advanced ages.

The great variety of age limits for voting employed in different countries is an indication that the particular age limit selected by a given country is likely to be arbitrary. The age requirements vary from eighteen years in the Soviet Union, Argentina, the States of Georgia and South Carolina, and the Swiss Canton of Schwyz, to twenty-five years in Iceland, and thirty years for women in Hungary prior to World War II.[2] The most common age is twenty-one years, the age at which, in Anglo-Saxon law, the male acquires certain legal rights. This is also the age at which education or apprenticeship is likely to be complete.

One of the distinguishing characteristics of the human race is the long time that it takes the individual to mature. This period of growth reaches its peak from the physical standpoint at about the age of eighteen or nineteen years. Although mental growth con-

---

[1] W. McLeod, *Origin and History of Politics,* New York, 1931.
[2] Woytinsky, *Die Welt in Zahlen,* Vol. 7.

tinues throughout life, some psychologists contend that mental capacity reaches its maximum at an age earlier than that at which physical maturity is attained. This would mean that the age limit of twenty-one years is based upon social and historical considerations rather than upon scientific determinations regarding maturity.

In the United States, the application of the Selective Service Act to young men eighteen, nineteen, and twenty years of age raised the question about lowering the age limits for voting. The State of Georgia amended its Constitution in 1943 so as to permit the lowering of the age limit to eighteen years. South Carolina followed suit in 1945. Public sentiment throughout the country, as indicated by the Gallup polls, changed sharply from a negative to an affirmative position on this issue. Whereas only 17 per cent were in favor of lowering the age requirements for voting in 1939, 52 per cent were in favor of doing so in 1943.[3] If a man can fight for his country at the age of eighteen, why should he not be able to vote at the same age?

The figures regarding the participation of the voters of different age groups in elections are far from complete, but they uniformly indicate that the youngest voters do not show as much interest in casting their ballots as the voters in the middle age groups. When the older age brackets are reached, there is a decline in participation. These trends are shown by scattered figures obtained in Sweden, Switzerland, Weimar Germany, Denmark, Holland, and the United States.[4] The differences between the youngest and the middle age groups varied from 5 per cent to 28 per cent in the different jurisdictions reporting figures. The most common difference was about 10 per cent.

A few figures are available on the party affiliations of the youngest voters as compared with the older age groups. Official election returns have been broken down in this fashion for a number of Swedish towns and for Amsterdam. According to these data, the youngest voters are more inclined to support the left-wing parties and less inclined to support the right-wing parties than are the older voters.[5] As persons grow older, they acquire more property and they

---

[3] Public Opinion News Service release of September 5, 1943.
[4] H. Tingsten, *Political Behavior*, London, 1937.
[5] *Ibid.*, p. 116.

come to have a vested interest in maintaining a conservative political order. In the United States there are no official statistics on the voting behavior of different age groups, but Gallup polls taken in 1940, 1942, and 1944 show that the youngest age group was 10 per cent more Democratic than the voters fifty years of age and over.[6] This differential would certainly retard any movement to lower the age limits for voting, since many of the States are under Republican control.

While the usual practice is to enfranchise citizens who are twenty-one years of age, much higher age qualifications are imposed by law or by custom upon those who run for elective office. It is true that in Great Britain and the British dominions a citizen may run for the lower house on attaining the majority, twenty-one years of age, but in most states there is a much higher age requirement. Thus, in the United States, a member of the House of Representatives must be twenty-five years of age, and a member of the Senate thirty years old; in France, under the Third Republic, senators had to be forty years of age; and in Czechoslovakia members of the upper house had to be forty-five years old.

The low age requirement for British legislators has meant that some of them have begun distinguished careers at an early age, and have had a long period during which they could serve their country. Gladstone was elected to the House of Commons when he was twenty-four years old, and he remained in Parliament (with the exception of a short time in 1846) for the next sixty-one years. The Czechs, with their high age requirements, have deprived themselves of the possibility of any such record.

The battle between age and youth is an old one. On its own side, age has experience, an established order, tradition, and vested interests. To meet these assets, youth has flexibility, hope, impetuosity, and vigor. The problems facing modern governments are such that the assets of both groups are needed. In practice, age requirements for elective office are not needed. In England the average age of the members of the House of Commons was fifty-one years in 1929.[7] The young man who can commend himself to the

---

[6] G. Gallup, *Gallup Political Almanac for 1946*, Princeton, 1946.
[7] H. Finer, *Theory and Practice of Modern Government*, London, 1932, p. 720.

electrate is a rare person. If there are a few such, why not give them a chance.

Residence Requirements

As the Austrian jurist, Braunias, has put it, the requirement of special residence for the exercise of the franchise is not compatible with the pure equality of democracy. From the standpoint of the government it is necessary because only those will look after the consequences of their policies who have to face them. The homeless agitator, now here, now there, will not assume such responsibility.[8]

There are four general types of residence requirements: (1) requirements as to the actual time the voter must reside in a specific political jurisdiction in order to gain the right to vote; (2) requirements applying to voters who are removing from one political subdivision to another within a given jurisdiction; (3) requirements applying to the loss or gain of residence due to military stationing, service for the government, confinement in institutions publicly supported; and (4) residence in a territory which is politically recognized.

In respect to the first type of residence requirement, a year's residence in the political jurisdiction concerned is the most common requirement. In Great Britain it is only three months. The United States is in a peculiar position, since each State can set a different requirement. In order to vote for President, an American citizen has to live only six months in one fourth of the States, but in six States two years' residence is required. All the States requiring a longer period of residence are in the South, except Rhode Island. Of those States requiring only six months, all but two are in the western part of the United States.

There is no question that the residence requirement disfranchises large elements, particularly in a period of economic depression when there are many migratory laborers seeking jobs, or in a war boom period when workers are attracted from their former homes to war industry centers.[9] In the southern part of the United States the longer residence requirement is specifically designed to place an ob-

---

[8] K. Braunias, *Das Parlamentarische Wahlrecht*, Berlin, 1932, Vol. 2, p. 97.
[9] *Editorial Research Reports*, August 6, 1943, estimates that war industry centers had increased by 4,400,000.

stacle in the way of the Negro's voting. It is notorious that the Negro agricultural laborers are in a precarious economic position in the South, and that they seek to improve their lot by making changes. Each change constitutes a barrier to voting.

The second general type of residence requirement applies to residents removing from one place to another within a given jurisdiction. In Great Britain the registration-for-voting system is such that there is no requirement of this sort. Any voter who is registered as a Parliamentary elector at one place may return to that place and vote if at the time of the election he has removed to another location. This is called in Britain voting on a "stale" register. In the United States, on the other hand, there are residence requirements for minor subdivisions and for the polling district itself. Thus, county residence requirements, as specified in the American State constitutions, vary from one year to six months, the most common requirement being six months. Residence requirement in the election district varies from one year, as in Mississippi, to one month, the latter being the most common provision. In Britain this requirement does not present a serious problem, since the country is small and the elector may return to the polling area where he was registered. In the United States, "stale" registers are not used, and the voter must be enrolled in the polling district where he lives at the time of the election. Thus it might happen in Mississippi that a voter moved across the street into the adjoining polling district and as a result found himself disfranchised for a year. Such a high residence requirement serves no true democratic purpose. It is a device to discriminate against the more mobile elements of the population.

Closely related to the residential requirement is the regulation that the voter must cast his vote in person. This rule is usually mitigated by provisions for absent voting. Most democratic countries have laws which permit voters who are going to be absent from their residences on election day for specified reasons to vote in some other manner. Thus, in Great Britain, a voter who expects to be away from his polling place on election day may name a close relative as a proxy to cast his vote for him; in Weimar Germany a voter who anticipated absence from home on election day could get a special electoral card which permitted him to vote in national elections wherever he happened to be on election day; in the American States a voter may cast his ballot in advance of the regular election at some central polling place, or by mail from some distant point, in accordance with the provisions of his particular State law. Absent voting laws are not used to the extent that they might be, since they are sometimes surrounded by burdensome regulations.[10] However, they constitute a recognition of the democratic theory that a person should not be deprived of the vote just because he does not happen to be at home on the day of the polling. Absence from voting residence on account of business is usually a valid justification for asking for an absent-voter's ballot. In some jurisdictions sickness is also a valid excuse.

If members of the armed forces are going to vote, especially in time of war, it is necessary to make special provisions for them, exempting them from the usual residence requirements and from appearance at the polling place on election day. The French, under the Third Republic, deliberately disfranchised all those in the armed forces. The British, on the other hand, with their proxy voting system, had a ready-made provision which fitted the needs of the armed services. No British sailor or soldier serving overseas had to worry about being disfranchised because he could not get back to his home base on election day. In time of war British general parliamentary elections are usually suspended, but by-elections are still held to fill vacancies. These elections sometimes have considerable importance.

In the United States, Presidential and Congressional elections have never been suspended during a war. The question of the vote of the armed forces therefore assumes considerable importance. With no proxy voting as in Britain, and with inadequate absent voting laws, it is necessary in time of war to make special provisions for the casting of the soldier and sailor vote. In 1942 Congress passed a law at the last minute which suspended the usual residence requirements for registration, but left each State to provide a method of absent voting. The State laws lacked uniformity and flexibility, and the result was that the estimated soldier and sailor vote was only a negligible proportion of those qualified. In New York State it

[10] J. P. Harris, *Election Administration in the United States*, Washington, D. C., 1934.

was estimated that only 3 per cent of the qualified voters in the armed services took advantage of the belated absent voting privileges conferred upon them. In 1944 Congress passed another law which purported to facilitate the voting of the soldiers and sailors, but this law did not go much farther than the 1942 law. It did, however, stimulate action on the part of the States, and the result was a higher participation on the part of the armed forces in the 1944 election than in 1942.[11] The clerical and administrative work involved in the handling of over four million applications was well organized by the armed forces. In a few States a failure on the part of the legislature to act in time disfranchised many persons who were in active military or naval service.

Disfranchisement of Residents of the District of Columbia

One of the most bizarre of all the residence disqualifications is that imposed upon citizens who happen to live in the District of Columbia. Federal employees and others working in the District who live across the District line may vote in near-by Maryland or Virginia, but the District residents have been disfranchised since 1874. In theory, the inhabitants of the District may be voters in the State where they lived before they removed to Washington, D. C., but there are many persons who were born in the city and who therefore never qualified as voters in one of the forty-eight States.

The United States is the only democratic country which deprives the residents of the capital city of any voice in electoral affairs, either national or local.[12] This has not always been the case, since in the early part of American history the residents of the District voted on local matters.

The anomalous position of the city of Washington makes it possible to raise some theoretical questions about the effects of disfranchisement. Has the government of the District been less responsive to public demands than governments of cities of comparable size that

---

[11] According to the *Statistical Abstract of the United States for 1945,* the percentage of military ballots in general elections to total popular vote for President was 5.6. According to the United States War Ballot Commission *Report* (Washington, D. C., 1945, p. 52), about one third of the persons in service of voting age in ten reporting states cast effective ballots.

[12] U. S. Advisory Committee on Fiscal Relations Study, *Fiscal Relations between the United States and the District of Columbia,* Washington, D. C., 1937, Section 15.

have local self-government? Has the government of the District been more or less efficient than the government of self-governed cities? In other words, has disfranchisement made a difference in the status of the residents of the District?

An Advisory Committee analyzing the fiscal relations between the United States and the District of Columbia reported in 1937 that field observations and available statistical information indicated that the residents and property owners in the District were receiving services roughly equal to the average of seventeen comparable cities.[13] There were two variations reported: First, the relief burden of the District was half that of the other cities, on an average; second, park facilities and services in the District were considerably above the level of the other cities. On the basis of this evidence, a superficial observer might conclude that disfranchisement in the District made no difference, and that the citizens are just as well off as if they had the ballot.

While the residents of the District have no vote, this does not mean that they have no voice in the affairs of the city. Neighborhood associations are much more active in Washington than in other American cities of its approximate size. These local organizations have officers elected by the membership, and though they lack legal powers nevertheless they are consulted by the three commissioners who govern the District under a grant of powers from Congress.[14]

Satisfactory as the situation may appear to be on the surface, a closer examination reveals that disfranchisement does make a difference. A considerable proportion of the residents of the District, the estimated population of which was over eight hundred and forty thousand in 1945 and thus exceeded that of ten different States, have in various ways expressed dissatisfaction with the existing situation. A number of petitions have been presented to Congress pointing out that if "taxation without representation" was tyranny in 1776, it is no less so today. In favor of suffrage for the District have been a number of neighborhood associations, labor unions, Negro organiza-

---

[13] *Ibid.*, p. 113.
[14] United States 78th Congress, 1st Session, Senate, Subcommittee of the Committee on the District of Columbia, *Hearings on Reorganization of the Government of the District of Columbia on S 1420, S 1527, and S. J. Res. 87*, December, 1943.

tions, the League of Women Voters, and some trade and commercial groups.

Opposed to local suffrage for the District are certain reform groups which have pointed to corruption and boss rule in large American cities which had local self-government. These groups have expressed the view that the large Southern population of the District, composed of antagonistic white and colored elements, would furnish a poor foundation for a stable local government of the national capital.

Negroes compose almost a third of the population of the District; their position is an anomalous one. So far as discrimination is concerned, they are not as badly off as the Negroes in some of the cities farther south, but on the other hand they are not as well off as the Negroes in New York, Chicago, and some of the other northern cities. The District has a segregated school system, but there is equal pay for white and colored teachers. In New York and Chicago the schools are not segregated, as a matter of law. The health facilities of the District are also separate, but they are approximately equal for both whites and Negroes. There is no segregation on the local transportation lines, but hotels, restaurants, and theaters discriminate against Negroes. Improvements could be made in the District in the way in which the police treat Negroes as compared with the way in which the police treat Negroes in cities farther north.

The question of suffrage for the District is thus tangled with the larger question of Negro disfranchisement. There are some who contend that the Negroes would be worse off under local self-government because of the large Southern white element in the population, and there are others who contend that the granting of suffrage to the residents of the District would put the Negroes in a better position to defend themselves against various types of discrimination.

There are special considerations which mark off Washington from other American cities. Many senators and some representatives become residents of the District and thus are vitally interested in its affairs. Whatever the form of government, it is clear that the Federal Government would want to exercise some special supervision over an area containing so many of its buildings. Some have expressed doubt as to whether statehood would be advisable for the District under these circumstances. Such a change would require a constitutional amendment which would meet hard sledding. From the standpoint of democratic principles, however, there is no question that the present arrangements are unsatisfactory.

Literacy Tests for Voting

In parts of the American hemisphere and in some of the British self-governing dominions, literacy tests have been used as qualifications for voting. The theory underlying these tests has been that modern representative democracy is so dependent upon written communications that those who are unable to read cannot be fully informed regarding their voting obligations. In some of the South American countries, as for instance, Brazil, literacy tests have in the past disfranchised a majority of the population. With the improvement of the educational facilities this is no longer so, but the proportion disfranchised is still large.

In the United States the constitutions of some twenty States specify literacy or educational qualifications for voting.[15] An examination of the geographical distribution of the States having educational qualifications shows that about one fourth of them are in the Northeast, one fourth in the West, and one half in the South. The most common literacy requirement (found in the Alabama, California, Delaware, and New York constitutions) specifies that "no person shall be entitled to vote unless such person is also able, except for physical disability, to read and write English."

The effectiveness of the educational qualifications depends in large part upon the methods by which they are enforced. In the State of Massachusetts the voters are given slips of paper which contain sections of the Commonwealth constitution, and they are asked to read these sections. In the State of New York the educational authorities are responsible for the enforcement of the provision, and simple reading tests are given to all new voters who cannot furnish a diploma from an accredited high school. In recent years 7 per cent of the applicants in New York State failed to pass these simple

---

[15] New York State Constitutional Convention Committee, *Constitutions of the States of the United States,* New York, 1938.

literacy tests.[16] On the other hand, the election inspectors in the State of California merely ask the prospective voters if they can read and write, and it is likely that many illiterates answer "yes" to this question.

In the Southern States the educational qualifications are used for the purpose of disfranchising Negroes, and many of them require both literacy and the ability to "understand" or "explain" sections of the State constitutions. For example, the Georgia Constitution permits all those to vote who can correctly "read in the English language any paragraph of the Constitution of the United States or of this State and correctly write the same in the English language when read to them by any of the registrars . . . and give a reasonable interpretation of any paragraph of the Constitution of the United States or of this State that may be read to them by any one of the registrars." [17] The constitutions of the States of Georgia, Louisiana, and South Carolina are the only ones which specifically indicate that the administration of the literacy qualifications is to be handled by the registration officers. No matter how correct an interpretation of a provision a Negro applicant might make, it would always be possible for the registrar to hold that it was not "reasonable."

Because there are no satisfactory statistics on literacy, it is extremely difficult to estimate the number of persons who have been disfranchised in the United States by these requirements. One estimate places the number at two million adults.[18]

The operation of the literacy requirements is also difficult to evaluate. When illiterates have the right to vote, do they exercise it? Two field studies made in the city of Chicago in the twenties indicated that a larger proportion of the persons who could not read and write English failed to register and vote than of those who could do both.[19] Later studies made on the basis of census data indicated that there was an inverse relationship between the percentage of total population completing high school and interest in voting, as shown by the percentage of the adult citizens that registered.[20]

[16] New York State, *Legislative Manual*, 1943, p. 1143. From June 1, 1942, through May 31, 1943, there were 47,341 citizens who applied for certificates and 3,457 of these failed to pass the test.
[17] Article 2, Section 1, Paragraph 4.
[18] *Editorial Research Reports*, August 6, 1943, No. 5.
[19] H. F. Gosnell, *Getting Out the Vote*, Chicago, 1927, p. 117.
[20] H. F. Gosnell, *Machine Politics: Chicago Model*, Chicago, 1937, p. 109.

When the influence of mobility was eliminated, however, the findings tended to substantiate the earlier survey. In other words, it may be assumed that illiterate persons tend to neglect their electoral duties in larger numbers than do educated persons.

No figures are available showing the political attitudes of the illiterate voters as compared with the literate. It may be inferred, nevertheless, that there is some relationship between the amount of education received and economic status. The persons who have had superior educational opportunities tend to vote for conservative candidates and policies.[21] Persons who read no papers published in English tended to support candidates who were in favor of liberal public spending. Such voters were also more likely to be under the guidance of political bosses and machines.

When the literacy requirement is accompanied by universal compulsory education and adequate schools, it is not a serious disqualification. In small rural countries and in isolated villages, literacy is not so essential a requirement as it is in a huge representative democracy where newspapers, books, periodicals, and pamphlets are important sources of information regarding issues and candidates.

A General Evaluation of the Franchise

Only when a group in a democratic country possesses the weapon of the suffrage can it guard its political position. Just how much difference the suffrage makes in the status of a group it is difficult to ascertain, since the group must achieve a position of some power and influence in the community in order to win the suffrage. The experience of the lower income groups, women, foreign-born groups, and different caste groups supports the proposition that the ballot itself may be used as a means for advancing the interests of the group. The ballot may be a means for securing more equal justice in the courts, more equal sharing of the educational, recreational, health, and welfare facilities of the state, and more equal opportunities for economic advancement.

The suffrage may be employed as one of the chief defenses against intolerance. A group which lacks the vote may find itself unable to fight back effectively against discrimination and bigotry.

---

[21] *Ibid.*

When an unpopular group holds a share of political power, it can bargain for more tolerant treatment. In a country where democratic ways of reaching decisions are accepted, the presence of conflicting interests makes for tolerance, since each group can perceive what would happen if the other groups had their way. The opposing groups expose each other, and thus each group is shown its own weaknesses. In such an atmosphere intolerance does not thrive.

After a given group has won the right to vote, it finds that it is just beginning its struggle for a fair share of the benefits conferred by the state. When great expectations have been built up regarding enfranchisement, this is sometimes a disillusioning experience. It must be learned that suffrage gives a group an opportunity to formulate programs and choose leaders. Suffrage does not automatically produce either programs or leaders. A newly enfranchised group must learn in the hard school of experience how to use the tools of democracy. It must learn how to organize, how to develop leaders, how to prepare workable programs, how to disseminate information regarding these programs, and how to form winning combinations.

Chapter 8

VIEWS OF REPRESENTATION *

In the realm of theory, the most important question confronting the Western Democracies is whether representation does or does not make a difference. If representation is irrelevant to democracy, it can be abandoned. If it is necessary to democracy, it must be preserved and fostered.[1] If certain types of representation are more conducive to democracy, they must be preferred to others. The nature of representation, therefore, must be considered at some length.

Tentatively, we can list what we should like to find out about representation.[2] First, how is representative power gained and held? What are the techniques of gaining and holding power in a representative government? What manner of men become leaders of a representative government? Secondly, we should like to know the relationship between popular government and representation. Their mutual dependence and interacting effects must be discovered. Then, thirdly, we shall examine the peculiarities of the different devices and systems of representation as they have sprung up in various countries. The problem here is to determine whether or not there is only an inconsequential relativity. Are systems of representation, like the domiciles of different ant tribes, merely equivalent and effective ways of doing the same thing? For the consideration of these questions

---

* Alfred DeGrazia assisted in the preparation of this chapter.

[1] This question is reflected in the discrepancy between two schools of thought. One believes that representative government is a poor but necessary substitute for a direct democracy, and seeks to introduce popular governmental devices such as the initiative, referendum, and recall. The other group believes that democracy can only work through representation because leaders must develop to prevent mob rule and govern efficiently. The "Founding Fathers" exemplify the latter train of thought.

[2] Herman Finer lists those problems which he thinks most important in a study of representative government. They are: "(1) What entities shall the government represent? (2) Who may choose representatives? (3) How shall candidates for the assembly be chosen? (4) How far is it permissible to influence others in the election of candidates? (5) To what degree is the representative obliged to obey the directions of the electors?" *The Theory and Practice of Modern Government*, London, 1932, Vol. 1, p. 398.

there must be an adequate definition of representation, with parts capable of being sliced off, in turn, to give further illumination, like a splinter from a flaming log.

The ostensible source for a definition is the existing literature. But an examination of the most frequently occurring references to "representation" reveals no definition which suffices for our purpose. Most of them exclude significant bodies of data. Some of them contain veiled preferences for democracy or a certain system of representation. It is simple to get what one wants by using a definition as a top hat, from which preinserted rabbits may be extracted. Some examples will illustrate this practice.

Hobbes, in building up a monarchical system, strove so hard to take advantage of the positive coloration of the word "representative" that he deprived it of much meaning. In the *Leviathan* he said:

> A commonwealth is said to be instituted when a multitude of men do agree and covenant, every one with every one, that to whatsoever man or assembly of men shall be given by the major part the right to present the person of them all, that is to say, to be their representative, every one, as well he that voted for it as he that voted against it, shall authorize all the actions and judgments of that man or assembly of men in the same manner as if they were his own, to the end to live peaceably amongst themselves and to be protected against other men.[3]

It may be stated that Hobbes, with his mechanistic theory of man as an animal urged by irrational drives to make rational efforts towards their achievement, would regard representative action as any action which helped realize man's efforts to escape from the state of nature which Hobbes regarded as a state of strife. A king, no matter how tyrannical, was "representative" of the people because the people felt that, left to their own devices, they would be more destructive of one another than he would be destructive of them. This definition makes representation almost synonymous with political power.[4] In history, representation has always implied a measure of consent. Hobbes' definition practically eliminates the consent element. It imposes an acceptance of paternalism.

---

[3] Sir Thomas Hobbes, *Leviathan*, New York, E. P. Dutton & Company, Inc., Everyman's Library, 1937, p. 90.
[4] K. Friedrich, *Constitutional Government and Democracy*, New York, 1941, p. 260.

A century and a quarter later, James Wilson, in the midst of the American Revolution, defined representation as "the chain of communication between the people and those to whom they have committed the exercise of the powers of government."[5] Here the consent element is emphasized, and if "communication" is defined broadly enough to take care of informal influences which the people exercise on their representatives, this definition has merit. One might pertinently ask if the people must perform the act that transfers powers of representation. Moreover, in many cases there is communication but not representation. What good did the huge petitions of the Chartists do in England? What effect did the testimony of the ranking American economists have upon the Smoot-Hawley Tariff Act of 1928?

Lord Brougham wrote that "the essence of representation is that the power of the people should be parted with, and given over, for a limited time, to the deputy chosen by the people, and that he should perform the part of the government which, but for the transfer, would have been performed by the people themselves."[6] Here again no account is taken of the fundamental changes which take place in the constitution of power when the change is made.

Thomas Hare, "father" of proportional representation, stated that "Representation is the vicarious performance of duties which cannot be personally executed. . . . In a multitude of circumstances people are compelled to place themselves and their interests in the hands of others."[7] This definition is faulty because it does not include some of the more significant aspects of representation. It says nothing of the power relationships which result from the new structure. Obviously, important changes take place which make the substitute assembly far different from the direct meeting of the people. Furthermore, Hare's definition limits representation to assemblages. Other writers point out that representation can exist with reference to the judiciary, the executive, or the bureaucracy.[8] Representation

---

[5] *Lectures on Law,* Vol. 2, pp. 120-123.

[6] *Works,* Glasgow, 1860, Vol. 11, pp. 35, 36.

[7] Thomas Hare, *The Election of Representatives* (3rd edition), London, 1865, Chapter 35.

[8] Among others, see Carl J. Friedrich, *Constitutional Government and Democracy,* New York, 1937, pp. 261 ff.; Otto von Gierke, *Political Theories of the Middle Ages,* translated by F. W. Maitland, Cambridge, 1900; John of Salisbury, *Policraticus* (1159), translated by Dickinson, New York, 1927, Vol. 2, p. 64,

can occur, in fact, wherever there is an exercise of power.[9] Because
he was primarily interested in assemblies which could use his system,
Hare failed to notice this. If no change in the character of the power
exercised occurs in representation, proportional representation is
more desirable. The interests of all are on an equal basis, and all
must be represented. Thus Hare and others, through gymnastic
definitions, accomplish remarkable feats of problem-solving.

Robert von Mohl, in the middle of the nineteenth century, defined the word as follows: "The process through which the influence
which the entire citizenry or a part of them have upon governmental
action is exercised on their behalf by a smaller number among them,
with binding effect upon those represented." [10] This appears to exclude direct influence of people upon governmental action. It ex-
cludes lobbying, petitioning, and the control brought by premonitions
of elections. An American political scientist commented on this:
"Such a large body of people is not very likely to participate in or effectively to control governmental action." [11] Mohl implies that "on
their behalf" is something objectively determined by the representatives, which again has a faint scent of Hobbism. His definition is
too normative for one who wishes to describe what representation
is without question-begging through the use of terms like "true representation" and "false representation."

Edward McChesney Sait limited his definition strictly, without
some of its meaningful connotations, when he said that representation "occurs whenever one person is authorized to act in place of
others." [12] This includes legal agents who certainly do not partake
of the characteristics of the complete representative. Also, a person
may act in place of another, but against the other's wishes, an act
which few would defend as being representation.

In their excellent article on "Representative Government in Evo-

---

where John maintains that the prince represents the whole body of the commonwealth and stands in its place. Also see Charles A. Beard and John D. Lewis,
"Representative Government in Evolution," *American Political Science Review,*
Vol. 26 (April, 1932), p. 227.
[9] William Paterson stated that "The principle of representation . . . is an expedient by which an assembly of certain individuals chosen by the people is sub-
stituted in place of the inconvenient meeting of the people themselves." Wm. Seal
Carpenter, *Democracy and Representation,* Princeton, 1925, p. 39.
[10] *Staatsrecht, Völkerrecht, und Politik,* 1860, Vol. 1, pp. 8, 9.
[11] Friedrich, *op. cit.,* p. 260.
[12] *Political Institutions, A Preface,* New York, 1938, p. 476.

lution," Charles A. Beard and John D. Lewis decided that "The modern idea of representation can be broken into three component parts: (1) a representative person or group has power to act for, or in place of, another person or group; (2) the representative is elected by those for whom he is to act; (3) the representative is responsible for his acts to those whom he represents."[13] But not many would agree that the representative is only to act for his group which elects him. Many representatives act for themselves or for others who did not elect them. Shifts in the composition of majorities are not unknown. Many people shift their votes when acts by a representative affect them positively or negatively. President Franklin D. Roosevelt did not represent the same people in 1936 that he did in 1933. The lower income groups had swung more preponderantly in the direction of the New Deal.[14] A final criticism of the above definition is that it is a definition of representative government and not of representation. One evidence of this is a quotation following the above one from Beard and Lewis.

> . . . when we define representative government in simple terms, as above, we arbitrarily lay out a little land of rational certainty and speak in the language of autonomy. This is not enough, for representative government is merely one phase of the whole process of civilization, and those who speak of it as if it were a Victorian bustle, to be put on or entirely discarded at will, display a woeful ignorance of its history.

Thus writers have intertwined representation with representative government. The distinction must be insisted upon. Since we have not as yet defined representation, we must arrive at the distinction by showing a frequent lack of correlation. On a purely *a priori* level, one easily sees that a man can act in agreement with another man, using powers which might belong to the second man, without any electoral process. Of course representation may be defined to include only the agreement which follows election. We do not insist upon the "truth" of definitions. But the failure to solve some of the most important problems of representation has been due to a neglect or

---

[13] *Op. cit.*, p. 228.

[14] Harold F. Gosnell, "How Accurate Were the Polls?", *Public Opinion Quarterly*, Vol. 1 (January, 1937), p. 97; *ibid., Grass Roots Politics*, Washington, D. C., 1942; E. H. Litchfield, *Voting Behavior in a Metropolitan Area*, Ann Arbor, 1941; W. Clark, *Economic Aspects of a President's Popularity*, Philadelphia, 1943.

refusal to distinguish these two concepts which ought to be distinguished for the sake of clarity and scientific value. Friedrich, Luce, Sait, and others have discussed the distinction.[15] Coker and Rodee described the history of early representation and declared, "There were no necessary democratic implications in this older idea of representation."[16] And they add, "The typical democratic doctrine is that popular election serves at least as well as any other system in securing representative leaders and serves better than any other system in confining the latter to their function of leadership."[17] This is a conclusion and remains to be shown.

Much of the criticism directed at past definitions and discussions of representation involves a criticism of the "rational man" theory of government. To read some of the material on the subject, one would gather that the writers are concerned primarily and almost exclusively with those few individuals who are sophisticated critics of legislation.

This attitude seems to have arisen naturally from several aspects of nineteenth century thought. There was the "economic man" who functioned with omniscience in the field of supply and demand. There were the extreme democratic doctrines of persons like Rousseau, who thought each man could judge what were his peculiar wants, and that he needed no society to define or implement his interests. Rousseau significantly denounced representation as a specious principle which deprived the people of sovereignty. Then the bourgeois liberal thinkers saw society in terms of their social set, and visualized a representative system judged by individuals of their ilk. Each rational man could criticize, instruct, and learn from his representative. "Interests," as they conceived them, were patent and explicit. Each man was supposed to know what his representative was doing, and so could judge the latter's actions adequately. Add to this omnipotent "political man" a system of elections, and the problems of representation resulting therefrom might be solved without delving into the mysteries of nonrational and noninformed behavior.

---

[15] Friedrich, *op. cit.*, Chapter 16, on "General Problems of Representation"; Robert Luce, *Legislative Principles,* Boston, 1930, Chapter 9, on "Representation"; and Sait, *op. cit.*, Chapter 20, on "Representation."
[16] Francis W. Coker and Carlton C. Rodee, "Representation," *Encyclopedia of the Social Sciences,* Vol. 13, p. 309 ff.
[17] *Ibid.*, p. 312.

The great confounder in the study of representation is not the rather simple distinction between representative government and representation, nor the manipulative problem of getting everyone represented.[18] It is, rather, the large number of cases of power-wielding where the subject feels no desires, where acts of the power-wielder are done without consultation with the subjects. Many of the difficulties come in cases where there is no mode of communication between ruler and subject except unconscious thought processes and patterns.[19] A working definition of representation should include the possibilities of delving into these cases. One way of avoiding the difficulty is to define the term so as to exclude any unconscious representation. This may be done explicitly or implicitly. Avid democrats tend to avoid such cases because they define representation in terms of other institutional structures of democracy. Such an approach only confuses the basic issues. In order to be adequately studied, representation must be viewed apart from the complex of concepts which create any particular political ideology.

The definition we shall take here is thus analytical rather than historical. History has defined representation "not wisely but too well" to suit the times and man. In terms of the body of data which presents itself for analysis, the following definition is submitted: *Representation of an individual in a society is a condition which exists when the characteristics and acts of a person in a position of power in the society are in accord with the desires, expressed and unexpressed, of the individual.*

Before explaining the terms of the definition, two noticeable characteristics of it should be indicated. It has subjective aspects, and it is conceived from a quite individualistic standpoint. The "act" is an individual act occurring at a certain time and place and over the single individual.[20] Each act and each individual it affects are taken

---

[18] The latter problem concerns those writers who see in proportional representation a cure-all for the ills of democracy, to the neglect of more basic factors than "paper representation." Coker and Rodee, we might add, also consider the problem of representing all interests and everybody the most important one.

[19] The elite may frequently assert its right to rule without advice or consent, but just as frequently it "keeps both ears to the ground." The absence of machinery of expression is sometimes immaterial to the presence or absence of representation, as we shall see later.

[20] Thus, Congressman Jones votes for a sales tax of 1 per cent for one year on the people, of which John Smith is one. By the definition, the act of voting is either representative or nonrepresentative.

together in determining whether representation exists. There are many cases where an individual is subject to an exercise of power which he dislikes, though the power-wielder represents a majority of the society. There representation does not exist, so far as concerns this person. Whether or not representative government exists is another matter.

The word "act" is chosen deliberately instead of the phrase "act of power." If the latter were used, it would have to be expanded indefinitely to the obliteration of its customary meaning. To take an example: State Representative Doe, from a nondescript district, delivers a speech with which few members of the House sympathize or to which few even listen. The speech is not an act of power in any functional meaning of the term "power." But it offends a minority group in his district. They feel unrepresented, though no power has been directed against them. They probably feel strongly enough because of the mere speech to overweigh favorable impressions they may have gained from Doe's previous acts of power on their behalf. Likewise, a number of constituents may like his picture with a pretty wife and child, though they dislike his voting $50,000 to construct a useless dam. They may desire a handsome family in public position more than they dislike the dam.

The desire for a handsome family to represent them would fall under that part of the definition which concerns the "characteristics" of the person in a position of power. To use a definition confined to "acts" would violate some basic conditions of representation. A person may be ignorant of the acts of the officeholder, but yet see a remarkable similarity to himself in the physiognomy and social characteristics of his representative. In fact, he sees a mirroring of himself. He will feel as though he himself were present in the seat of power. One of the primitive, literal, and persistent meanings of the term representation is to "present again," and "from this it has come to mean to appear in the place of another." [21]

The idea of agency which clings to the term also substantiates the inclusion of the word "characteristics." It is true that the only interest of the principal in his agent is in the latter's acts. But those acts are supposed to be, and legally must be, based on the assumption

[21] John A. Fairlie, "The Nature of Political Representation," *American Political Science Review*, Vol. 34 (April and June, 1940), pp. 236, 456.

of certain characteristics of the principal. The agent is supposed to look through the eyes of his principal.[22] Can we then say that the reverse is not true, and that the person seeking representation should not judge the acts of his agent by his characteristics?

An interesting etymological fact bolsters the idea that representation should include "characteristics" of the power-holder. The development of the Latin word *persona* (person) evolved offshoots with different meanings.[23] One of the meanings of *impersonare* (to impersonate) was "to represent" as in a corporation. In other words, "to possess the characteristics of" someone or something seems to have been all the time a connotation of the word "representation."

Even when representation has a wider meaning than agency, it includes more than "acts." Beard and Lewis found that the idea of representation is more than mere agency; it reflects the whole movement of social forces in the community.[24]

On the basis of what others have thought about the nature of representation, there is no startling novelty about including characteristics as well as acts. Who is to say that representation is not truly obtained through identical or desirable characteristics, but is acquired through acts? That would be equivalent to stating that causation can be ascertained in the latter case but not in the former. Already it has been shown that "acts" include not only acts of power but expressive acts. We must admit that a person judges whether he is being represented by (*a*) acts of power, (*b*) expressive acts, and (*c*) characteristics of the representative. How can we possibly study representation if we arbitrarily decide what the people whom we are studying should think it is?

So far as acts of power are concerned, the subject must agree with the act when done, but not with the manner in which the power is executed. A man may like a large army and gladly consent to be

---

[22] A appoints B as his agent to purchase Blackacre for him. B thinks Blackacre is a great bargain and buys it for himself. A can recover the land from B because B violated his agency. Thus the law prevents B from acting in his own interests when he should be acting as A would.

[23] Gordon F. Allport, *Personality: A Psychological Interpretation*, New York, 1937, pp. 25-28.

[24] *Op. cit.*, p. 225. Burke is quoted as saying, "The value, spirit, and essence of the House of Commons consists in its being the express image of the feelings of the nation."

taxed for its creation, but dislike its use for aggressive warfare. The last act is a separate act of power and would be unrepresentative in this person's case. This disseverance of subsidiary acts from the main act of power is important in the study of bureaucracy. A large though varying amount of power seeps into the remote reaches of the power hierarchy. The degree of importance of this fact to a study of representation depends upon the quantity of power possessed in the lower levels of the hierarchy.

The judgment as to whether representation exists must be made while looking at the act at the time it was done. A later judgment by an outside observer, that the act was really for the best interests of the subject and was therefore representative, is improper. Nor does later rejection on the part of the subject of the act negate the representative quality of the act, though it affects his later feeling of unrepresentation.

Danger undoubtedly exists in the subjectivism of the definition. But even more danger exists in excluding subjectivism. Subjective elements cannot be denied. They can only be concealed. It is far better to be conscious of them. Furthermore, it is doubtful whether many definitions of representation can escape the accusation of subjectivism in a subtler and more aggravated form. In his work on *Representative Government,* Henry Jones Ford declared: "The essence of the term [representation] is plainly the fact of representation, however it may be arranged. The idea is that the people, while not in person present at the seat of government, are to be considered as present by proxy." [25] Ford and others (Willoughby, for example) [26] see representation as a delegation of the job of performing acts of power by the people who retain sovereignty. Then the question becomes, what is sovereignty and what is power? What do the representatives do to the people, and what do the people do to their representatives? What mutual concessions are necessary? When is the ability of the representative to wax strong dependent upon certain incapacities in the minds of the constituents? In the classifications under our definition, we shall be able to segregate and isolate these elements.

---

[25] New York, 1924, p. 3.
[26] W. F. Willoughby, *The Government of Modern States,* New York, 1936, Chapter 8.

The words "expressed" and "unexpressed" are used rather than "conscious," because "conscious" suggests invariably "unconscious" which is ill-adapted to the purpose. "Unconscious" more irreconcilably contradicts the noun it modifies than "unexpressed."

Talk of "unexpressed desire" is useful in making the definition consistent and embracing. A representative, as we shall see, will frequently act in a manner which is approved only when later it comes to the attention of the represented person. It is really an *ex post facto* recognition of what was hitherto nonapparent. But when he learns of a past power act of power-holder A, of which he disapproves, a person will feel as unrepresented as if his desire had been plain all the while.

Expressed desires are manifested in speech and actions. The varieties and extent of expression are indices of the significance of the act to the existing power equilibrium. Forms of expression are the usual means of communication, plus those associated ordinarily only with the peculiar structure of the state, as for example, the channels of communication established in a representative government (elections, etc.).

Unexpressed desires are frequently prevalent in a large part of society. Their presence is often known by the stimulation which an unusual or stringent act affords. In the absence of ready means of communication, unexpressed desires may be mistaken for disinterest and "apathy of the masses." That which a despotism considers inertia is often the result of lack of freedom for communication under a despotism. The expression of attitudes on political questions is suppressed, and energies are diverted into nonpolitical activities.[27] What would be "worth while bothering about" under easy conditions of expression is not worth while where expression is difficult. Unexpressed desires may be diagnosed by reference to history or in future retrospect. What is now subject of consideration may have come up for consideration before, when the idea was more violently debated because of its novelty or stringency. Past expressed attitudes can be used to predict present desires, though unexpressed. Unexpressed desires may later be expressed, and thus be discovered.

---

[27] Harold Lasswell, *Politics, Who Gets What, When, How,* New York, 1936, Chapter 8 on "Personality."

They can then be used to describe the character of representation at the time the act was done.

Desires may also be divided into those which are *ascertainable easily* and those *ascertainable only with difficulty*. This distinction is important from the standpoint of the representative, and for making a judgment on the rationalizations the representative gives for his behavior.[28] No matter how a representative may strain his faculties to devise methods for allowing the expression of desire by his constituent, a number of persons, for one reason or another, will never express their attitudes.[29] The extent to which different representatives go in probing unexpressed desires varies widely and may be used as an indication of the extent to which they adopt the "deputy" or "leader" function.

Desires are not expressed because they lack importance,[30] because the subject is ignorant of the act,[31] or because he cannot conceive of them by reason of the complexity and number of acts.[32] In some cases of unexpressed desires, the way the subject would have acted can be predicted. The presence or absence of representation can here be determined.

Like expressed desires, *unexpressed desires* may be divided into ascertainable and unascertainable. Unexpressed desires are not the stuff of politics at the time of the act in question. They may concern a matter regarding which the politicians want to develop active and felt wishes. There is a similarity then with the expressed desires

---

[28] Note that both expressed felt desires and unexpressed felt desires may be ascertainable only with bother. *E.g.*, a representative can know the felt desires of group AB by reading countless letters from the A section and by predicting the attitudes of B section through knowledge of their past attitudes.

[29] Charles E. Merriam and Harold F. Gosnell, *Non-Voting*, Chicago, 1924. The chart of reasons for non-voting shows why many people refuse to express demands or attitudes in the electoral process.

[30] The private act of Congress pensioning Mrs. Smith makes no difference to Mr. A., who has more important things to think about.

[31] A grows sugar beets. Congress passes a tariff on sugar imports. A is ignorant of the act (though it is important to him) and remains ignorant up to the time the act is repealed.

[32] B knows of an act of the state legislature which imposes specifications for .e construction of houses. He cannot decide whether he desires the act, because ￬ cannot understand structural engineering. Inertia prevents B from ever learning whether the state legislature had correctly prevented structural defects.
"The subject-matter of legislation has become so highly technical that much of its meaning is unintelligible to the multitude; and its extent is so great that there is rarely time for its essential principles to be illuminated by public discussion." Harold J. Laski, "The Present Position of Representative Democracy," *American Political Science Review*, Vol. 26 (August, 1932), p. 631.

which are only ascertainable with difficulty. The same political devices may stimulate both categories into some sort of change.[33]

To resume our concern with the whole definition of representation, we can divide it again into *basic representation* and *ostensible representation*. There are cases where the application of power is considered desirable by both parties, but where such a decision is arrived at through different modes of thought. This is a new type of representation we have not considered up to now. Both the new and the old forms are representation because the representative and the represented agree on the exercise of power and its mode of exercise. They do not agree in the reasoning by which they arrived at their conclusions. A man may want the Communist Party dissolved and declared illegal because he hates radicals' threats to his vested interests; because he believes in a two-party system; or because he would like to see William Z. Foster, whose face he dislikes, humiliated. Other men agree with his conclusion regarding the Communist Party, but not with his reasons. This situation, if it occurs between representative and constituent, results in ostensible representation.[34]

Voting and attitude studies of people have often shown the prevalence of conflicting reasons for the same attitude.[35] A vote, after all, is a most extreme way of simplifying reality.

Representation of this sort is a matter of coincidence rather than of sympathetic ideologies. It is disturbing and distracting to any "rational" theory of representation. But it is something for which allowances must be made in the institutional structures of representation. A party system may be such that a great number of divergent viewpoints have to be harmonized at any cost. The party

[33] A has all the positive attitudes necessary in order for him to favor a law allowing tort actions to be brought by next of kin to a deceased person. (His father was killed in a locomotive explosion while working for a railroad company and he cannot recover under the existing law.) His state senator backs a wrongful death bill. The senator already is representing A's unexpressed desire into an expressed desire, and at the same time making it of that class of expressed desires hitherto ascertainable with bother.

[34] Of course, not only acts of power, but other acts and characteristics of the power-holder, are liked or disliked for different reasons by different people. Examples might be cited *ad infinitum*.

[35] For example, Southern Democrats in many cases are only Democratic because of the Civil War and Reconstruction. See the study of Merriam and Gosnell, *American Party System*, New York, 1940, pp. 79-81. Also the work of Samuel P. Hayes, Jr., "Inter-Relations of Political Attitudes," *Journal of Social Psychology* (November, 1937), pp. 503-552.

symbols must be made broad enough to encompass people who follow the symbols for different reasons. One can say that there is a direct relationship between the vagueness and generality of party symbols and the amount of ostensible representation present in the Congressional debates and in legislation. The amount of basic representation occurring in a state is directly dependent upon the kind of representative structure established. Whether basic or ostensible representation is more conducive to a stable society is a matter for later discussion.[36]

A final distinction should be made in the concept of representation. Most thought concerning representation does not consider the unconscious elements in it. Too frequently it is assumed that all that is important is the omnipresent riddle of whether the representative shall do as he thinks best, or that he should seek in a most painstaking way to ascertain the popular will of his constituency on each act he commits. Whole sections of books deal with the rationalizations of philosophers who were warped by predilections for "mass" or "elitist" theories of history.

Common observation shows a number of situations where agreement exists between representative and represented without any conscious interchange of ideas or beliefs. Many laws are unpremeditated at the time of the election, if such is the method of selecting representatives. An individual law, even when premeditated by the constituents in electing their representative, is most frequently amended. This allows the representative to avoid the mandate of the people if he is extremely desirous of doing so. It affords him excuses to rationalize his failure to follow promises. Furthermore, we must remember that the only pressures and expressions of opinion on many acts of power come from minority groups. The representative, a good part of the time, fumbles in the dark so far as knowing his constituents' minds through external communication. Finally, a large number of constituents vote on the basis of the personality of the representative, on his general record, or as a protest to acts of his opponents.[37] The sum of these behavior patterns means that any

---

[36] See Chapter 10 below.

[37] In like vein, Harold J. Laski wrote, "It is sometimes suggested that a member of the legislative assembly must be either a delegate or a representative, must either vote as he is instructed, or use his best judgment upon the issues he is called upon to decide. That is, in fact, a wholly false antithesis. For no member can

agreement, if there is to be such, must come about through identity of outlook between representative and constituent. As some writers have stated, a person judges his representative on the general, vague sum of the latter's power acts. A general impression is all most voters have to go on. More exactly stated, this proposition can be divided into *unconscious representation* and *conscious representation*.

Unconscious representation is the condition which exists when an act or a characteristic of an official is in accord with an individual's expressed or unexpressed desire, and when that accord is the result of environmental influences of which neither representative nor represented is aware. Conscious representation exists when the conformance of desires is credited to come from expressed and acknowledged causes. The latter might be said to be arrived at on the "rational" level of social communication. Orthodox treatments of representation give far too much attention to this phase of representation, sometimes assuming that it is the only body of data worth bothering about. The first is sometimes commented on in an absentminded and unsystematic manner. An example of it acutely stated is found in Leslie Stephen's famous description of the powers of the English Parliament.

> Lawyers are apt to speak as though the legislature were omnipotent, as they do not require to go beyond its decisions. It is, of course, omnipotent in the sense that it can make whatever laws it pleases, inasmuch as a law means any rule which has been made by the legislature. But from the scientific point of view, the power of the legislature is of course strictly limited. It is limited, so to speak, both from within and from without; *from within, because the legislature is the product of a certain social condition, and determined by whatever determines the society;* and from without, because the power of imposing laws is dependent upon the instinct of subordination, which is itself limited. If the legislature decided that all blue-eyed babies should be murdered, the preservation of blue-eyed babies would be illegal, but legislators must go mad before they could pass such a law, and subjects be idiotic before they could submit to it.[38]

state his total views; partly because there is not the time to do so, partly because new issues are bound to arise." *Grammar of Politics*, London, 1925, p. 319.

[38] *Science of Ethics*, p. 143, as quoted in Albert Venn Dicey, *Introduction to the Study of the Law of the Constitution*, New York, 1889, p. 77. (Italics ours.) The frequency with which this passage is cited is an indication of the importance of its analysis and of the lack of any more systematic treatment of the problem elsewhere.

In the final resolution, the agreement that makes representation consists of all the similar intellectual, economic, social, and moral forces that shape the personality of the two individuals. Certain elements in their backgrounds have so much in common that by a sort of "independent invention" their minds reach the same results. This is done without conscious communication in the case of unconscious representation.

One particular resolution of a power situation may contain both conscious and unconscious elements, both struggling for representation. There may easily be a conflict between them. Suppose the desires of the constituent to be antipathetic to those of the representative. How he arrives at his decision to act in a certain manner is a result of the basic character and the quantity of the conflicts. All the forces of politics enter into the picture. The deciding factor in many cases may be the threat of election defeat, yet to call that final would be to ignore the forces of rebellion and independence in many a man's character, and to belie many an historical incident. It would be a specious study of representation which neglected the underlying psychological aspects of character. Individual studies of political leaders have shown how popular stimulus of a certain kind causes different reactions in the different political types.[39] The difference between conscious and unconscious representation appears strikingly in the game of politics. Almost everything seems to be fought out in the open with frank recognition of clashing wills and interests. How the representative and represented agree and disagree is known, and is at issue in the political sphere, but why they do and do not is little discussed. Little attention is paid to unconscious factors which are so great as to be basic to all the superficial politicizing. Writers, more concerned with the apparent than the real, describe representation as they would a sporting event — a few sketchy histories of the players, a play by play account, and a box score.

Both conscious and unconscious representation may be divided into *actual* and *virtual* representation. On the conscious level, representation occurs when agreement and conformance are associated with the conscious modes of eliciting social consensus. In conscious actual representation, the representative and the represented may use

---

[39] Harold Lasswell, *Psychopathology and Politics,* Chicago, 1930; *Politics, Who Gets What, When, How,* New York, 1936.

domination, persuasion, or the conscious assumption of the characteristics of the other party or parties in order to arrive at a use of power consistent with their ends. We may call the third device "conscious reflection." A power-holder can get agreement to his acts by the utterance of commands, which, if they have behind them the sanctity of legality, will frequently be agreed to by the subjects apart from any intrinsic merit in the exercise of power. Another form of this, frequently found in the sphere of political parties, is agreement on the basis of past decision. John Smith, loyal constituent of Congressman Jones, may have as his first reaction to Jones' voting for a bill, "Anything Jones does is good enough for me." The dominant type of representative would include men like Jackson, Bryan, and the two Roosevelts. Despite Theodore Roosevelt's admiration of domination as a form of arriving at agreement with the subjects of political power, he admitted persuasion as another tool. A leader is one who "fights openly for principles and who keeps his position of leadership by stirring the consciences and convincing the intellects of his followers, so that they have confidence in him and will follow him, because they can achieve greater results under him than under anyone else." [40]

In the realm of actual conscious representation, the fact that a political leader reflects qualities of the subjects of which they are cognizant causes them to agree with his acts through reasoning by analogy. Whereas in actual conscious representation by domination the subject "follows wherever Jones may lead" because he reveres, respects, or admires Jones, and whereas in actual conscious representation by persuasion the subject follows Jones because he thinks Jones is proceeding along rational lines to the accomplishment of the subject's ends, in actual conscious representation by reflection the subject agrees with Jones because "Jones is a man of the people" or "a fellow Mason" or a "good dirt farmer like me." In practice the three are intermingled in the individual personality.

Conscious representation may also be "virtual" or spurious. Virtual representation would exist in those cases where agreement is reached through coercion or threat of coercion, where an impression

---

[40] *Autobiography*, New York, Chas. Scribner's Sons, 1920, p. 148.

of similarity is created though none really exists; it is associated with force, manipulation, and imitation. A totalitarian "election" of "representatives" is designed to create the illusion of complete representation. In sections of the American scene where boss-control is present, the same devices masquerade beneath the garments of representative structures. We would also use virtual representation to cover those cases where politicians falsely assume the character of their constituents, *i.e.,* a conscious attempt to fall under the categories of positive traits which their minds recognize. Observers of the American scene are all too familiar with the farcical attempts of politicians to identify themselves with the community's largest common positive characteristic. American history shows many a "rustic, barefoot Wall Street lawyer."

We must admit that the division between actual and virtual, so far as regards these conscious mirrorings of the subjects, is far less clear and therefore not very useful. One can easily tell the difference between force and persuasion, but can hardly distinguish between persuasion and propaganda. The former can be objectively ascertained with universal agreement; the latter can hardly be agreed upon.

The same difficulty occurs when we divide unconscious representation into actual and virtual. We can define actual unconscious representation as behavior on the part of actor and subject which agree because of unnoticed elements of common origin in the personalities of both parties. The representative is bound under any system of selection to be typical of some sections of the population. These sections he mirrors and represents.

We have to make some form of subjective judgment on the difference between virtual and actual in unconscious representation. Virtual unconscious representation would be an appearance of representation resulting from an assumption of traits valued by the subject, but which really are unrepresentative traits when objectively considered in the light of history. Thus we find in England, over a long period of time, an elite class, possessing socially valued traits which were used for the perpetuation of the interests of the class, but which were regarded by the masses as prerequisites for representing them.

An excellent illustration of this situation is given by Aye:

> Last in our survey of candidates comes the extremist, a common type being the candidate who puts up for a poor constituency and goes to live among his constituents in order to get atmosphere. This is how an East End costermonger summarized the qualifications and prospects of one gentleman, who, in following his Fabian precepts, had adopted this role. "Vote for 'Arry Gusher. Wot, 'im as lives at Buggin's Rents, close agin' the docks? Gentleman, is 'e? And lives at Buggin's Rents. 'Oo's a-going to vote for 'im? Why, 'e must be barmy, and 'is friends ought to look after 'im." [41]

We have now delineated a sufficient number of categories and distinctions to form a basis for a comprehensive study of representation. Any limited discussion of representation must be confined in most of its materials to its milieu. A student of Nazi government would study the representative elements in the German state under the Third Reich. A student of American and British democracy must confine himself mostly to representation as it is found under representative government, embracing other "undemocratic" systems only occasionally to add point to a generalization. When a total survey is impossible, one must seek the materials relevant to his society and purpose.

---

[41] John Aye (pseudonym), *The Humour of Parliament and Parliamentary Elections*, London, Universal Publications, Ltd., 1931, p. 20.

Chapter 9

THE STRUGGLE FOR REPRESENTATION *

In the previous chapter, representation was defined as the condition in a society which exists when the characteristics and acts of a person in a position of power in the society are in accord with the expressed and unexpressed desires of the individual. From the theoretical point of view this definition has certain advantages, but when an attempt is made to apply it historically a number of difficulties are encountered. It is sometimes not feasible to classify the acts of individuals in a given time and place as expressed or unexpressed. In fact, it is difficult to determine what are the desires and acts of leaders and followers in a given time-place situation.

Discussion of the historical evolution of representative institutions must be approached in a practical fashion. The definition was in terms of the individual, but it is the behavior of the group which determines whether or not the government is representative. Group action has been made possible by the invention of the device of majority rule. According to this convention, a group is represented when a majority of those composing it are represented. Hence to say that Andrew Jackson represented the American frontiersmen means that a majority of the people living on the frontier felt that Jackson's characteristics and acts were in accord with their wishes and ambitions. A rough way of measuring the desires of the frontiersmen would be to examine their votes. The elections of 1828 and 1832 left no doubt on this score.[1]

The second element concerns the timing of a series of acts. Generally, when it is said that "A" represents the farm hands, a number of acts are involved. In an ideal construction, it may be said that a

---

* Alfred DeGrazia assisted in the preparation of this chapter.
[1] C. O. Paullin, *Atlas of the Historical Geography of the United States,* New York, 1932. The majority rule principle and representative government grew up together in English Parliamentary history. See Maude V. Clarke, *Medieval Representation and Consent,* London, 1936.

single farm hand is or is not represented in every act of "A"; the sum of "A's" acts causes the farm hand to feel that he is or is not represented. Practically, it is impossible to divorce each one of a maze of acts from the general mass, and it is also impractical for the farm hand to keep an up-to-date list of all the acts of "A." One unrepresentative act may be highly significant to the farm hand, while many representative acts may seem insignificant. The highly significant act will have much to do with making him feel unrepresented or represented.[2] To farmer "Brown," a vote against one bill sponsored by the farm organizations is more significant than a hundred votes in favor of other measures designed to benefit farmers but not in the way prescribed by his organization. To Negro "Jones," a vote on the Antilynching Bill is much more important than a vote on the Reciprocal Trade Agreement Act.

From the standpoint of an individual over a period of time, the sum of the representative's acts gives the individual a general impression of being represented or of not being represented. This is what we mean when we say that any individual is represented. Actually, the individual may not know much about the behavior of his representative, but he thinks that he knows something, and his thinking is important. Multiply the individual by others, and we can then decide whether or not the group is represented. To adopt an all-knowing attitude regarding the "best interests" of the group would be futile if we wish to discuss how people act rather than how they should act. If some people prefer to let their representative judge what their best interests are, they will still be represented according to the definition of representation given in this book. Such is the problem of political leadership.

Having shown that the definition of representation used in the previous chapter does not exclude the possibility of working with a group of people over a certain time period, we shall proceed to a summary of the theories regarding the origins of representation, with special emphasis on theories of the origin of representative assemblies. Historically, representation, representative assemblies, and elections have been divorced at some times and united at others.

---

[2] It would be unrealistic to talk of a majority of representative acts making a person represented.

Through the use of historical materials, we hope to bring out more strikingly the difference between representation and representative government, and also that between representation and election systems. At a later time an attempt will be made to put all three into relationship to one another.

Before specifically detailing the classical development of representative government, it is well to discuss how the idea of representation might arise in any society. Maude V. Clarke wrote that the representative principle manifested itself in three ways: "They may be classified broadly as personification, specific acts undertaken for reasons of administrative convenience, and political action bearing directly upon public law." [3]

An example of the first would be the sacrifice of a person by a primitive society under the belief that the person represents the sins of the society. "But I, as my brethren, offer up my body and life for the laws of our fathers . . . that in me and my brethren the wrath of the Almighty which is justly brought upon all our nation, may cease." [4]

Representation for administrative convenience is exemplified in the early English inquest jury: "Twelve men, therefore, were chosen from each county and these in the king's presence swore to make known the provisions of their laws and custom, so far as they were able, omitting nothing and changing nothing by description." [5]

When the change was made from giving information to acting, there was the third kind of representation through "political action bearing directly upon public law." Thus the English presentment jury was a representative sample of the men of substance in the county. They were the official accusers of persons suspected of crime. As such, they acted positively and were part of the earliest public judicial machinery of the whole of England. [6]

The use of these last two examples should not imply that similar developments have not occurred in other societies. The fact of representation is almost universal because of its fundamental contribu-

---

[3] Clarke, *op. cit.,* p. 289.
[4] II Maccabees 6: 37, 38.
[5] *Leges Edwardi Confessoris* (prologue).
[6] Julius Goebel, Jr., *Development of Legal Institutions*, New York, 1937. The practice of presentment by jury was formalized by the Assize of Clarendon in 1166. See pp. 56, 120.

tion to an organized society. John Dewey put it well when he declared, "In itself it [the public] is unorganized and formless. By means of officials and their special powers it becomes the state. A public articulated and operating through representative officers is the state. . . ." [7]

Any specialization of functions involves the idea of representation. This is true of early societies which supported medicine men and chiefs. A specialist is one who takes better care of certain of the peoples' interests than they could if they assumed the task themselves. The people may lack magic or other skills; they may not wish to spend the time to undergo the inconvenience. There is the general need for someone to direct or assume the public energies. An engineer represents his clients in his work, as does a doctor his patient; and all specialists would fall under our definition but for the fact that political representation also involves a position of general political power.

The reason for the peculiar interest in representation in power situations is due to the disagreement over the solution of political problems. An engineer knows specifically his clients' desires. A doctor knows his patient wants health, and the patient knows either that the doctor can restore health or at least that he himself could do no better. The political situation establishes different attitudes. Selfishness is not nearly so detectable, nor altruism so obvious. A brief can frequently be made for the theory that the public knows not what it wants. Specialists in government are necessary, but proof of their representative quality is buried in the intricacies of the social situation. Wants are indefinable, unascertainable; means are debatable and numerous. For these reasons, in politics there are more problems of representation than in other specialized fields. It is relatively easy to find out whether a doctor is a good practitioner, but it is much harder to tell whether a representative is a good legislator. Medical knowledge about the physical aspects of birth-control is fairly complete, but the information about the moral and social consequences is not, and therefore the question is controversial and political. Significant it is, that whenever a problem of the specialized sciences is debatable among its practitioners and likewise important

[7] *The Public and Its Problems,* New York, 1927, p. 67.

to the public, it is hurled into the political sphere, there to become a problem in the solution of which people desire representation. Then the question becomes: How can the desire for representation be implemented?

From what has gone before, it is clear that representation can be found to a lesser or greater degree in all societies. A king may represent his dynastic interests, if nothing else.[8] What is then important is how many people are represented. Assuming the majority principle as the dividing line, we might say that a group is represented when more than half of the individuals in it are represented.

Harking back to Miss Clarke's trichotomy of representation — personifications, administrative acts, and political action — a comparison may be made with the terms "characteristics and acts" in the definition presented in the preceding chapter. Accord in characteristics would doubtlessly be in agreement with her idea of personification. Characteristics and expressive acts are often closely allied, the latter naturally emanating from the former. They would both in large measure be included under the idea of personification.[9] Miss Clarke's administrative and political acts would fall under the acts of power in our classification. In fact, of all definitions, hers is most akin to ours. She says: "We recognized the representative principle as at work when one or more persons stand or act for others in such a way that, at least for the matter in hand, an identity of interest between them is assumed." [10]

In recognition of the prevalence of the representative principle in various societies, any theory of an absolute origin of representative assemblies in one country must be viewed with raised eyebrows. Any description of the conditions necessitating and prerequisite to the growth of representative government must consider numerous causes. Henry Jones Ford believed the English Parliament arose because the English monarch was absolute,[11] but E. M. Sait pointed to the long centuries of French absolutism with no sign of waxing

---

[8] Oscar Jaszi, *Dissolution of the Hapsburg Monarchy,* Chicago, 1929, Chapter 2, "The Hapsburg Empire as a Family Estate *(Fidei Commissum).*"

[9] Miss Clarke, however, would not include the element of desire in her principle, whereas our definition demands (1) accord in characteristics and (2) accord in desiring the characteristics.

[10] Maude V. Clarke, *Medieval Representation and Consent,* London, Longmans, Green & Company, 1936, p. 289.

[11] *Representative Government,* New York, 1924.

parliamentarism.[12] A survey of the work in the field of representation shows no agreement on the meaning of the problem, and it cannot be expected that any conclusions would be agreeable to all.

Since the fact of representation could easily be present anywhere, the formal political structure which embraced the fact can be treated historically as conditioned by environmental circumstances. The idea will be brought down to date, and the object of the history is to get a perspective on how the modern form of representative assembly happened.

The influence of (1) legal traditions, (2) the institutions of the Greeks and Romans, (3) the practices of the barbarians, (4) the Roman Catholic Church, (5) the spread of the corporate theory, (6) and the English and (7) American situation will be examined in order as antecedents of the present.

Many writings on representation have utilized various legal analogies to elucidate their point. The danger in the use of terms like "agency," "proxy," and "guardian" as synonyms for "representative" lie in their limited implications.[13] They are too connotative and circumscribed to describe representation adequately. There is no use for them except to belabor a point. Why the term "agency," for example, should be used rather than another term from another specialized field is the result of historical connections between legal practice and the growth of representative theory. Suppose the function of the representative is to formulate new policies. Obviously, "proxy" fits his capacity no more than "postman." A proxy delivers a vote for a man — a postman delivers a letter for him which might contain a vote. The end result is the same. In this case, if the representative were called a proxy, he might also be called a postman.

In the beginning of representative government in England, the "representative" was an agent in the strict legal usage of the word. It was not until some time afterward that the representative process became so complicated that more than agency was involved. We discussed above the type of unconscious representation through reflection, as found in the English jury. The origin of this type of representative must be distinguished from that of the agency type

---

12 *Political Institutions: A Preface*, New York, 1938.
13 For a brief definition of these terms, see F. E. Luepp, "Do Our Representatives Represent?", *Atlantic Monthly*, Vol. 114 (1914), p. 433.

now under discussion. The distinctive origins of these two, and of other kinds, lead us to believe that the representative function is performed in a number of different ways, and that it springs from independent founts. The legal source will be discussed first.

An assembly of agents is not a representative assembly in any realistic description of the term. Nor is a congress of ambassadors a representative assembly. Elements of the representative assembly are possessed by both, but they are strictly limited.

The structure of feudalism in England after the Norman conquest made the king supreme overlord. His sovereign perquisites by no means overwhelmed his feudal limitations before the system of representation began.[14] Consequently the embryonic Parliament was composed of the nobles and their proxies. Any deputation of powers that did exist was strictly controlled by the individuals possessing those powers. There was no idea of representing the nation. Feudalism was a system of the individual rights of each man in his own sphere.[15]

On behalf of the idea of representation, however, and against the legal idea of agency, several forces were evolving. First were the sovereign powers of the king which made him presentable as the representative of the whole nation. He had public jurisdiction, an oath of fealty, a bureaucracy, and public revenues. The theory of the sovereignty of the king came from Anglo-Saxon and Roman legal sources. About 1256, the English jurist, Henry de Bracton, wrote on the position of the king as vicar of God and guardian of the people. Since the king did what was good for his subjects, any later

---

[14] Goebel, *op. cit.,* pp. 39 ff. "William's politics in England may be considered from any one of three angles: (1) as feudal overlord, (2) as conqueror, (3) as King."

[15] "Representatives of this description [legal agents] were the deputies anciently chosen in England by the counties and boroughs to treat with the King concerning the amount of money required for the service of the state and the wants of the crown, which the several bodies, of whom there were the several organs, would agree to grant to the King. So completely was this transaction considered in the light of a bargain between two parties, that in early times the grant was made in the form of an indenture, each estate granting separately; and the King's assent (in the case of a common grantee) was presumed without being formally given. This proceeding less resembled the making of a law, than a contract between an individual on the one part, and the committee of a company or a body corporate on the other part.... They [first Parliaments] granted subsidies for his immediate use and advantage, and not for the advantage of the whole community, of which they were members." There was no idea of the "common good." Sir George Cornwall Lewis, *Remarks on the Use and Abuse of Some Political Terms,* Oxford, 1832 and 1898, pp. 105, 106.

dispersion of sovereignty to underlings had to be at least in theory for the good of the whole body politic. Thus, in a representative are the notions of agency and of general welfare. The two conflict and form an area of doubt which may resolve in either direction.

Another nonagency source of the representative idea was the system of suretyship which also was a product of the nonindividualistic and tribal Anglo-Saxon custom. "It is of this sort," wrote a twelfth-century writer, "namely, that all men in every vill of the whole realm were by custom under obligation to be in the suretyship of ten so that if one of the ten commit an offence the nine have him to justice." [16] This was a system of collective compulsory bail fixed before the crime. Here again is a general responsibility of one man to the community. An act of the one binds all the rest. Hobbes, interestingly and significantly, saw the relationship of suretyship to representation. The bailors are the represented person, or authors, as he calls them, while the bailee is the representative or actor.[17]

It is notable that the word "representation" was first given a political meaning by the Latin writers, and that it came into general use in England by the opening of the seventeenth century to describe Parliamentary deputation.[18] Before that time various other Latin terms were used to describe the representing of one by another. Whereas the magnates needed only the idea of proxy to describe their parliamentary representation, the groups whose consent was required developed new ideas.

The lower clergy, in the fight to establish the right of consent to the king's taxation of them, used as their slogan the private law maxim of Rome: *Quod omnes tangit, ab omnibus approbetur.* The Chronicler of Malmesbury was the first to read a wider political application into the doctrine of consent through the use of this phrase.[19] Needless to say, the phrase had influence only to the extent to which it was backed up by material factors strengthening the clergy.[20]

---

[16] W. A. Morris, *The Frankpledge System*, New York, 1910, p. 1.

[17] *Leviathan* (Everyman's Edition), London, 1914, p. 86.

[18] C. A. Beard and J. D. Lewis, "Representative Government in Evolution," *American Political Science Review*, Vol. 26 (1932), p. 223.

[19] *Vita Edwardi II*, (1325 A.D.), p. 170, quoted in Clarke, *op. cit.*, p. 16.

[20] Their material forces would include such things as the Pope's support, their use to the King in counterattacking the nobility, their perquisites under the ancient Anglo-Saxon and canon law.

The growth of both juridical machinery and the House of Lords from the Curia Regis made legal influences on the thinking about Parliament frequent and prolonged. The phrase, *Delegata potestas non potest delegari,* is a maxim which may have had force in the private law of agency and appointment, but it should not have been taken over by analogy into the field of representation. This doctrine was very similar to the Continental medieval writers' doctrine of complete or "absorptive representation," which held that power once delegated remains always delegated. It originated in the medieval commentaries on the Digest and Decretals. It was picked up by the English jurist, Edward Coke, without due care in delimiting its roots, and received wide vogue. The American jurists, James Kent and Joseph Story, regarded it as a principle of public law. Applied by the courts to the delegation of powers by the legislature to other agencies or to the public only on the flimsiest logical grounds, it "rises as a ghost to hamper the efficient and proper distribution of the functions of government." [21]

There is no space here for an extended discussion of what changes the judicial frame of reference has brought to the representative idea. Certainly, in numbers of cases, representation and representative assemblies have existed without conscious analogies to the legal system. It is safest to assume that both representative "imperative mandates" and agency are aspects of the same type of situation, a situation which exists when a man or a group of men have simple, direct, conscious, and strict control over the actions of another person.

Some time might be spent discussing the embryos of representative government in the ancient world. Such attention would presumably be guided by the search for origins of the modern systems. That a search for representative governments need not be confined to Greece and Rome was demonstrated by the interesting discussion of the Iroquois Federal Republic by an American anthropologist.[22] The Indian type of government was used to bear out the thesis "that what we call modern representative government is essentially and

---

[21] P. W. Duff and Horace E. Whiteside, "Delegata Potestas non Delegari," *Cornell Law Quarterly,* Vol. 14 (1929), p. 168.
[22] William P. McLeod, *The Origin and History of Politics,* New York, 1931, Chapter 17.

historically in fact a league or confederation pattern; that this pattern represented an adaptation to league purposes of the idea and practice of representative government previously existing within the tribe or city state: that in the course of development in medieval Europe, the league pattern was modified so as to become a pattern of government suitable to any type of political consolidation." [23]

Our thesis is that representation can take different forms, depending upon different conditions, and that the league pattern of representative government arises from one of several situations. McLeod believes that the original type of representative government was to be found in the tribe or city state. With the statement that government through representation existed in many tribes and city-states, we have no argument. It was pointed out earlier that representation is a phenomenon arising from various specialized situations. When an attempt is made, however, to relate English representative government to the league pattern, which was derived from the city-state or tribe type, we must be wary. If American Indians could develop a representative confederation without borrowing from Greece, the English might conceivably be expected to do likewise, barring convincing evidence to the contrary. There does not seem to be enough evidence to warrant any generalization that, after long diffusion, England received her government from Greece. The evidence is insufficient to say that England's government is of the league or confederation pattern, or that France under the Directorate and Napoleon had a Venetian, tribal, or city-state pattern, or that even the Greek confederation came originally from the city-state pattern. Nor can we ever "conclude that our modern patterns are mostly English rather than Venetian because Napoleon lost the Battle of Waterloo." [24]

In the first place, English political institutions can be explained on fairly substantial grounds without tying them unnecessarily to Greek city-states in origin. So can French and Venetian institutions. And the Greek confederations were not derived from the city-states according to the best evidence that is available. All that is known exactly is that representation is used in the city-state and also in the confederation. But, in the former, representation is the

---

[23] *Ibid.*, p. 308.
[24] *Ibid.*, p. 362.

result of the need for specialized statesmanship, whereas in the latter, representation is the result of the inability of the scattered peoples to get together, and the obvious advantages of having machinery for the compromising of differences. The city-state was designed for ruling, the confederation for the making of compromises. As Freeman has pointed out regarding the Amphictyonic Council, "The Council was representative, just because it was not a Government." [25] It was a Congress of Ambassadors each of whom tried to carry out his particular instructions. The city-states had only delegated a minute portion of the ruling powers to the Council. Freeman adds, "But a really representative Senate would be just as great an anomaly in an ordinary Greek constitution as a representative Assembly." [26] There was no real representative government by assemblage of city delegates. The examples of Vinogradoff show how cities were occasionally represented by groups of prominent citizens for the purpose of raising public loans or making treaties.[27] No one would call the Holy Alliance or the League of Nations a representative government of Europe. There were no national ties to hold the Greek cities together as there were to hold the parts of England together. As Tenney Frank put it, "In the ordinary (Greek) league it was the primary assembly of the populace which had the power of deciding all important questions of war, peace, and membership. The synedrion was usually a counseling body only, which shaped the ordinances and recommended them to the populace." [28]

Frank, however, finds some evidence of a convincing sort that the Romans established representative governments in Macedonia after conquering that region. In each state set up, there was a representative senate which was the predominant lawmaking body whose ordinances "resembled in their binding force the laws of modern states." [29] The primary reason for establishing these states was to have a machinery to pay tribute levied by the Romans.

---

[25] Edward A. Freeman, *History of Federal Government in Greece and Italy*, London, 1893, p. 109.
[26] *Ibid.*, p. 108.
[27] P. Vinogradoff, *Outlines of Historical Jurisprudence*, London, 1920-1922, Vol. 2, pp. 107 ff.
[28] Tenney Frank, "Representative Government in the Macedonian Republic," *Classical Philology*, Vol. 9 (1914), p. 49.
[29] *Ibid.*, p. 50.

The quality of evidence offered by McLeod does not convince one of the inescapable evolution of representative government all over Europe from the Greek city-states. The later political innovators could see in the Greek city government something which even the greatest Greek philosophers failed to recognize is very unlikely without positive evidence to that effect. We must content ourselves with saying that like conditions produce like manifestations of the representative principle.

For example, the common Diet of the Holy Roman Empire was virtually a Congress of Ambassadors when the Princes ceased to attend and sent proxies instead. There were independent states, with no chance of central government because of the weakness of the whole as compared with each part, and the lack of a great national tradition. In several of the Greek leagues, however, there was the beginning of a central government. The same may be said of the Iroquois Nation. In the United States and in Switzerland, the states released some of their powers and a federal government was formed.

It can be affirmed that the ancient world was basically nonrepresentative in form. Exceptions to the rule of direct democracy, oligarchy, or tyranny are to be found here and there inside the city-state where specialized tasks demanded representatives, chosen by lot, election, or social position. Among the cities were found leagues which wielded a few meager powers. The Roman consul was elected, and, if the theory of democracy is correct, he was "representative," but a representative assembly by election was utterly lacking. The Macedonian assemblies were true representative types, and these states of the hinterland may well be thought of as the modern type. But no great body of evidence is to be had regarding them.[30] The provinces of the later Roman Empire had provincial assemblies which wielded powers of no great importance. For the most part their function was advisory.[31]

When the invasions came, it is probable that not all representative structures became only of reminiscent value. Some writers have de-

---

[30] Frank, *op. cit.* See also his *History of Rome*, Baltimore, 1923. On p. 209 he states that Caius Gracchus is credited with contemplating a representative government for the whole of Italy.
[31] E. G. Hardy, "The Provincial Concilia from Augustus to Diocletian," *Studies in Roman History*, London, 1906; George F. Stokes, "Home Rule Under the Roman Empire," *Macmillan's Magazine*, Vol. 47 (1882), p. 52.

clared their belief that these provincial assemblies survived and were projected into the Middle Ages, there to form the basis of a type of government which later diffused to England and became the English Parliamentary system.[32]

Before leaping too far ahead, however, certain tenacious contributors to the idea of representation and representative government should be discussed. Whereas in ancient times we had only structures to inform us, there being no conscious reflection on the nature of political representation, the Middle Ages brought the first writings on representation as a concept, and consequently a greater emphasis on certain structures as being more conducive to representation. The chief contributing sources to medieval representative theory were the Church and the corporate idea. The extent to which ancient Mediterranean practices persisted into the beginnings of modern representative government cannot be ascertained with any degree of certainty. The once-vaunted barbarian contributions are likewise indeterminate and no longer vehemently publicized.

The Teutonic myth has been dispelled with such finality that only a word about it need be said here.[33] To the inquiring mind, hints of representation can be found in many situations. To the person who perceives these hints, and who has a bias in favor of the "Anglo-Saxon freedom of spirit," the jump from the hints to representative government is easy. The German barbarians' approval of the chief through "the clashing of spears" seemed to be some sort of popular assemblage approving the tribal officials. But to one who knows of modern Fascism, this situation also has connotations of the perfunctory acclaim of a totalitarian election.[34]

---

[32] E. M. Sait, *op. cit.*, pp. 480-499, states: "It was not in the Teutonic north of Europe that medieval representation originated, but in the Roman south, where it found a basis in tradition and in surviving municipal self-government."

[33] The person interested in the steps in the dissolution of the myth might consult: Thomas Wright, *The Celt, the Roman, and the Saxon,* London, 1852; Thomas Nicholas, *The Pedigree of the English People,* London, 1868; Henry Hallam, *Constitutional History of England,* London, 1865; Numia D. F. Coulanges, in *Revue des Questions Historiques* (April, 1889); H. Munro Chadwick, *The Origin of the English Nation,* Cambridge, 1907; *The Heroic Age,* Cambridge, 1912; Henry Jones Ford, *op. cit.;* C. A. Beard, "The Teutonic Origins of Representative Government," *American Political Science Review,* Vol. 26 (1932), p. 28; E. M. Sait, *op. cit.*

[34] The theory held that the German tribes were free communities. This free community was territorially designated a "mark." The men of the "mark" held assembly to which all free men belonged, and this assembly governed the local community. From the "mark" government, representative government developed,

The chief evidence of representative government before the Norman Conquest is the existence of the Hundred Court, with the reeve and four members of each tun in attendance. These men undoubtedly held some power, and acted in place of the rest of the tun. The Hundred Court in those times, too, was more than a judicial body; it had administrative functions as well. Here was a weak shadow of things to come. But no great importance should be attached to it. For representative government to come about, drastic changes had to occur in England. Foreign inventions had to be introduced.

The medieval Roman Catholic Church was both the initiator and the carrier of political innovations in representative government. Its role at particular times is hard to define. In the earliest period, the Church functioned through assemblies in the different dioceses and provinces. There was no conscious democratic mode of selection at first. Leadership came from the top. The bishops attended the provincial councils by virtue of their office, without any express mandate from the people. The elective mode of achieving representation was not applied. The elite, or ruling class, were recruited because of their "blessedness, saintliness, or asceticism," and it was not until the conciliar movement in the twilight of the Middle Ages that democratic assemblies were proposed, with control reaching even to the Papacy.

Most writers find the beginnings of the Church's contributions to representative government in the various monastic orders which grew up in the twelfth and thirteenth centuries.[35] Of these, the most famous and influential was the Order of Dominicans. Its constitution, which was probably drafted at the first general chapter in 1221, followed the general lines of that of the Cistercian order. The friars of each convent elected a representative to speak their views at the provincial chapter. Members of the provincial chapter elected the pro-

---

covered at one stage in history by the Norman feudalism. Absolutist systems in Europe destroyed the germs of democracy, except in the obscure forest customs of Switzerland.

All of this spinning is neat but not fact. There is no evidence of there ever being a "mark" in England.

[35] See Ford, *op. cit.,* Chapter 10; Clarke, *op. cit.,* Chapters 12-14; Ernest Barker, *The Dominican Order and Convocation,* Oxford, 1913; R. W. and A. J. Carlyle, *A History of Medieval Political Theory,* New York and London, 1903-1936.

vincial prior who represented the province in the general chapter. The importance of the Dominicans lay, not in the novelty of their organization, but in their sojourn in England at a crucial period for representative purposes. The Fourth Lateran Council of 1215 had employed the principle of representation extensively, over eight hundred priors and abbots being present to represent their orders. But the Dominicans between 1221 and 1236 established nearly a score of houses in England. A principle made evident by other factors in English history which we have mentioned, stimulated by the example of the Cortes of Spain and the assemblies of Southern France and Italy, was impressed more strongly with the stamp of universality by its use in Church organization on a permanent and widespread scale.[36]

King John of England expressed the idea of representation by summoning four knights from each shire to consult with him on affairs of the realm in 1213. This body, however, seems never to have met. In 1226 there was an assemblage at Lincoln of elected knights, four from each shire, to draw up complaints against the sheriffs who were engaged in their customary sharp practices. Elected knights were summoned; these met with the Curia Regis in 1254. In 1264, Simon de Montfort called three knights from each shire to Parliament, and in 1265 summoned two knights and two burgesses from each shire to his second Parliament.[37] The practice of de Montfort continued after his death.

At a period whose intricacies are little known to us, these specific dates do not mean much in trying to trace the evolution of so abstruse a concept as representation. The numerous conditions for rep-

---

[36] Clarke does not think the example of the Dominicans was widely known, *op. cit.,* p. 304. Barker wrote: "the Dominicans and their institutions were well known in the central places of England, at Oxford and at London, we can see that the heads of Church and State, Langton and Kilwardby, de Montfort, and Edward I, were familiar with the Order." See his *Dominican Order and Convocation,* Oxford, 1913, p. 25.

[37] Before 1265, the King in Council summoned representatives of specific towns to meet him for special purposes. See A. B. White, *American Historical Review,* Vol. 19, p. 742. Before 1265 there was representation, but only after that date was there the foundation for representative government. May McKisack, *The Parliamentary Representation of the English Boroughs during the Middle Ages,* London, 1932, p. 2, says: "The whole assembly has been well described 'the convention of a party rather than a true parliament,' and to see in it evidence of de Montfort's wish to apply the representative principle to the summoning of the Great Council is to misunderstand the nature of his opposition to the Crown."

resentation which have been already suggested cannot be well tied to dates.

Different kinds of representation come from different sources. To trace "representation" to the Greek confederation pattern, as does McLeod; to the Dominican order, as does Barker; or to the family connections of Lockland, as does Sait, is like explaining Nazism solely in terms of Hitler's personality. Maude Clarke adopts a most sensible approach. She isolates the principle of representation from the principle of consent, and shows that permutations and combinations of both were being made during the twelfth and thirteenth centuries in both secular and ecclesiastical organization. Her idea is "that representation in itself could have achieved little, unless it had gained direction and reality as the vehicle for the doctrine of consent." [38]

Representation is possible without a doctrine of consent, but representative government through a parliament is not. Before a representative government can come into being, there must exist in practice an idea of representation and an idea of consent. Before the idea of consent can be made workable in accomplishing representative government, there must be applied the principle of majority rule. Ultimately, representation, consent, and majority rule depend upon a grasping of the essentials of corporate theory. The corporate idea implements both consent and representation. Consent is a means of attaining representation. It is basically connected with the idea of responsibility. It is necessary in laying the foundations of elections and assemblies. Consequently, Miss Clarke's discussion of representation and consent as two distinct principles is a significant contribution to the study of the origins of representative government.

The doctrine of consent means merely that the wishes of the ruled shall be followed by the rulers. The idea of popular consent was imbedded in Roman law from the days of the Republic, and not even the centuries of absolutism could dislodge it. It was part of the heritage the Church received from Rome, and the ecclesiastical scholars transmitted belief in popular consent to the early modern governments.

---

[38] *Op. cit.*, p. 276.

As for the doctrine of consent with reference to Church and state, the Church dignitaries claimed that the privilege against the monarch was representative of a universal body with independence of the temporal state. Consent had to be asked for taxation of Church property.

Even without any Church or Roman influence, the doctrine of consent would have prospered. Among the barbarians, a hint of consent was to be found in approval signified by a clashing of spears. More significantly, the doctrine of consent underlay the feudal system. The duties of one man to another were fairly well defined. Certain payments had to be made; they were part of the feudal "bargain." Frequently the lord or king asked for more than his vassals were required to give. These aids were gracious and voluntary, and for them, consent was necessary.

The doctrine of consent did not flourish unopposed. There was the impossibility of securing unanimity when consent was thought of as a private and personal right. All persons with the right could not be polled efficiently. Both Pope and Crown opposed the attempts of the lower clergy to work out a system whereby consent could be the basis for action.[39]

The solution through representation made consent a permanent feature of the English political system. Representation was evolved from consent expressed through the corporate body and the principle of majority rule. Both were at last intertwined.

In the beginning of the Curia Regis, a magistrate who was absent from a meeting was not bound by the laws of the meeting. Each lord would fight desperately for his privilege of declining any imposition of power upon himself. If the Curia was to function as a governing body, it could not pass laws which in origin were merely innumerable private bargains. During the first quarter of the thirteenth century, laws of the Curia were only such. Ideas of majority rule and of power to bind the absent were found in the monastic orders of that period, but not in the Curia.

As influences towards this innovation in the Curia, there must be listed the Church, the incorporated borough, and the representation of many by one in the shires (*i.e.,* the knights). All factors weaken-

---

[39] Clarke, *op. cit.,* p. 266.

ing feudal ties and making the magnates in the Curia group-conscious tended towards the corporate spirit. As Gierke put it, "the concept of a real Group-Personality, [which] will, unreservedly and in all aspects, replace the idea of mandate by the idea of an appointment to a specialized political function, and the idea of Agency (that is, the representation of one person by another person and thus of the whole by the whole) by the idea of Organism." [40]

Medieval German and Italian political theorists and jurists were writing about "complete and absorptive representation" wherein there was no responsibility of ruler to ruled. The Church had used the corporate idea in describing its own constitution. The medieval town gained independence and effectiveness through its conception of itself as a body with a mayor as head. Medieval theories of politics, wrote Gierke, "borrowed from corporation law, besides the conception of the ruler as a representative of the community, and the derivation of the principle of majority rule from the representation of all by the majority, the theoretical formulation of the idea, long current in the Middle Ages, of the exercise of the rights belonging to a community by an assembly of representatives." [41]

In England there was great hesitation in accepting corporate theories. Towns struggled along for decades without heads, bodies, or limbs. They were encumbered by the limited belief that all who made up the town must act for it on all occasions.

Various substitute fictions and analogies were used for dealing with embarrassing cases that involved aggregations of men. The courts tried the idea of agency, of guardianship, and even of family law; e.g., "the abbot is held for the torts of a monk, as a husband for the torts of the wife." [42] This state of legal theory persisted until after the first parliaments, though the latter were based upon representative principles. But note that in Parliament, it was the idea of agency which prevailed, not that of organic representation which Gierke speaks about. A smooth-working assemblage needed more than a feeble theoretical framework. Unless a conception of integrity and cohesion were established, Parliamentary business would be encumbered by individualistic interpretations of its nature.

---

[40] Otto Friedrich von Gierke, *Das Deutsche Genossenschaftsrecht,* p. 248.
[41] *Op. cit.,* p. 241.
[42] Goebel, *op. cit.,* p. 530.

Indigenous precedent and hostility to foreign and canon law made the courts reluctant to accept corporate fictions.

Not until about 1345 does one find cases such as the one where a court considered London a "commonalty like an individual person that might have an action in its common name the way a single person can." [43] Once the precedent was established, English parliamentarians clung tenaciously to the corporate idea. Sir Thomas Smith, Sidney, Burke, and others preached that Parliament was the nation; the theory of "virtual" representation was based upon the idea, and even Bagehot held that the suffrage did not need to be extended to the workers, who were spoken for by the middle class in Parliament.[44]

When this occurred, the ground was prepared for the principle of majority rule. It was to the King's interest to have a group that could act as a unit so that "the royal right to demand competent subsidies was resolved, not on personal, but on corporate lines. For this reason, Parliament took shape as *communitas communitatum.*" [45]

Miss Clarke found that "the theory of the corporate existence of the council was developed in order to meet the difficulty of taxing subtenants." [46] The King assumed the burden of collecting taxes from the men of the magnates, instead of having each level of the feudal structure collect from the next lowest. This procedure, done in the name of royal authority, rendered insecure the bargaining position of the subtenants, but it gave the council a corporate character, for the King was authorized by that body to go directly to the subtenants. By 1226, the Curia Regis was acting as a corporate entity by binding absent members to its decisions. Since the magnates of the realm acted only for themselves, they might utilize the doctrine of consent and majority rule in the council, but they had no need for the principle of representation except insofar as some men sent proxies to represent them on various occasions.

The clergy seem to have been the first to put together the ideas of representation and consent.[47] But the proctors of the clergy never became part of the English national assembly. They held their assemblies separately from the Commons and the Lords.

----

[43] *Ibid.,* p. 573.
[44] Walter Bagehot, *The English Constitution,* New York, 1882, pp. 241-242.
[45] Clarke, *op. cit.,* p. 370.
[46] *Ibid.,* p. 258.
[47] *Ibid.,* p. 317.

By the end of the thirteenth century, the Crown had lost the power of being financially independent of Parliament, and so was dependent upon the latter's consent for revenues. The struggle between Crown and barons strengthened the Commons, whose support was sought by both sides. The political situation was such that the King depended upon the support of the knights and burgesses, while the Commons could not control the King's actions unless they gave a *quid pro quo*. Each needed the other, and representative government resulted.[48]

The *Modus Tenendi Parliamentum* (*circa* 1322) saw Parliament as a unified whole, its members as peers, but the Commons as most worthy and deservedly foremost of the estates.[49] The doctrine of consent and representation found in it became extended into fictions, until, in 1583, Sir Thomas Smith could write that Parliament

> . . . representeth and hath power of the whole realme, both the head and the bodie. For evere Englishman is entended to be there present, either by person or by procuration and attornies of whatever preheminence, state, dignitie, or qualities soever he be, from the Princ (be he king or Queene) to the lowest person in England, and the consent of Parliament is taken to be everie man's consent.[50]

It was about this time that the English colonies were forming in North America, with political structures based upon the English to a great extent. But local peculiarities evolved significant differences. The colonies drew upon British eighteenth-century experience with Parliamentary institutions, but they also drew upon their own experience as British colonies. The colonial charters emphasized the corporate theories and also the doctrine of consent. Many of the charters provided for governments which were more democratic than that of the home country. Following the American Revolution, State governments were established which were based upon the colo-

---

[48] Charles H. McIlwain, *The Growth of Political Thought in the West*, New York, 1932, p. 373, says: "If the king in all cases could appropriate *de jure* his subjects' goods without their consent, this constitutional development would have been impossible and is now incomprehensible. . . . What is not so generally understood is the fact that the subjects would have had no need to buy redress if they could always demand it as a right. Redress was in large measure voluntary on the King's part, supply was in the main voluntary on the part of the subject."

[49] Clarke, *op. cit.*, p. 11.

[50] *De Republica Anglorum*, ed. by L. Alston, London, 1906, p. 49.

nial charters, the English Parliament, and the revolutionary doctrines.

This meant that after 1776 Americans did not regard their representative assemblies in the light of the primordial use of Parliament in wresting concessions from the Crown. The Revolution meant to them the end of the struggle with the Crown. The State legislature was the organ of a sovereign people. The doctrines of natural rights which had been used to justify the Revolution were now used to furnish the theoretical foundation for the new governments. As William Seal Carpenter has put it, "The representative body was not conceived to be an agency for the control of government; it was to be a part of the government itself. . . . This conception of the representative body (on the part of the 'Founding Fathers') sprang from the notion of the state as a compact." [51] At the beginning of their existence as a separate nation, the people of the United States regarded the legislature as their instrument to be used to advance their safety, comfort, and happiness.

The framing of the United States Constitution was another step forward in the development of representative government. A new device, which was called the "federal system," was invented to grant a large measure of local autonomy and yet at the same time provide for a national government strong enough to defend the states collectively, command the respect of foreign countries, and prevent internal strife whether of a commercial or violent character. The new Congress of the United States was not a gathering of ambassadors from the several States, but a national legislature whose powers were to grow as the country expanded. At the same time, the Constitution protected the rights of the States in those matters which the "Founding Fathers" thought should be left to the localities. The Supreme Court of the United States gradually evolved as the guardian of the Constitution and the latter's system of a territorial division of powers. Thus the Americans developed a system of representation which gave a maximum of freedom and self-determination to the localities, and also provided the framework for a vigorous nation.[52]

---

[51] *Democracy and Representation,* Princeton, The Princeton University Press, 1925, p. 48.

[52] Robert Luce, *Legislative Principles,* Boston, 1930, pp. 82-333.

Chapter 10

DEVICES FOR ACCOMPLISHING
REPRESENTATION

In the III Epistle of *An Essay on Man*, where (according to his own "argument") the author discusses various forms of government, and the true end of all, Pope says:

> "For Forms of Government let fools contest;
> Whate'er is best administered is best:"

If Pope were alive today he would find a world of fools, because men have inevitably formalized their governmental structures whenever they became complicated and specialized. From then on, changes in form were debated in a vigorous fashion. Despite Pope, it is also a truism that governmental forms under certain conditions do make a difference. As an American political scientist has put it, "Political institutions have a twofold function; they favor the accession of men of particular attributes to positions of effective influence, and they continue to operate upon the personalities of the influential." [1] It is the problem of this chapter to consider some of the effects of different devices for representation.

There are two principal forms of representation, the single-member-district plan and the multi-membered-district system. Each type has a great number of subvarieties, and the relative merits of this or that system have been hotly debated by political scientists as well as by public men. In fact, there are few governmental subjects which have been more bitterly debated than the system of representation. [2] Scholars who have no difficulty in maintaining calmness and objectivity on most subjects become emotional when this or that scheme of representation is defended or attacked.

---

[1] H. D. Lasswell, "Types of Political Personalities," in *Personality and the Group*, edited by E. W. Burgess, Chicago, 1929.

[2] For two sides of the proportional representation controversy see F. A. Hermens, *Democracy or Anarchy: A Study of Proportional Representation*, Notre Dame, Indiana, 1941, and G. H. Hallett and C. G. Hoag, *Proportional Representation*, Washington, D. C., 1937.

The single-member-district plan is the older, since it has had a long history in England, the Mother of Parliaments. When only two candidates are nominated, it secures majority representation. Even in England, however, the two-party system has not been continuously in operation, and the presence of three or more candidates in a contest for one seat is likely to lead to plurality election if the candidates are about even in popularity. Attempts to reconcile the theory of majority rule where more than two important contenders are likely to appear have led to the invention of a variety of devices for combining the votes for different candidates so as to produce a majority for one. Among these devices should be considered the different forms of preferential voting, the alternative vote, and the double-balloting plan.

The single-member-district system may be used to elect a legislator or a chief executive officer from a large or small area. In the United States, examples of the above purposes would be in turn: the election of a State representative, the election of a United States senator, and the election of a mayor, a governor, or the President.

The fundamental theory behind the multi-membered district is that in a democracy the varieties of opinion in the electorate should be represented. One man cannot reflect all shades of opinion that might be found in a given constituency. While the plan is used to select a plural-headed executive, as in commission-manager cities in the United States, in general it may be said that the plan is part and parcel of democratic theory that legislation should be the product of a body of representatives, and not that of a single representative. The multi-membered system, then, is not in complete accord with the presidential plan under which the executive tends to increase his legislative powers.

Another characteristic of the thinking behind the multi-membered-district plan is the emphasis upon large electoral areas as compared with small ones. It is contended that the electoral process functions at a higher level if the constituency is larger. The logical conclusion to be drawn from this contention is that elections should be at large for the governmental unit concerned, *i.e.*, a city council should be elected as a body from the entire city and not by wards.

As in the case of the single-member-district plan, so in the multi-membered there are the problems of majority and minority representation. If a block system of voting is used, then it might happen that all the candidates elected would be the candidates of a particular party. If there were more than two well-disciplined parties, then the block system might not secure the election of a body which had behind it a majority of the voters. Such a possibility has led publicists and mathematicians to devise plans for securing majority and minority representation. Proportional representation, as these plans are called, is designed to secure a mathematical reflection of the strength of the various groups in the electorate which are politically articulate. Great ingenuity has been shown in devising schemes to accomplish this. There are various list systems with different quotas which were popular in continental Europe of the Weimar period, and then there is the famous English-Danish single transferable vote plan which has been employed in English-speaking jurisdictions.

After treating the details of these plans, we shall compare the advantages and disadvantages of the various forms. Emphasis will be placed upon the political and intellectual controversies which have waged around the single-member-district plan and this or that type of proportional representation.

One of the questions to be considered is whether or not the man who initially represents only a minority of the electors can truly be said to be a representative of his constituency, that is, of a majority of his community. This question can only be answered by a knowledge of the demands men make of their representatives, whether they ask the complete fulfillment of their specific demands, whether they know what they want, whether they are prepared to stand by their original ideas against any and all alternatives, and whether a choice between two men is just as satisfactory as a choice among more than two men. Answers to these queries would help determine whether the single-member district is the proper answer to the desire of representation.

Single-Member-District Plan

If we combine the single-member-district plan with the theory that large constituencies are better than small ones, then we come to the conclusion that the electors should choose a President but not a Congress, a governor but not a State legislature, a mayor but not a city council. On the other hand, if we assume that small constituencies have a place in the democratic system, then a case can be made out for the election of a legislative body by small units. As a matter of fact, these are the only kind of national elections to be found in England, with its long experience with representative government. There is a body of opinion which contends that the American practice of electing a single representative-at-large and setting him off against the body of locally elected representatives is highly objectionable. The merits of these different positions will presently be considered.

Majority or Plurality?

Where the two-party system prevails, the single-member-district system automatically insures that the successful candidate will have a majority of the votes cast. Of course it will not necessarily mean that a majority of the eligible voters will be behind him. This would be possible only when his majority was large, and when the amount of non-voting was negligible.[3] This is an extremely difficult situation to bring about, since interest in voting declines when the contest is not an even one.[4]

The presence of more than two candidates, even though one of them may not have much chance of election, means that the successful candidate may have only a plurality of the votes cast. If the contest were a close three-cornered one, the successful candidate might win with 34 per cent of the vote cast.[5] The more candidates in the running, and the closer their vote, the smaller would be the proportion of the total vote cast that went to the winning candidate. To take an extreme case: If there were ten evenly matched candidates, the successful one would need only one vote over one tenth of the vote cast. Under such circumstances it might be hard to say that the result gave "representation" to the district.

Such are the possibilities according to simple arithmetic. What are the facts? In England, Parliamentary elections produce many

[3] For example: Let 10,000 = the total electorate.
Let 6,000 = the vote cast.
If the successful candidate receives 4,000 votes, this is only 40 per cent of the total electorate. To get a majority of the electorate, he would have to win 5,001 votes, but this is 5/6 of the vote cast. Such a one-sided election would discourage later participation.

[4] H. F. Gosnell, *Why Europe Votes,* Chicago, 1930, pp. 14, 50.

[5] A good example is to be found in the gubernatorial election in the state of Kansas in 1932, when Alfred Landon won in a three-cornered contest.

three-cornered contests. The winning candidates frequently receive only a minority of the votes cast. Though the Proportional Representation Society in England was greatly concerned about the non-representation of majorities in three-membered constituencies, there is no evidence that the voters were particularly alarmed. Their attitudes were determined largely by their political preferences. If their party stood a chance to gain by the division of the forces of the opposition, then they did not mind the plurality system. The Conservatives and Labourites took this point of view. If the plurality system squeezed a given party between two overpowering tendencies, then the supporters of that party were unhappy about it. This was the position of the British Liberal Party after the election of 1918. Before 1914, the Liberals had not been particularly critical of the single-member-district plan. After the dissolution of the Lloyd George coalition government, it became obvious that the Liberal Party was to be the victim of a squeeze between the Conservative and Labour parties. Liberal leaders became ardent advocates of proportional representation.[6]

In the United States, the single-member-district plurality plan has systematically discouraged third-party movements. The Progressive movement in 1912 split the Republican Party, brought about a Democratic victory for President, and aided in the election of Democratic congressmen in many districts. The Progressives were not satisfied with this negative result, so they soon drifted back to the major parties where they would have a chance to vote with the majority.

In the state of Wisconsin, the Progressive Party launched in 1934 by the LaFollette brothers, Robert M., Jr. and Philip, resulted in many plurality victories in the election of the State legislature. In the Wisconsin senatorial and gubernatorial contests between 1934 and 1940, inclusive, on only two occasions did the successful candidate receive a majority of the votes cast.[7] Plurality elections were the rule, and in 1940, Heil, a Republican, was elected with only 40.8 per cent of the total vote cast.[8]

---

[6] Prime Ministers Asquith and Lloyd George.
[7] Robert M. LaFollette, Jr.'s election as U. S. Senator in 1934 and Heil's election as Governor in 1938.
[8] H. F. Gosnell, *Grass Roots Politics,* Washington, D. C., 1942, p. 150.

Since the winning of a majority is regarded as highly desirable in itself, every effort is made to bring about this result automatically. On the continent of Europe a common device employed in the presence of the multiple-party system was the double-balloting system. If no candidate received a majority at the first balloting, then a second balloting was held. In Germany prior to 1918, the rule at the second balloting was that only the two highest candidates on the first balloting would be eligible to run. This rule insured a majority election. In the United States it is employed by a number of states having the run-off primary.[9] In France from 1870 to 1919, and again from 1928 to 1936, this rule was not employed. Just as many candidates could run in the second balloting as had run in the first. Actually, however, many candidates dropped out at the second balloting. Under the Weimar Constitution the Germans employed this system for the election of the president. This was of significance in 1932, since the Communist candidate, Ernst Thalmann, refused to withdraw, and Hindenburg was elected rather than Marx. If Thalmann had been eliminated from the second balloting, then it is probable that Marx could have won.[10] Marx would not have given Hitler the opportunities which Hindenburg did. Whether this characteristic of the German election system can be held to be responsible for Hitler's coming to power, we cannot say. Hitler might have seized power in some other fashion.

In several American jurisdictions, systems of preferential voting have been employed in order to secure majority elections. Some of the plans have been defective from the logical point of view, and consequently they have not brought about the desired result. This can be said of the so-called Bucklin system, named after its founder, James W. Bucklin, of Grand Junction, Colorado.[11] From the theoretical point of view, the most perfect plan is the alternative (single transferable) vote plan, which has the advantages of the double-ballot system and yet involves the trouble and expense of only a single election. Under this system, instead of putting a cross mark or some other standard marking, the voter places a number opposite

[9] Georgia, Louisiana, Mississippi, North Carolina, South Carolina, and Texas.
[10] Hindenburg, 53 per cent; Hitler, 36.8 per cent; and Thalmann, 10.2 per cent.
[11] It was used in Grand Junction, Colorado, from 1909 until 1923. The system is defective, since the later choices may count against the first choice. See Hoag and Hallett, *op. cit.*, pp. 485-492.

the name of the candidate which represents the order in which he would rank that candidate. The voter puts the figure 1 opposite his first choice, the figure 2 opposite his second choice, the figure 3 opposite his third choice, and so on until he has expressed as many choices as he wishes to make among the candidates running. When the ballots are counted through the first time, only the first choices are considered. If a candidate receives a majority of the first choices, then he is declared elected. If no candidate receives a majority in this first count, then there are additional counts based upon the second and later choices. The next step is the elimination of the low man on the first count, and the distribution of his ballots according to the next available choices. If the second balloting system were used in a three-cornered election, one could obtain practically the same result as under the double-balloting plan. The principal difference is that the voter under the alternative-vote plan indicates in advance how he would vote if it should turn out that his candidate has no chance of being elected.[12]

The alternative-vote plan has been used with satisfactory results in parts of Canada, Australia, and the United States.[13] The system does not have greater vogue because under the plurality plan the major parties may squeeze minor parties as in England and the United States. Politicians in jurisdictions which have the double-balloting system do not favor the alternative vote because it would compel them to make their bargains and do their maneuvering before a single election. The time between the first and second ballotings is usually employed by the candidates and party leaders in political intrigue. The first balloting gives the politicians a view of their bargaining power. Under the alternative-vote plan, they would be working in the dark to a greater extent.

Large or Small Districts

One theory of democracy holds that the electoral districts should be small so that voters may have a chance to get acquainted with the candidates. The tiny Swiss electoral units, the *Landesgemeinde,* are

---

[12] See Appendix B.
[13] C. E. Merriam and L. Overacker, *Primary Elections,* Chicago, 1942, pp. 83-85; Hoag and Hallett, *op. cit.,* pp. 483-485.

looked upon with favor because they illustrate what democracy means when it is based upon primary contacts. All the voters come together in a common meeting place to elect officers and pass upon measures. In thickly populated centers it would be obviously ridiculous to try to elect a legislature on such a basis. The electorate would be so large that no place large enough for it to meet in could be found. In a large country, then, physical difficulties rule out the small arena where national candidates and constituents can meet each other commonly in face-to-face situations. If the democratic system in the modern state must operate largely upon the basis of secondary contacts, then the question is: How large should the electoral district be under these conditions?

If a large area is to be used, say, the entire United States, then it would be difficult to elect an entire legislative body from this unit. In Ireland, the attempt to elect an upper house from the entire country was not a success. It follows that from such a large constituency a much more workable system is the single-member plan. Carried to its logical conclusion, it would mean the election of a president or governor and no other representative. It would be a one-man rule, but a popular (representative) not a hereditary one. In history, the representative system has always been closely identified with a legislative body. Experience with elective monarchs has so frequently resulted in the abandonment of the popular feature that it might be said that this system is highly unstable. Cromwell, the Napoleons, and, if we may call him an elective monarch, Hitler, abolished the electoral control aspects of their regimes soon after coming to power.

Assuming, then, that a legislative body is to be chosen, what is the proper size of the districts? The answer depends upon the size and distribution of the electorate, the size of the resulting legislative body, and the character of the means of communication between representatives and constituents. If the population is large and widely scattered, small districts would produce an unwieldy legislative body. Within certain limits, the smaller the legislative body, the easier it is for the body to function. To take an example, it is commonly agreed that the American Senate, a body of ninety-six, is a more effective legislative agency than the American House of Representatives, which has four hundred and thirty-five members.[14] It is also agreed that the New York City Council of from seventeen to twenty-six under the 1936 charter is more effective than the old Board of Aldermen of sixty-five.[15]

Small districts give rise to what is called in America, "peanut politics." The relationship between a representative and his constituents in a small area may be closer, but on that account it may be less wholesome for the body politic. This is a paradox of modern democracy. The ideal democratic system of Rousseau was based on primary contacts. Yet, in the machine age, primary contacts may be corrosive. Life has become so complex, and interests so varied, that it is difficult to find that identity of interests in a constituency which characterized the rural areas of Rousseau's or Thomas Jefferson's days. The modern politician in a small area can make primary contacts, but these contacts are based upon "bread-and-butter" arguments. They are casual contacts, likely to be based upon the granting of favors. Voters may support candidate "A" because the party worker of "A's" party fixed a traffic ticket or did some other petty favor for him which was not related in any way to major political questions which faced the body politic. Primary contacts do not have to be corrosive. Sidney Webb, when he was the parliamentary representative for a Newcastle mining constituency, did a splendid job in educating his constituents on the issues of the day.[16] Demands made upon the modern legislator, however, are such that he does not have time to make many primary contacts, so he has to leave this to others. While British politicians have a high code of ethics, the victory of a Frank Gray and his final defeat by a football hero in the Oxford constituency can hardly be regarded as great triumphs for democracy. Gray prided himself on his ability to make primary contacts. His methods were those of the Fuller Brush Man and not those of a. Socrates in the market place.[17] "Fuller-Brush politicians" are all too common in the American municipal scene.[18]

---

[14] L. Rogers, *The American Senate*, New York, 1926.
[15] F. A. Hermens, *Democracy or Anarchy*, Notre Dame, Indiana, 1941, p. 401.
[16] S. Webb, "The Story of the Durham Miners," in *Labour Year Book* (1919).
[17] Frank Gray, *Confessions of a Candidate*, London, 1925.
[18] J. T. Salter, *Boss Rule*, New York, 1935; H. F. Gosnell, *Machine Politics: Chicago Model*, Chicago, 1937; D. H. Kurtzman, *Methods of Controlling Votes in Philadelphia*, Philadelphia, 1935.

Some of them push their way into the State legislatures and into Congress. It is significant that Huey Long got his start in Louisiana as a door-to-door salesman.[19]

Contacts between the politicians and the voters in a modern city are too superficial to furnish the basis of communication regarding policy matters. The smaller the area, the more unfortunate may be the results. The election of precinct committeemen in Philadelphia has produced many abuses.[20] It was not that the voters were venal. They were too busy with their own affairs, the election was too insignificant, and the scoundrels running for office were too smooth. The voters failed to realize that they were selling their democratic birthright for a mess of pottage.

In the rural areas, the small electoral unit still functions more effectively than in the urban. The election of school boards in the United States by tiny school districts, however, can hardly be regarded as a success. The school boards have lacked vision for coping with the problems of education. Modern life can no longer be based upon isolated self-contained communities. Larger areas are necessary for providing the education needed in our technological age. Local school boards may reflect the views of isolated communities, but these communities no longer reflect the spirit of the modern age.

The election of a representative from a larger area means greater dependence upon the means of mass communication. Those who control those means are in an advantageous position. The candidate who has access to the press, the radio, and the motion pictures has a big head start in a campaign which covers a large number of widely scattered voters. If the opposing candidate does not have the same opportunity to use these facilities, he must rely upon pamphlets, meetings, and canvassers. Where the stakes are large, it is feasible to recruit persons to do these tasks. In the United States it is possible to get volunteer workers for Presidential campaigns, but it is extremely difficult to do so for the election of precinct committeemen.

Especially in the larger cities the contrast between the results obtained in the large and small districts stands out. In Detroit much

19 Hartnett T. Kane, *Louisiana Hayride,* New York, 1941; Carlton Beals, *The Story of Huey P. Long,* New York, 1935.
20 Salter, *op. cit.,* Kurtzman, *op. cit.*

better results were obtained under the plan which provided for the election of the councilmen-at-large for the entire city than under the old ward plan.[21]   The same can be said for New York City, although the election-at-large brought with it a new system of marking and counting the ballots.[22]   There is no question that the trend in American cities has been toward the larger municipal electoral constituencies and away from the old ward plan with its emphasis upon localism and petty politics.   The larger area will not insure good results, and there have been outstanding city fathers chosen from wards; but looking at general tendencies it is safe to say that it is easier to uproot rascals who face city-wide publicity than it is to uproot those who have their tentacles on local graft, local favors, and local friendships.   City machines may be uprooted, but ward bosses are the most difficult persons to defeat in the entire American electoral system.[23]   Even when their city leaders are deposed they cling to the control of their party in their bailiwicks, waiting patiently for a shift in party fortunes.

Apportionment, Gerrymandering, and Rotten Boroughs

In order to carry out the theory of "one man, one vote" in the selection of representatives by geographical areas, some system of fairly equal apportionment must be employed.   There is no problem of apportionment where a representative or a group of representatives is chosen from the whole society, as in the case of the American President or the New York City Council under the charter of 1936. The framers of the United States Constitution, and the framers of every State constitution, were faced with the problem of apportionment, since the initial decision had been made to recognize localities in the selection of legislators.   In the various post-war international organizations it has been necessary to work out elaborate rules for the apportionment of expenses.

Apportionment is the allotting of representatives on the basis of geographical or sociological considerations.   The geographical basis is the one most commonly used.   In Soviet Russia a rough grouping system was employed under the constitution of 1918.   Geography

---

[21] W. P. Lovett, *Detroit Rules Itself*, Boston, 1930.
[22] See below, pp. 185-87.
[23] H. F. Gosnell, *Machine Politics*, Chapter 2.

as the basis of apportionment is a reflector, in some cases, of a low group cohesion. The surveyor's lines may cut across social, class, economic, religious, occupational, age, racial, and sex barriers. Within an arbitrary area, any reflection of group sentiment is bound to be less vivid than if some concerted effort were made to isolate sects and parties. Basically, of course, the mere fact of dividing a society into geographical areas is in response to the demand for greater representation of local interests.

Since the matters of apportionment and system of representation are generally treated separately, we shall follow that practice here. Apportionment is a treatment of society numerically, a treatment which ignores social differences for the most part and uses the idea of "rugged individualism" instead. It assumes and fosters the idea of great social mobility, of a lack of crystallization of status, and of a perfect equality of participation. The two requirements which make apportionment a truly neutral device, and which divorce it from all except purely coincidental relationship to social groups, are equality of population for each district and purely geometric drawing of district boundaries.

Originally, places and not persons were recognized as the units to be considered in making an apportionment. Each British borough sent its representative to the House of Commons. Variations in the size of the borough were not considered to be of importance so far as the composition of the House was concerned. The Reform Act of 1832 was a partial recognition of the number of inhabitants. Even the 1928 Representation of the People (Equal Franchise) Act was not exclusively based upon the equal population theory.

In the United States, counties or towns were first used as units for forming legislative districts. Later on, population became the basis, but never to the exclusion of local political lines. What parts of the population should be counted? Should it be the entire population, the citizen population, the registered vote, or the actual vote? Arguments can be adduced for any one of these bases. The total population is the one which is most commonly used. The citizen population would be as fair as any.

The two evils of apportionment are "rotten boroughs" and gerrymandering. To gerrymander is to make an arrangement whereby the dominant political party in a legislature preserves or augments its power over the State by drawing district boundaries so as to maximize the voting potential of its own constituents and minimize that of its opponents. This is effected by massing its opponent's voters in a few districts and its own voters in such a manner that they are in a small majority in as many districts as possible. "Rotten boroughs" are disproportionately small electoral districts of declining population which retain their membership at the cost of districts of increasing population.

Gerrymandering is a deliberate act; "rotten boroughs" are historical accidents retained by a deliberate inactivity. The first violates the requirement of apportionment, that the boundaries of districts be geometrical; *i.e.*, contiguous and accidental. The second violates the requirement, that equal populations should send an equal number of members to the representative body.

The "rotten borough" is found in English history and in present-day American legislatures. Any distinction between the two is a matter of defining the degree of "rottenness." In England, the decline of once populous towns accounted for the growth of "rotten boroughs" at an early date. From the sixteenth to the nineteenth century the process continued. In 1793, one hundred and fifty-seven members of the Commons were chosen by eighty-four persons, and the majority of the Commons was responsible to fewer than fifteen thousand electors. In 1827, two hundred and seventy-six seats were held by the sole grace of patrons. The Reform Act of 1832 dealt a fatal blow to the system of "rotten boroughs," but it took the Acts of 1867 and 1884 to restore the democratic character of the franchise which had existed at the beginning of the borough system.[24]

The gerrymander is typical of American politics, but it has also been practiced in France.[25] In Europe, the experiments in democracy brought the list system of voting and proportional representation, under which gerrymandering is well-nigh impossible on any significant scale. But where the single-member-district system prevails, it is an effective tool of the ruling party. When France

---

[24] See May McKisack, *The Parliamentary Representation of English Boroughs,* Oxford, 1932; E. and A. G. Porritt, *The Unreformed House of Commons,* 2 vols., Cambridge, 1903; Charles Seymour, *Electoral Reform in England and Wales: 1832-1885,* New Haven, 1915. Also see the chapter on "The Gaining of the Suffrage." For a treatment of American "rotten boroughs," see below, pp. 177-83.

[25] Walter R. Sharp, "The New French Electoral Law and the Elections of 1928," *American Political Science Review,* Vol. 22 (August, 1928), pp. 684-698.

changed from *scrutin de liste* to *scrutin d'arrondissement* in 1927, the committee in charge of redistricting flagrantly violated the canons of equality and accident in favor of the Center bloc. The metropolitan region of Paris was greatly discriminated against. The Communists were gathered into a few districts with great majorities, while the Radical Socialists were spread out thinly where they would do the most good for their party.[26]

In America, some examples of gerrymandering are still in evidence. The salamander-like "gerrymander" of Governor Gerry, in Massachusetts, was the forerunner of many later manipulations of geographical areas.[27] The "shoe-string" district of Mississippi is another example, while the "saddlebag" and "dumbbell" districts resulted from other operations. Flagrant gerrymandering frequently violates public opinion and incurs animosity at the polls, but any watered-down form of gerrymandering will persist as it exists in many American apportionments until the difference between Democrats and Republicans is great enough to result in bitterness at the injustice of the practice and brings a threat of retaliation.

Article I of the United States Constitution prescribed no intrastate scheme of apportionment; but the growth of population, the large distances to travel for members with whole-state constituencies, and the general disfavor at the six states which were electing representatives-at-large resulted in the Apportionment Act of 1842 in which Congress declared that there were to be as many districts in each state as there were representatives from that state. Though effective in combating the major inconveniences of election-at-large, the Act did not include measures to prevent gerrymandering on the part of the State legislatures.

Concomitant with the problem of districting was the difficulty of restricting membership in the House of Representatives to a workable number of persons. No Federal law governs the physical shape of the districts or the size of the population of the districts. Any such requirements that are incorporated into an apportionment act expire with the coming of a new apportionment.[28] As a consequence,

---

[26] G. LaChapelle, *Les Régimes Electoraux*, Paris, 1934. Familiar was the excuse: to maintain "an equilibrium between the representation of the cities and the countryside."

[27] Luce, *op. cit.*, pp. 397, 398.

[28] Wood *vs.* Broom, 287 U. S. 8 (1932).

in many States, the size of Congressional districts has varied widely. In the forties, the largest district in Illinois was 191.4 per cent above the average, and the smallest was 54.7 per cent below the average. The Illinois apportionment of Congressional districts for that period was based upon an act of 1901, which even then was unequal in its effects. Michigan Congressional districts varied about 34 per cent above and below the average population. In New York, the most populous district was 173.1 per cent above the average, the least populous 69.0 per cent below it. "Five districts have populations more than 100 per cent above the average; these are all in or adjacent to New York City. In Congress, as in the State legislatures, the cities have not increased in power as they have in population over the country as a whole. Congress has not seen fit to force the States to comply with rules of equity in laying out districts." [29]

Present Congressional apportionment counts the whole population, including the politically inexpressive sector of the population — aliens or Southern Negroes who do not possess the ballot. Thus, in areas of equal population, but of unequal proportions of aliens or Negroes, the number of voters per representative differs considerably.

The automatic "recurrent" Reapportionment Act of June, 1929, as amended, provided that within one week of the reassembling of the first regular session of the 77th Congress (January, 1941) and of each fifth Congress thereafter, the President should submit to Congress a statement of the apportionment population of each state, together with an apportionment of representatives to each state according to the then existing membership of the House using the method of equal proportions.[30] If Congress fails to pass a new apportionment act, representation in the second succeeding Congress shall be according to the number of members shown by the last preceding Census.[31] In 1941 the President's plan was transmitted to the House, no action was taken by that body, and, in consequence, the plan went into effect in the election of the next succeeding Con-

---

[29] L. F. Schmeckebier, *Congressional Apportionment,* Washington, D. C., 1941, p. 171.

[30] For a discussion of this and other methods see Schmeckebier, *op. cit.,* Chapter 3, on "Modern Methods of Apportionment."

[31] An amendment of 1940 allowed the promulgation of the automatic apportionment sixty days after the transmission of the report, if Congress had not acted.

gress, the 78th, elected in 1942 and convened in January, 1943. This act allots the members among the States, but it leaves the drawing of district lines to the States.

The condition of apportionment of American State representative districts is much worse than the apportionment of Congressmen among the States. Although almost all State constitutions require reapportionment of the membership in their legislatures every ten years or less, the dates of the last reapportionments in nineteen States range from 1890 to 1925.[32] Mississippi made its last apportionment in 1890, Kentucky in 1893 (amended in 1918), and Delaware in 1897. Illinois, Alabama, and Tennessee completed apportionments in 1901.

The reasons for failure to reapportion are several. They include (1) the difficulty and size of the reapportioning task, (2) the struggle for legislative supremacy between rural and urban areas, (3) the efforts by areas of relatively or absolutely declining population to retain a disproportionate representation, and (4) the reluctance of representatives to deprive some of their own number of offices.

It should be noted that in some States, even if the constitutional provisions for reapportionment are carried out, there may still be inequalities in the population of the various districts. In fifteen States, constitutional provisions are primarily responsible for inequalities in Senate membership; fourteen States discriminate against certain districts in the lower house by their constitutional law.[33] The most common producer of inequalities is the provision guaranteeing at least one representative per county. This is found in nineteen States; it is similar to the Federal provision that allows each State at least one member in the House of Representatives.

---

[32] Figures from the Council of State Governments in *News Bulletin* of Public Administration Clearing House, Chicago, Illinois, Release No. 1, February 3, 1941. Forty-two States require reapportionment every ten years or after each U. S. Census. Kansas requires one every five years, Indiana every six, Arizona six months before any general election when the vote for governor at the preceding election entitled any county to more representation. Delaware's Constitution does not provide for reapportionment, while those of Idaho and Nevada state that such action shall be "as provided by law." The reapportionment may be executive, executive-legislative, or, most commonly, legislative, in its procedure.

[33] David O. Walter, "Reapportionment and Urban Representation," *Annals of the American Academy of Political and Social Science,* Vol. 195 (January, 1938), pp. 11-20. Also see V. O. Key, Jr., "Procedures in State Legislative Apportionment," *American Political Science Review,* Vol. 22 (December, 1932), pp. 1050-1058.

The problems presented in several States by legislative failure to reapportion are exemplified in the case of Illinois. The Illinois Constitution of 1870 provides a fair system of apportionment on the basis of population. The senatorial ratio of representatives is obtained by dividing the whole state population by fifty-one, the fixed number of senators. Furthermore, no district may contain fewer than four-fifths of the ratio, or more than one and three-fourths times the ratio. In 1901, the last reapportionment was made on this basis. Since then, Cook County has increased in population far out of proportion to the rest of the State. But it still has only nineteen senators, rather than the twenty-six which its 52 per cent of the population should accord it. All four of the reasons for failure to reapportion are found in Illinois. Most prominent is the hostility between urban and rural areas.

The making of the reapportionment is rendered all the more difficult since the drafters attempt to preserve vested interests as much as possible. The usual provision that county lines are to be followed, and that the districts must be compact, may make it impossible for the districts to be nearly equal. In Illinois, near Chicago, all the counties are so populous that there is little opportunity to juggle them around in order to fulfill the equality requirement. By itself, one county may be too small; and when two counties are added together, the proposed district is too large. The strength of local lines as embalmed in State constitutions is such that the splitting of counties is not ordinarily permitted, except where one county far exceeds *twice* the ratio. A senator does not like to change his constituency or get an enlarged one. And the denial of apportionment has been made more vehement by the presence of legislators who would lose their jobs. A senator once declared before the Illinois Senate, "This resolution [to reapportion], if passed, means decapitating the political heads of eight senators and twenty-four representatives, all downstate. Who will volunteer to lay his head on the block?" [34]

The farmers' fear and dislike of the metropolis occasions much of the opposition to reapportionment proposals in the legislature. City scandals, gangsterdom, and the bosses, have overshadowed the

[34] R. L. Mott, "Reapportionment in Illinois," *American Political Science Review*, Vol. 21 (August, 1937), p. 598.

crude fumblings of the small-town politicians. The Board of Trade is a little Wall Street to the farmers. The city is teeming with strange people, unneighborly and unfriendly. It has grown and grown, and the farmers have become outnumbered.

As a result, Chicago is hampered and discriminated against in legislation. The introduction of beneficial legislation is abandoned when the sectional boomerang is foreseen. The main job of the office of the Corporation Counsel in Chicago is to find ways of circumventing or changing provisions in the State laws which hamper the city. Chicago has been unable to deal with public utilities in an effective fashion. Zoning ordinances have been delayed. Relief plans, housing plans, licensing, and assessment regulation have been delayed and circumvented by an indifferent and often hostile legislature.[35] And inside the city itself, the failure to apportion has meant an overrepresentation of blighted and socially disorganized areas.

The lack of response to the popular will reminds one strongly, again, of the resemblance between apportionment and the forms of representation. It is as if a minority of representatives were able, inside the house, to block the acts of the majority. The rationalization of the rural folk is that of the proponents of proportional representation. "We demand our privilege of stopping the action of the majority on matters which affect the majority and minority, because we do not constitute or agree with the majority." Certainly this obvious failure to "play the game fairly" may furnish rationalization, too, for opponents of the whole democratic framework of elections and representations.

New York City, St. Louis, Detroit, and other cities have similar difficulties in their respective States. New York City contains 59.3 per cent of the State's population, and controls 44.6 per cent of the total membership of the House and 47.0 per cent of the Senate. The corresponding figures for Detroit are 39.0 per cent, 21.0 per cent, and 21.8 per cent; for St. Louis, 22.6 per cent, 12.6 per cent, and 17.6 per cent.

Not only is faulty apportionment at the basis of party differences and party majorities (*e.g.,* Chicago and New York City are fre-

---

[35] For the many problems besetting Chicago's relation with downstate Illinois cf. C. E. Merriam, S. D. Parratt, and A. Lepawsky, *The Government of the Metropolitan Region of Chicago,* Chicago, 1933, pp. 176, 177.

quently Democratic when the rest of the State is Republican), but inside the parties themselves, it makes a difference. Since in many States representation of State party committees is based upon representation in the legislature, rural voters may have more to say about the structure of the party platform. In the so-called "one-party States," as in the Solid South, the effects are even more noticeable. It is an axiom that in those States the party nomination is equivalent to election; it is not always emphasized that control of party nominations is in the hands of delegates from the rural, sparsely populated sections of those States. In Alabama, Georgia, and Louisiana there are conflicts between rural and urban areas as bitter as those fought out along party lines in other States.[36]

The failure to make a fair apportionment has serious consequences to democratic institutions. It reveals some of the fundamental weaknesses of the system of popular representation. The theories of equality and tolerance do not work because human beings in favored positions do not find it to their personal advantage to put them into operation. Elected representatives and their constituents who benefit from a gerrymander or a "rotten borough" situation do not perceive that fundamental democratic theories are at stake. Their particularistic attitudes when carried to an extreme produce the kind of factionalism which contributed to Fascism in Germany. Their actions deny the convention of the majority rule, and substitute a system of veto by minority blocs.

Can those who are interested in preserving democratic institutions employ some safeguards against the weaknesses of the apportionment system? Some of the American States have much fairer systems of apportionment than others. The vesting of the power to make a reapportionment in some body other than the legislature is a scheme which has rectified abuses in several States. This power may be given to the executive, the courts, or to the electorate as a whole. In Maryland, Ohio, and South Dakota the executive system is used; in Arkansas, the judicial; and in Colorado and Washington, the popular. In Ohio the executive system has worked well. The forcing of a reapportionment by a popular initiative is feasible, but

---

[36] Walter, *op. cit.*, p. 15. Cf. H. F. Gosnell, *Grass Roots Politics,* Washington, D. C., 1942, Chapter 8 on Louisiana.

it has the limitations of the popular lawmaking devices. It is cumbersome, rigid, and expensive.

If the single-member-district system is to be employed, there is no good reason why it should not provide virtual equality in voting power. If the democratic system is to thrive, it is necessary that this principle of equality and its corollary, the majority-rule convention, be respected.

Multimembered Districts

Block System

The election of more than one representative from an area presents a number of problems. If each voter has as many votes as there are candidates to be elected, and if he is permitted to choose freely among the candidates running, the votes of the successful candidates may vary widely. The most popular candidate might receive an overwhelming majority, whereas the last one elected might have a mere plurality and a slim one at that. If party lines were sharply drawn, all successful candidates would receive approximately the same votes, and the minority party or parties would elect no representatives whatsoever. If there were more than two major parties, the successful candidates could win with a plurality of the votes.

In securing majority representation, the block system has serious limitations; nevertheless it has been employed without arousing undue criticism. In Detroit the system has some ardent defenders.[37] Of the city-manager cities in the United States, about three fourths elect their councils in this fashion, and the results have been regarded as satisfactory.[38] The plurality block plan will work where party strife is not bitter, and where minority groups are willing to abide by the results.

Minority or Proportional Representation

Statesmen and mathematicians have been interested for at least a hundred and fifty years in schemes which would give an accurate reflection of the electorate. This and that quota system, and a variety of methods of counting the ballots, have been proposed. As early

---

[37] Lovett, *op. cit.*
[38] *The Municipal Yearbook*, 1943, p. 132.

as 1770 a Frenchman by the name of De Borda devised an ingenious system for weighting votes so as to give minority representation.[39] In the French National Assembly the subject was mentioned. It was in the nineteenth century, however, that the subject gained general attention and the first trials were made. American, Swiss, Danish, and English inventors had thought out plans by approximately the half-century mark. When the great British philosopher, John Stuart Mill, took up and defended vigorously the plan which was discovered almost simultaneously by the Danish and British inventors, the subject became one which has been hotly debated in legislative and academic halls ever since. Mill pronounced the plan as one of the greatest of all political inventions.

Granting the hypotheses on which Mill based his case, his arguments are reasonable. If it can be assumed that the voters are well informed and act rationally, then an attempt should be made to consider the wishes of as large a proportion of them as possible. These are not assumptions which modern psychologists and political scientists are willing to make. Furthermore, it is clear that Mill failed to recognize the need for positive leadership in a legislative body. The assembly might be a reflection of the electorate, but the electorate might have such diverse views that common action would be extremely difficult. The legislative body might find itself incapable of action. This is precisely what happened in Germany under the Weimar system.

Single Transferable Vote Plan

The system which Mill sponsored has been called the "single transferable vote plan." In English-speaking countries it has also gone under the title, the "Hare plan," from the name of the English inventor, Thomas Hare, a London barrister.[40] Mill found that it was an uphill fight to get the politicians to adopt the system. He did not see any English jurisdiction try the plan in his day. In the twentieth century, however, the plan was adopted for the English university constituencies, for use in Irish national and local elections, and for the election of city councils in several American cities, includ-

[39] Braunias, *op. cit.*
[40] See above, p. 126, for a discussion of his theories of representation.

ing New York City. Experience under the plan will be discussed after the details of the system have been presented.

The fundamental rules for the single transferable vote plan are similar to those of the alternative vote, which has already been discussed in these pages.[41] As a matter of fact, the alternative vote was derived from the single transferable vote. The ballots are marked in exactly the same fashion, with numbers instead of cross marks. Under the Hare plan there are as a rule, more candidates and the indicating of preferences is therefore more difficult. The principal differences between the two systems are that the Hare plan calls for the determination of a quota and for handling of the so-called surplus ballots. Under the alternative vote plan the quota is determined in advance, since the number necessary to elect under the majority rule is one more than one half. If we generalize this rule, we have the quota which is ordinarily employed under the Hare plan. In other words, if the total valid vote cast is divided by one more than the number of seats to be filled, and if the resulting quotient is completed to the next round number, we have the quota used in many Hare elections. This is the smallest number which will elect the number of representatives to be chosen, and no more than this number. The determination of the quota may be illustrated by a simple example. In Cincinnati, Ohio, a council of nine is elected by the voters-at-large in accordance with the Hare plan. In any election, the quota is obtained by dividing the total number of valid votes cast by ten.

The framers of the New York City charter, having decided to simplify the quota system, set a fixed quota at seventy-five thousand votes, and left the size of the city council dependent upon the size of the vote cast. This method produced a city council of from seventeen to twenty-six members. The election was held by city boroughs and each borough was entitled to as many seats as the number seventy-five thousand was contained in the total vote cast in that borough.

After the polls are closed, all the ballots are brought to a central counting place, where they are sorted according to first choices. All candidates whose first-choice votes equal or exceed the quota are de-

---

[41] See above, pp. 169, 170.

clared elected. Those ballots which a candidate receives above and beyond the quota are called "surplus" ballots. Such ballots are transferred to the next available choice marked on them, beginning with the ballots of the candidates having the largest surplus. If, after the distribution of the surplus ballots, there are still seats to be filled, the candidates having the smallest number of ballots are eliminated in turn, and their ballots transferred to the next available choices. This process continues until all the seats are filled.

The enthusiastic supporters of the Hare plan make the following claims for their system: it gives the maximum amount of freedom to the individual voter, it insures that a majority and any important minority will be represented, it improves the caliber of candidates and raises the tone of campaigning, and it avoids the defects of the single-member-district system, such as "rotten boroughs," gerrymandering, landslides, complicated nominating systems, and excessive localism, all of which is conducive to machine rule under American conditions.

The adoption of the Hare plan has proceeded sporadically. In the United States it was first tried out in the city of Ashtabula, Ohio, located on Lake Erie, near Cleveland. The secretary of the Proportional Representation League got off the train by mistake at this point, and in trying to make the best of his time convinced the local authorities of the need for proportional representation in their town. The plan went into operation in 1915 and was employed for eight elections. The politicians were never reconciled to the plan, and twice tried to repeal it before they finally succeeded in 1927. The system was criticized because it secured the representation of unpopular minority groups. The intolerance of the majority led to a return of the plurality plan.

The Hare plan was then tried in a number of jurisdictions: Boulder (Colorado); Cleveland, Cincinnati, Hamilton, and Toledo (Ohio); Wheeling (West Virginia); New York City and Yonkers (New York); Cambridge and Lowell (Massachusetts). The passage of a new city charter in Cincinnati in 1925 was hailed as a great victory for the advocates of proportional representation. The so-called Charter Group which had backed the change, won the majority in the city council for five successive elections. In the sixth election it lost this majority, but there was no substantial change in the city administration on that account. The Cincinnati city councils chosen under the Hare plan have contained many distinguished citizens. Whether they would have been chosen under another system of representation is problematical. A wave of civic reform which is sufficiently strong can sweep over governmental structural barriers.

Proportional representation in Cincinnati has secured the selection of councilmen representing minority groups. From time to time there have been Negro, foreign-born and labor members. The count of ballots shows that there has been a tendency for the voters who mark their first choices for candidates belonging to given racial, religious, and income groups to mark their second and other choices for candidates of the same or similar background.[42] This tendency has been decried by certain writers who contend that competency should be the guiding consideration, and that the important function of representation is to secure a working majority, not to insure this or that minority a chance to hold up the majority.

The largest scale experiment with proportional representation has been in New York City under the charter adopted in 1936. The old ward plan resulted in overwhelming majorities for the dominant political party in the metropolis. There can be no question that the new system ended this one-sided situation and produced a city council of more distinguished membership. That the plan would be unpopular with the politicians of the dominant organization was to be expected. In operation, the plan presented some difficulties. Too many candidates were nominated, so the voters were confronted with very confusing ballots; votes of the independents were so scattered as not to be effective. These defects could be remedied by limiting the number of candidates and providing a method of grouping candidates.

The single transferable vote has also been employed in certain Canadian cities, parts of Australia, and in the Irish Free State for local and national elections. It was first put into operation in Ireland

[42] J. P. Harris, "The Practical Workings of Proportional Representation in the United States and Canada," *National Municipal Review*, Vol. 19 (May, 1930); H. F. Gosnell, "Proportional Representation," in *Encyclopaedia of the Social Sciences*, and "Proportional Representation: Its Operation in Cincinnati," *Public Affairs*, Vol. 2 (March, 1939), pp. 133-135; and "Motives for Voting as Shown by the Cincinnati P. R. Election of 1929," *National Municipal Review*, Vol. 19 (July, 1930), pp. 471-476.

in the municipal elections of Sligo in 1919. It was extended to the Irish Free State elections in 1920. An attempt was made in 1926 to use the nation as a whole as the constituency for the election of the upper house (Seanad Eireann). This election indicated that the plan was unwieldy when there was a mixed urban and rural constituency of considerable size and a large number of candidates. There were seventy-six candidates, the vote was widely scattered, and the count took six weeks. The method of electing the Seanad Eireann was changed in 1928 from a direct to an indirect one. For the election of the lower house (Dail) the Hare plan is still employed. While the Dail constituencies are smaller than they need be (some are three-membered), the system has been generally accepted. It has accurately reflected the political views of the Irish voters, a majority of whom favored the Fianna Fail in the thirties. President Eamon de Valera said, "Whether it benefited us or not, I would be in favor of the principle because it is justice." The experience of the Irish Free State furnishes a clear answer to the question raised as to whether proportional representation would prevent the election of a majority in the legislative body. If a majority of the voters are organized, proportional representation will reflect this situation accurately.

The experience of various countries with the single-transferable-vote system enables us to draw the following conclusions regarding its operation:

1. It insures the representation of an existing majority and of every well-organized and sizable minority. In the Irish Free State there has been a majority party and the Hare plan has brought it to power. On the other hand, in New York City the minorities which were unrepresented under the plurality plan are now represented.

2. The plan, involving as it does election from a larger constituency than the district plan, has improved the caliber of local representatives. Whether it is the larger constituency or the transferable vote feature that has brought this result is very difficult to determine.

3. While in some jurisdictions there have been higher ratios of spoiled ballots than under the plurality plan, the method has been reasonably well understood by the voters. It is necessary to keep up a program of education as to how the system works, but this is one

of the essentials of the democratic system. An uneducated electorate does not function under any circumstances, even under the single-member-district plan.

4. The plan has not been more expensive than the plurality system, since it has eliminated expensive nominating systems, particularly in the United States.

5. Where a coherent majority does not exist among the electorate, this condition will be reflected in the results of the proportional representation election. The legislative body so chosen may not contain a working majority if the members elected show a lack of the spirit of compromise.

6. The system reflects accurately the presence or absence of effective civic organization. It gave expression to civic uprisings in Cincinnati, Hamilton, Toledo, and Wheeling; but it did not prevent the Republican party in Cleveland or the Democratic organization in New York City from electing a majority of the representatives.

7. The time consumed in attacking and defending the plan has been diverted from more fundamental issues. Extravagant claims made by both sides have confused the issue.

List Systems of Proportional Representation

On the continent of Europe, except in Denmark, where a very limited use of the single-transferable-vote was made, the list system of proportional representation has been far more popular. While the first trial of a list system was made in Serbia for local elections in 1888, the plan in the Swiss Canton of Geneva, which went into effect in 1891, has attracted more attention.

The chief differences between the list plan and the Hare plan are the method of marking the ballot, the freedom of choice as among candidates, and the method of counting. Instead of the numbering system, a cross mark or some other simple designation is used. In the Canton of Geneva (Switzerland), the voter put his official stamp on the ballot of his choice. Each party furnished its own list of candidates, and this printed list did not become an official ballot until the voter had affixed his stamp. Under most list systems, the voter is not given an opportunity to pick and choose among all the candidates running. He has to choose between lists presented by well-organized parties. It is obvious from this that the counting of the ballot is much simpler than under the Hare plan. The seats are apportioned among parties and not among individual candidates. Within a given party list, the successful candidates are chosen in a variety of ways. The party leaders may determine the order of selection of candidates from their list. In Switzerland the voters are given a little voice in the matter, but not much. In general, we can say that the list system is one which glorifies the party leaders and depreciates the role of the individual voters.

A list system of proportional representation was first tried in local elections. After it was shown to operate successfully for several years in the Swiss Canton of Geneva it spread gradually to some of the other cantons. The first country to employ a list system for national elections was Belgium, which incorporated the plan in its constitution of 1899. Prior to 1918 the plan was also adopted by Finland, Cuba, Sweden, Portugal, Bulgaria, and Denmark.

President Wilson's Fourteen Points gave an impetus to the spread of proportional representation. Granting the assumptions of self-determination, what was theoretically more perfect than a system which reflected accurately the composition of opinion in the electorate. The defeated powers, Germany and Austria, adopted the plan and so did Poland, Czechoslovakia, Latvia, Lithuania, Esthonia, Rumania, Italy, Switzerland (for national elections), and Norway.

In some of the countries which adopted the list system of proportional representation, political conditions were such that the plan was doomed to hard sledding. The system assumes a literate electorate which accepts democratic ways of thought and which is united on some long-range objectives regardless of party differences on issues of the day. These conditions were, in the main, not fulfilled in Italy, Poland, or the Balkan and Baltic states. Although Germany had a highly literate population which included many articulate groups, there was no general acceptance of the democratic method.

There are many different types of list system, varying from the Swiss plan, whose founders had some faith in the intelligence of the average voter, to the German plan under the Weimar Constitution, which thoroughly regiments the individual voter.

In Switzerland the list plan of proportional representation, first put into operation in the Canton of Geneva in 1892 and then adopted for the entire country in 1918, provides for a limited amount of discretion on the part of the individual voter. When he goes to the polls, the voter must select a party list, but he may also write the name of his favorite. candidate twice. This is called the *cumul*. The party itself may exercise this right by printing the name of the favored candidate or candidates twice. After the polls are closed, the number of votes cast for each party list are counted, and the quota is obtained by dividing the total number of votes cast by one more than the number of candidates to be elected. Party lists may be joined for purposes of the application of this quota. If the original division does not distribute all the seats, then the remaining seats are assigned to the list which would have the highest average vote per seat if it received that additional seat.[43] After the seats are distributed among the parties, the next step is to determine who are the successful candidates within each party. If the party has twice printed the names of certain of its candidates on the ballot, then these candidates will be sure of election. The voters' private *cumuls* might affect the result, but the order determined by the party leaders usually prevails. The Swiss plan gives the voter far less freedom than he enjoys under the single-transferable-vote plan.

The experience of Switzerland with a list system of proportional representation is extremely useful, since other conditions were substantially the same before and after the elections of 1919, when the plan was first put into operation for the election of the national council. The suffrage was the same, the parties were substantially the same, and the general form of the government was the same. We can, then, say that whatever changes followed the adoption of proportional representation were probably the result of the adoption and not due to some other factors.

Two outstanding consequences followed the introduction of proportional representation in Switzerland. One was the multiplication of political parties. Before the introduction of the system there were six or seven main parties, but the Independent Democratic Party managed to secure a majority in the Federal Council. The members of this party bitterly fought the introduction of proportional representation, but the minority parties rallied against them and, using

---

[43] C. G. Hoag and G. H. Hallett, *Proportional Representation,* New York, 1926, p. 421.

the direct initiative, changed the Federal Constitution. The minority parties could not control the Federal Council elections, but their supporters constituted a majority of the electorate on the issue of the plurality plan versus the proportional plan. After the new law went into effect, the Independent Democratic Party lost its majority in the Federal Council, and an important new party, the Peasants' Party, came into existence.[44] The threat of the rising power of the Social Democratic Party united the parties which rested largely upon middle-income-group support under the provisions of the law which permitted such united lists, so that as far as economic questions were concerned the old conservative majority still controlled Swiss affairs.

The other consequence of the law was the increased participation in voting. It has been argued that a fair system of representation would increase interest in voting, since the voters would feel that their votes would count in determining the result. In Switzerland there was such an increase in participation, and this increase has been sustained. On the average about 20 per cent more of the voters take part in national council elections since 1919 than did so before that time.

The Belgians adopted a system of proportional representation in 1899, along with a number of other electoral reforms, including plural voting and universal adult manhood suffrage. The Belgian electoral law did not give the individual voter the same amount of freedom enjoyed by the Swiss voter. Under it a voter could choose a list, or he might name a candidate, but such a naming would only affect the final choice slightly. In essence, control over the selection of successful candidates for the seats assigned to a given party was largely in the hands of the party leaders, but a revolt of large proportions might make some difference. The quota system was similar to the Geneva (Switzerland) system, but parties were not permitted to join together for purposes of the original allotment, and there was a crude system of adding together remainders for small groups of districts which went part way to correct some of the errors of the original apportionment of seats to districts.[45] The Belgian plan, in other words, accomplished proportional representation within the

---

[44] H. F. Gosnell, *Why Europe Votes*, Chicago, 1930.
[45] *Ibid.*

districts selected, but in the country at large there were some discrepancies. These discrepancies were small as compared with those which arise under the single-member-district plurality plan in other countries.

The Belgian system of proportional representation produced majorities for the Catholic Party during the period from 1899 to 1919, when the system of plural voting was in operation. The introduction of the "one man, one vote" rule after World War I meant that the Catholic Party no longer was able to secure a majority of all the seats. Proportional representation under the new suffrage conditions revealed the fact that opinion in Belgium was divided among three main groups, the Catholics, the Laborites, and the Liberals. It was contended that under a single-member-district plan the Liberals would have been squeezed between the two larger parties, just as the Liberal party in England was squeezed in the period following 1919. Elections would have then resulted in Catholic or Labor governments, and not in the unsatisfactory coalitions which characterized the twenties and thirties. One writer goes so far as to claim that the unstable ministries in Belgium resulting from the lack of decisive results at the elections contributed to the defeat of Belgium in World War II, since it gave the King greater power.[46]

The reasons for the military collapse of the democratic countries in Europe in 1940 are many and varied. Disaster came to Belgium, as it did to France, because of the shortsighted policies of her diplomats and military experts. The Belgian government failed to provide adequate national defense, one of the minimum essentials for survival of governmental institutions. To blame the system of proportional representation for the shortcomings of the post-Versailles leaders hardly seems to be reasonable. Neither France nor Great Britain had proportional representation during this time. It was Britain's island position which saved her in 1940, not the single-member-district plan.

The German law of 1920, which had some unique features, has been the subject of many heated discussions. Its quota plan and its method for counting remainders were looked upon as ingenious attempts to carry out the principles of proportional representation to

---

[46] Hermens, *op. cit.*

their logical conclusions. Instead of using complicated rules for determining a quota which might be mathematically correct, the German publicists who drafted the law worked out the fixed-quota plan. Any party which cast sixty thousand votes would be entitled to a seat. The number of seats in the Reichstag would depend upon the size of the vote cast. The country was divided into thirty-five districts, and a system was worked out for pooling the remainders, first for groups of districts and then for the entire Reich. Here was a plan which preserved large electoral districts and at the same time provided for national adjustments. The fly in the ointment was the way in which successful candidates were chosen from the lists. The individual voter had no choice as between individual candidates. He could merely choose between lists. No discretion was allowed to the voter either in his district or in the nation at large. All the candidates for the entire country were selected by the party leaders.

The German system of proportional representation has been the subject of many bitter controversies. Some anti-Nazis have gone so far as to say that this plan was responsible for the rise of Hitler to power. This view assumes that the system of government plays an extraordinary role in human affairs. Political scientists might wish that governmental practices were that important, but a more realistic view would negate this hypothesis. A voting system is of importance within certain limits. What are those limits? An examination of the German experience under the Weimar Constitution might throw some light upon this general question. The thesis of those who magnify the role of the German system of representation under the Weimar régime is to the effect that this system multiplied the number of parties and made it impossible for the resultant Reichstag to form a working majority. Under the single-member-district plan, it is contended, the Nazi Party would have been squeezed, and a working majority favorable to a democratic régime would have maintained itself in power.[47] To state this thesis is to refute it. There was a multiple party system in Germany under the Constitution of 1870 which provided for a Reichstag elected under

[47] Hermens, *Democracy or Anarchy?*, p. 293, says: "In Germany it was easy to follow the results of one election after the other, and to demonstrate that the various parties which destroyed the majorities existing in the pre-War Reichstag could never have arisen or never have become important under the majority system."

the single-member-district system. A multiple party system is the product of social, economic, and political influences. The German multiple party system before and after the Revolution of 1918 was the product of the economic system, the land tenure system, the labor unions, the religious differences, the sectional differences, and the ideological differences found in the country. Under any electoral system these various differences would have found one form of expression or another. While the Weimar parties had different names from the parties of the Kaiser's régime, their leaders and their members were about the same. The fortunes of the Weimar parties rose and fell with economic and social changes. The Democratic Party, a party made up of middle-income groups, could not survive the inflation, the stabilization, and other dislocations of the Weimar period. Hitler's Nazi Party throve upon the depression of the early thirties. The German system of proportional representation was not responsible for the stock market crash of 1929 in New York City.

Because of the bitterness of the controversy raging around the German system of proportional representation, it is worth our while to consider its operation more closely. There is no question that under the Weimar régime it was difficult to construct ministries which had workable majorities in the Reichstag. Looking back over the history of those ill-fated days, it is just as easy to say that had the party leaders of those days been able to see into the future, the Communists would have combined with the Social Democrats rather than fought them, that the Social Democrats would have been willing to sacrifice a few trade-union rules in order to preserve their very existence, that the Catholics would have collaborated more closely with those elements which were willing to fight for freedom of worship, that the German People's Party would have been willing to work more closely with the parties of the left in order to stave off the Nazis, and that the German Nationalists would also have clung to the Weimar régime rather than suffer the lessening of their power that came about under the Nazis.

A better case can be made for the theory that the rise of Hitler to power was due rather to the shortsightedness of the German political leaders than to a system of voting. Until the fateful day of January 30, 1933, the Nazi leaders were at the mercy of the opposition. If there had been more firmness on the part of the non-

Nazis, then Hitler would not have had his chance. Lack of vision, lack of character, lack of will power, cannot be blamed upon a governmental practice. It is the result of years of conditioning, of mental blindness, of smugness, of fear of change, of refusal to read the signs of the time. Hitler's will power was based upon desperation, upon the conviction that nothing could be worse than the Weimar régime, upon rage at the alleged "injustices" existing in the world as he saw it. The non-Nazis did not think that conditions were completely unbearable. The anti-Nazis were soon to learn how they could be made so. The rise of Hitler to power is typical of the years 1933-1942, the forces of the opposition were "too little and too late."

What role did the system of representation have in the spread of the paralysis which wrecked the Weimar régime? Would another plan of voting have prevented the deadly infection? This is a question, like many other historical questions, which cannot be answered in a final fashion. To deny that the system of representation had any influence would be to negate the importance of organization in human affairs. Proportional representation was tried under very unfavorable circumstances. The international situation, the internal economic conditions, and the confusion of social and political loyalties were a severe challenge with which to cope. The Weimar system did not meet that challenge. Would another system have met the challenge? The British system of single-member-district majority elections would not have prevented Hitler from staging his abortive Beerhall *Putsch*. It would not have prevented Hitler from organizing his brown shirts. In England, Oswald Mosely was unable to rally any considerable body of supporters to his Fascist standard. The British did not handle their political affairs in this fashion. Their system of government was not built in a day. It is largely based today upon conventions, upon traditions which are observed by those who engage in the game of politics. The Germans were without such traditions. Germany was a relative newcomer to the society of nation states.

The German system of proportional representation was defective in that it limited the freedom of action of the individual voter. Under the single-member-district plan, the voter chooses between individual candidates, and he has some feeling of participation in the selection of the legislative body. Under the Weimar plan, the individual voter was completely frustrated in his desire to punish or reward this or that individual member of the Reichstag. It is also clear that the Weimar plan did not stem the disintegrating influences which were at work in Germany. Whether the single-member-district plan could have done this is problematical. The *scrutin d'arrondissement* did not give wisdom to the French voters and politicians in the dark days of the thirties.

The early forties found proportional representation under severe fire. It was blamed for some of the weaknesses of democratic government. Now that the Allies have won, what will be the future of proportional representation? The Swiss and the Swedes, during a most trying period in their histories, retained the list systems which they found satisfactory in the prewar days. The Belgians and Dutch have reinstated the political practices which were suspended during the German occupation. The military weaknesses of these governments were more closely related to the deficiencies of the international world order than they were to deficiencies of the national governments. On the other hand, the Italians and Germans, who abandoned proportional representation without reference to external pressures, should have a more realistic attitude toward it. In the Axis countries proportional representation is not likely to be regarded as a panacea. While it might be possible to convince these people that their political woes during the twenties and thirties were not the product of proportional representation, the stark fact remains that proportional representation did not solve the problems of these difficult days. In coming back to proportional representation in 1945, the Italians adopted a system for electing a constituent assembly which was eminently fair. In such countries as Sweden and Switzerland where there is a high degree of likemindedness and a large amount of tolerance, the system has been accepted in a realistic fashion as a device which recognized political and group differences. The Swiss Executive Council provides a method for integrating the divergent elements found in the national legislative body. In Sweden the parliamentary system has operated successfully with a legislature chosen by proportional representation.

Proportional representation is a device for a politically mature people. Its successful use depends upon the will to make it work.

It must also be coupled with a mechanism for securing a government which can act. The majority principle was not sufficient in Germany under the Weimar régime, since party differences made the formation of a legislative majority impossible. No system will work if over half the voters support parties which are pledged to do everything to prevent its working. There must be a thorough repudiation of the Fascist position in all its forms.

This brings up again one of the dilemmas of the democratic system. Democracy involves freedom of choice and freedom of expression. Suppose one of the choices presented is an antidemocratic one. The democracies of the twenties and thirties permitted organizations to grow which were pledged to destroy democratic institutions. A government which is to survive must protect itself against subversive movements. The use of terror as a political weapon must be ruthlessly suppressed by a régime which is based upon discussion.

Chapter 11

THE REPRESENTATIVE *

O NE of the disputed points in the history and theory of representative government has been the position of the representative. The problem is well stated by the British philosopher, T. H. Green:

> There are two principal conceptions of the essential nature of the representative. According to one, he is a senator; according to the other, he is an agent or a delegate. The former theory holds that he is both, the election signifying that the constituency desires to entrust its affairs and those of the nation to the direction and management of his superior mind.[1]

The extreme position of the holder of the senator viewpoint would be that of Thomas Hobbes, who wrote: "Men who are in absolute liberty may give authority to one man to represent everybody."[2] Any act of the despot was thus justified.

Toward the end of the eighteenth century, Edmund Burke declared:

> It is not the derivation of the power of that House [of Commons] from the people which makes it in a direct sense the representative. The King is the representative of the people; so are the Lords. They are all trustees for the people, as well as the Commons; because no power is given for the sake of the holder.[3]

---

* Alfred DeGrazia assisted substantially in the preparation of this chapter.

[1] *Works* (1885-1888), Vol. 2, p. 170. This alternative is somewhat differently stated by Sir George C. Lewis: "Either a representative is a mere delegate, empowered to act according to the instructions of his constituents, and not concerned about the general expediency or inexpediency (as it may seem to him) of the course he is following; or he is morally bound, no less than he is legally able, to follow that line of conduct which he considers most conducive to the public welfare. Besides these two alternatives, there is no third: a representative must be either a delegate or a free agent; he must either follow the opinions of others, or his own; nor is it possible to distinguish between cases in which he should be his own master, and in what he should be the servant of his constituents."

[2] *Leviathan,* London, 1651.

[3] *Works* (World's Classics) 1906, Vol. 2, p. 50.

Edmund Burke could not maintain both his seat and his high ideal. His famous "Speech to the Electors of Bristol" showed that his abstract principles were tempered by a realistic view of what was needed to win votes.[4] To convince his electors of his assiduous labor on their behalf, he inscribed a list of fence-mending activities.

In the United States about the same time a writer in the *Federalist* took a less extreme position. Adopting a middle course, he declared that representatives were to follow "the deliberate sense of the community," but not to give "unqualified compliance to every sudden breeze of passion, or to every transient impulse which the people may receive from the acts of men, who flatter their prejudices to betray their interests."[5]

In the nineteenth century, John Stuart Mill, starting with the premise that man is a rational animal, glorified the electorate as follows:

> Let the system of representation be what it may, it will be converted into one of mere delegation if the electors so choose. As long as they are free not to vote, and free to vote as they like, they cannot be prevented from making their vote depend on any condition they think fit to annex to it. By refusing to elect anyone who will not pledge himself to all of their opinions and even, if they please, to consult with them before voting on any important subject not foreseen, they can reduce their representative to their mere mouthpiece, or compel him in honour, when no longer willing to act in that capacity, to resign his seat.[6]

Mill was thinking about an ideal electorate where reason prevailed. He did not state where such an ideal electorate could be found. Certainly it did not exist in the England of his day.

Thoroughly in the Mill tradition was the viewpoint of the English rationalist, T. D. Woolsey, who wrote:

> Each representative is to consider the whole state first, and then each part of the state as far as its apparent welfare does not collide with that of the whole. He can, therefore, lawfully place himself under no pledges nor receive any instructions which are binding upon him, for to do so would imply that he is bound, after being convinced that

---

[4] November 3, 1774. *Works* (World's Classics) 1906, Vol. 2, pp. 159 ff.
[5] No. 71.
[6] *Op. cit.*, pp. 315-316.

the general good requires a certain course, to take directly the oppo-site.[7]

In the twentieth century the revolt against rationalism is clearly marked in such statements as the following by Hilaire Belloc and Cecil Chesterton, two cynical Englishmen, writing about the British party system as they saw it in the days immediately preceding World War I:

Either the representative must vote as his constituents would vote if consulted, or he must vote in the opposite sense. In the latter case, he is not a representative at all, but merely an oligarch; for it is surely ridiculous to say that a man represents Bethnal Green if he is in the habit of saying "Aye" when the people of Bethnal Green would vote "No." If, on the other hand, he does vote as his constituents would vote, then he is merely the mouthpiece of his constituents and derives his authority from them. And this is the only democratic theory of representation.[8]

Unfortunately, the dicta of writers have little relation to behavior. The extremes and the mean are postulated, but are useless unless it can be known how the actions of the representative are fixed on the scale. One must jump from the "ought" to the "is." As an American political scientist put it:

As to whether the representatives should be guided by their own immediate constituencies, by their party, or by their own views as to the best interests of the country as a whole, it may be said that all of these factors are likely to affect their decisions, in varying degrees, according to the definiteness and intensity with which these elements are expressed and recognized.[9]

The task to be done is the analysis and the description of the representative system in operation. We shall point out, as far as possible, the conditions under which the characteristics and acts of a person of political power are in accord with the expressed or un-expressed desires of the constituents. Three different aspects of the situation will be considered: (1) the personality and reputation of

[7] *Political Science*, New York, 1905, Vol. 1, p. 295.
[8] *The Party System*, London, 1911, p. 17. Also note that the German Weimar Constitution of 1919 declared, "Members are representative of the whole nation. They are subject to their conscience only and not bound by any instructions." (Article 21.) Compare this with the constitution of the Old German Empire: "The members of the Reichstag are the representatives of the people as a whole and shall not be bound by orders and instructions."
[9] John A. Fairlie, *op. cit.*, p. 466.

the representative; (2) the types of duty — legislative, administrative, and political — which he performs as representative; and (3) the effect of different types of constituency.

Personality of the Representative

The subject of the representative's personality inevitably shades into the subject of leadership. We can only offer a few hypotheses on the origins of representation, garnered from the leading works on the subject of leadership. We can point to the existence of influences in the private lives of the representatives which give impetus to their behavior in the public field. We endeavor to discover plausible reasons why some representatives behave more independently than others in the same assembly.

In the first place, what is meant by an "independent" representative? A representative may be independent because he violates the majority sentiment of the people in his constituency more frequently than other representatives. He may be independent in that he leads his constituents to adopt his viewpoint on many matters. By utilizing the various means of domination, propaganda, and persuasion, he forms his own majority. Conversely, the delegate type of representative may never vote against his constituents' known sentiment, or he may never try to change that sentiment but will accept it as the final word. At any rate, we see that an independent representative, for a host of reasons — personal, social, and institutional — may vote against the majority or feel it necessary to teach or prod or dupe his constituency. Complete independence would mean nonrepresentation. On the other hand, it is possible to have a great amount of virtual representation combined with a strong machine which turns out the vote.

Most representatives, at one time or another, indulge in a fleeting revolt against their constituencies. There are many causes for such a revolt, most of which will be treated later.[10] When the revolt is the result of temperamental factors, it resists controls. When resistance to popular demands recurs very often, the representative may lose his position. Even if his position is held by fraud, forfeit, or appointment, frequent straying from the path beaten by his con-

---

[10] See below, pp. 205, 206.

stituents will render his place more precarious. In such case his independence will repay him little except to ease his conscience or bolster his ego. A significant incident in early life may well make a man an incorrigible independent in one matter, but of average passivity in other matters. Thus, the representative whose father was a drunkard might understandably be an ardent "dry" even though his constituents were "wet." There need be no great consistency in a man's attitude of independence. As soon as his constituents became aroused about his independent acts in general, he is liable to be overthrown.

There may possibly be innate or predisposing traits in a representative which, in addition to, or in spite of, institutional and social circumstances, cause independence or dependence. The psychologists have coined phrases for the contrasting types, and speak of the polarities of ascendence-submission, dominance-subordination, or aggression-passivity.[11] These terms may be used here as synonyms for the traits called independence-dependence.

Few books have systematically observed the conditions of the early environment of political leaders and connected such early experience with later political behavior.[12]

The terms "aggressive" and "submissive" have been applied to the acts of representatives without reference to whether the aggression or submission was caused by the kind of constituency, the party leadership, the political institutions, or private stresses and strains of the representative. It has been presumed that the amount of attention invoked by a legislator was indicative of his "aggressiveness" or "passivity" of character. The legislator who aroused great popular support and enthusiasm was called "a great leader"; the one who made little stir, "a delegate."

Suggestive classifications of personality traits are to be found in only a few scattered places. The American psychologist, A. H. Maslow, who has studied monkeys and infants, has submitted some highly suggestive hypotheses.[13] Mr. Maslow finds that the domi-

---

[11] For a comprehensive discussion of personality traits see Gordon W. Allport, *Personality*, New York, 1937, Chapter 15.

[12] H. D. Lasswell's *Psychopathology and Politics* (Chicago, 1930) is a noteworthy exception.

[13] "Dominance, Feeling, Behavior, and Status," *Psychological Review*, Vol. 44 (September, 1937), pp. 404-429.

nance-feeling may exist without desire for dominance status. It is the latter that he would call true aggressiveness. He also distinguishes between dominance-feeling, dominance-behavior, craving for dominance, feelings of inferiority or superiority, matter-of-fact inferiority or superiority, and compensatory dominance behavior. Needless to say, a great deal of study is required before any classification of this kind can be made.

Other studies have concentrated mainly on the typical traits of politicians who have succeeded in winning support.[14] A writer of importance to our immediate interest in defining the relationship between constituent and representative is the German scholar, Fritz Giese, who analyzed data contained in the German *Who's Who* of 1914. Significantly, for our purpose, he classified his subjects according to those who were honored because of high quality but mainly routine professional accomplishments, those who had made a distinct contribution to their field of endeavor, and those who were also creative but unrestricted in their creativeness.[15] He found that politicians possessed the most heterogeneous background and affiliations. They were, however, classified according to two general types: one seeking in politics distinction and enjoyment, and the other making a life work of organizing and agitating.

Undoubtedly, if professional politicians alone were to become representatives, our task of discussing the typical representative's personality would be made lighter. The corridors to the legislative halls, however, are open to the wealthy as well as to the "party mules."[16] The heterogeneity of political types makes the task of assessing the importance of personality factors a difficult one.

In considering the types of duties that representatives perform, it would be of great value to be able to classify politicians according to their creativeness or their routine efficiency. It is possible to say

---

[14] Aristotle and Machiavelli were followed by Michels, Munro, Christensen, Spranger, Conway, and Cowley in depicting what types of personality prevail in politics.

[15] *Die öffentliche Persönlichkeit.* Beihefte zur *Zeitschrift für angewandte Psychologie,* Bd. 44.

[16] The socially useless plutocrat who turned to Parliament in George Bernard Shaw's book, *Major Barbara,* is called to mind here, as in Haxey's comment: "It is probable that Earl Winterdon was selected as Conservative candidate while still an Oxford student mainly on the grounds that he was a wealthy young aristocrat. He was not one of the people, but a member of the privileged class." (P. 28.)

that such tendencies may be related to independence on the one hand and dependence on the other. But the wide variety of functions performed, the different modes of recruitment throughout the world, the nonpolitical nature of much of the representative's work make classifications hazardous. In the American scene, a representative may be much less of the true *homo politicus* than a businessman. T. V. Smith, Illinois congressman and legislator, wrote complainingly about the "covert warriors and overt businessmen who have crept into our fold." [17]

Representatives are more likely to be agitators than administrators. The agitator as a personality type has been distinguished from other types by a concern with interpersonal relations. He is interested in people and in how they respond. Administrators as a type are more interested in handling objects. They deal in figures and goods. Among recent political figures, Adolf Hitler was clearly the agitator type. In the world of objects he was a failure. His ambitions to become a painter or an architect were frustrated. As a mob ruler, however, he was a past master. His sensitiveness to audience responses, and his ability to inspire fanaticism in his followers upset the world. President Hoover would be closer to the administrative type. As food administrator, as Secretary of Commerce, as a manipulator of stocks and oil properties, he was a great success. On the other hand, as a political leader, he lacked warmth in his personal relationships and fire in his speeches. He could handle goods better than he could handle people.

Pure examples of these types, however, can never be found in politics. Only the impression left by the sum of his acts tells what category describes the representative. The aggressive representative continually evades conformance to his constituents' will. He may be domineering by temperament, believing the masses should be directed rather than followed. His constituents may respond favorably to this treatment. They may be swept away by his program of actions. Apart from his position, his personal qualities may arouse the utmost devotion in his followers. A large number of his acts are acts of power; he desires to manipulate and to coerce, legally. Among his number, one would find those whose personality develop-

---

[17] *The Legislative Way of Life*, Chicago, 1940, p. 62.

ment is similar to that of the agitator type described above. Whether we like it or not, Hitler was representative of the German people, many of whom, like him, felt frustrated during the days of the Weimar Republic.

The aggressive representative cannot be generally considered as either good or bad. For his type produces statesmen as well as demagogues. Huey Long was an aggressive representative, as was Winston Churchill. But their behavior in office can be classified to some extent under the types of representation which ensue. A noteworthy thing about Churchill is that his ideas were not acceptable to the English people for a long period of time. When the country was on the verge of disaster, it turned to the aggressive type. Churchill was looked upon as the man who could save his country, and virtually all his constituents laid their fortunes at his feet in the dark days of the early forties.

When the representative is aggressive, there is less tendency for the constituents to identify themselves with their leader. There is less mirroring of the constituency. The constituents do not want to tell their representative what to do; they want to be told. All of this is with reference to the overt representation. It is representation on issues about which people have expressed desires.

The representative who acts against his constituents' desires may act on his beliefs as to their best interests. He may act in accordance with what he thinks are his own best interests. He may act on behalf of the best interests of the nation as he sees them, or he may act according to the wishes of powerful interest groups either because they subsidize him or because he believes in them. Under any of these situations, the ideal functioning of a representative system breaks down. There is no direct pipeline between the sovereign people and their agent. Representation must depend on an accord between representatives and represented, which under a democratic system presumably is guaranteed to a large extent by the process of election.

Frequently, representatives do not think of themselves as acting in a representative capacity. Before each act they do not ask themselves: "Am I being representative in this act?" But they act as they themselves feel as individuals. It was said of Lloyd George in 1915: "He is, in fact, the most prominent and powerful crowd-exponent in our day. He is the visible and audible incarnation of popular tendencies. His emotions respond as sensitively to those of a crowd as ever a barometer to the changes in atmospheric pressure. He has never manifested any trace of an individual mind or of independent thought." [18] This is the logical corollary to what was earlier called actual representation by reflection, wherein a constituent agreed with his representative because of identical characteristics. Here, the representative behaves as though he were the dominant voice of the community. Such a representative would need to worry little about the opinions of his constituents in a particular matter. Most politicians pride themselves in this intuitive penetration of the popular mind.

The assumption of some of the members of the American Constitutional Convention of 1787 was that any seizure of power would be used chiefly for private ends — the acquisition of personal booty and the monopolization of power without popular consent. Controls were imposed on the selfish behavior of public officials. There seemed to be a general feeling that men in office behaved as individuals, acting selfishly. Some prominent exceptions to this attitude were expressed in the *Federalist*. Today these exceptions are much more commonly the rule. John Dewey expressed the more liberal view when he declared: "Those concerned in government are still human beings. They retain their share of the ordinary traits of human nature. They still have private interests to serve and interests of special groups, those of family, clique, or class to which they belong. The best that most men attain to is the domination by the public weal of their other desires. What is meant by representative government is that the public is definitely organized with the intent to secure their dominance. The dual capacity of every officer of the public leads to conflict in individuals between their genuinely political aims and acts and those which they possess in their nonpolitical roles." [19] This statement, however, makes the representative's distinction between his private and public capacities appear to be a conscious mental process.[20]

---

[18] M. Conway, *The Crowd in Peace and War,* New York, 1915, p. 107.

[19] *The Public and Its Problems,* New York, 1927, p. 76.

[20] For studies of the unconscious intrusion of the private aspects of the political personality's acts on his public life refer to Lasswell's *Psychopathology and Politics.*

The amount of independence shown by a representative may bear significant relationships to his environments as an infant and child. Thus, Woodrow Wilson was noted for his independence as a representative. When he was governor, and later when he was President of the United States, he defied the party organization and also the public on issues on which he had deep convictions. His early religious training left him with great confidence in his own moral judgments.[21]

Even such practices as "log-rolling" and mutual "back-scratching" may be defended on noble grounds. If one were to accuse a legislator point blank of pursuing his private ends, glib and sweetly reasonable would come the reply: "I represent the people of my constituency. They have a right to demand consideration of local interests. To these demands I must defer." The same representative, in a wave of patriotism, will abnegate his local role, and "represent the whole people, from the sun-kissed shores of California to the rock-ribbed coasts of Maine." The representative is not impervious to the spirit of the times, and neither are his constituents.

Types of Acts

The kinds of tasks performed by the different types of representatives throughout the world are extremely varied. They can be generally narrowed to the four categories of expressive, administrative, special legislative, and general legislative acts. The basis for this division lies in the amount of popular knowledge regarding the act, and the scope and intensity of effect of the act, though, of course, those elements are highly correlated in the political process.

1. KNOWLEDGE. The effects of the knowledge by a small or a large part of the constituents of an act of a legislator are important. When the vast amount of anonymous acts of the legislator are considered, every representative, whether he is aggressive or inert in publicly viewed activity, is his own critic. Since he acts without the knowledge or care of his constituents, he considers naught but his "conscience," i.e., he has no immediate dread of a baleful public

---

[21] President Wilson was strictly brought up as a Presbyterian. It has been established by psychologists that a thorough indoctrination in a given set of moral values at an early age leaves the individual with a *Weltanschauung* which is not questioned in later years.

eye. In this sense, an ordinary inert representative partakes of the characteristics of the aggressive individual on matters not generally known. To the extent to which his public is ignorant and therefore uninformed, a representative may be unhampered and unchastened. For the test of the aggressive representative comes in the treatment of his opposition from his constituency. If he knuckles under, like the aloof Burke did, when the opposition arises, he is either a good politician or an inert character, depending upon whether it is done in view of the greater end or for personal reasons. When a piece of legislation is before the legislature, a representative is interested in what portion of his constituents have knowledge of the activity. The proposed law may be well known to be demanded by a majority of the electorate through such techniques as a full canvass, a straw poll, an initiative, party platforms, or the degree of vociferousness of agitation pro and con. Under such circumstances the representative has two alternatives and several reasons for choosing either. Most representatives will immediately decide as their constituency would have them decide. The voice of the electorate will, in effect, be an imperative mandate, baneful to the "Founding Fathers," but agreeable to the progressives around the turn of the century who desired such things as direct legislation.

In the case of a proposed law which is known to his constituents, though their feeling regarding it is unknown, a representative may act as he believes his constituents would have him act or as he thinks they should feel. In many an instance of novel legislation, especially of the less important sort, the representative is faced with blankness in the ordinary channels of communication with his district. If he votes as he thinks they believe, what was said above about mandates applies. The representative is, if he is intuitive, a crowd exponent, or what Lord Bryce called a "conduct pipe" for the opinion of his constituency.

In practice, the representative may happily confuse the difference between what the people believe and what they ought to believe. When this happens he has no compunction about voting the way he feels, and no problem is presented to his slipshod mentality. He may, on the other hand, decide to act in accordance with how his constituents should feel. Then his position is most insecure. Whatever he does, he must do it holding constant the imponderable of public opinion which may crush him no matter how skilfully he has maneuvered through the shoals of all other factors involved.

2. GENERALITY AND INTENSITY. There is a continuum of power acts from one exercising small discretion over a minute group to one exercising great discretion over the whole nation. Expressive acts would not be included in the category, as they are a special case, more in the sphere of propaganda than of power relationships. Some factors tend to make the independence of the legislator vary directly with the greatness of the power act, holding constant such matters as changes in institutional controls (party systems, etc.), assuming that the acts relate to felt desires on the part of the constituents. Where desires are latent, the degree of independence varies inversely with the greatness of the power act.

Acts with reference to felt desires will be taken up first. The direct relationship between independence and amount of power is so for several reasons. There is a rough correlation between the power exercised by a proposed law and the amount of publicity the law received. The press disseminates discussion. By the universality of attention, one is convinced that the proposed act is nation-wide in significance and that it concerns everyone. The representative is subjected to the public beam or glare. Any desires he may have for independence are reinforced by the desires he may have for acting on behalf of the whole nation. In the light of the situation, he can be recompensed for loss of local esteem by the accrual of national esteem.

The local constituency, too, is affected by the widespread publicity given a major act. They see that the nation as a whole is concerned with the act, and in the face of overwhelming national sentiment they will reduce their claims on the allegiance of their representative. They become self-conscious about the pressing of local viewpoints, and do not care so much if their representative acts contrary to their desires. They have a tendency to leave felt desires unexpressed. In a way, the independent representative is a compensation for their sheepish selfishness.

An equal possibility exists, however, that the constituency will agree with the nation and demand strict control over its representative's behavior. Thus the first type of independence is inhibited, and the second type of independence encouraged, by an act of great power. The Ludlow War Referendum proposal was based upon a widespread belief that the nation might believe differently than its representatives on a very broad and important subject. But the same broad and important act is liable to hold a high place in the representative's hierarchy of values. The more crucial the issue, the more he is inclined to feel that his personal integrity and honor are at stake. It is no more a matter of give and take, of giving a little to get a little. The matter achieves a sacred status, where to compromise is to lose one's soul. The electorate can never feel so intensely on an issue. Public opinion is too unwieldy, communication too faulty. Each voter can explain away the result of a decision on impersonal grounds — the fault of the system, the representative's fault, or a general bewilderment that does not bother to find fault.

Other factors add to independence in important matters. There is the complexity of all-important legislation which the ordinary person has time to comprehend only at the price of his job and wife. Helpless and ignorant, he cannot avoid giving more rein to his representative, who, like a doctor, is at least supposed to have read up on what he practices. Also, the effects to be expected from an act are relatively unknown to the constituents when compared with more narrow acts for jobs, bridges, and post offices. The representative has been becoming less and less a delegate or proxy since the public business has been growing more and more complex. The public has been becoming more and more a superintendent. Bills are not so frequently striking and romantic, as Harold J. Laski has pointed out. And "to decide what issue of the many hidden in each bill one wants to vote upon is delicate, but to make certain that the vote will be actually on that rather than upon another issue is indelicate presumption." [22]

A "static," rather than "functional," division of acts on the basis of the amount of power they wield, the number of persons encompassed, and the duration of the acts, would result in the more traditional trilogy of administrative, special legislative and general legislative acts. The first affects a great many people, but in an accustomed and therefore expected manner. The second affects a

---

[22] T. V. Smith, "Custom, Gossip, and Legislation," *Social Forces*, Vol. 16 (October, 1939), p. 24.

very small number of people in an important way. But the third includes laws of greatest change, and duration, and scope, such as the Social Security Act or the Wagner Labor Relations Act.

We have seen that inasmuch as a representative exercises the first two, he is not subject to the scrutiny of a large part of the electorate. Nevertheless the awareness, and therefore pressures exercised by those most concerned in these acts, are proportionately greater. Under administrative acts may be included all of that species of acts which make politics an occupation of menials, performing petty services and token obsequences for egoistic constituents. Many legislators are inhibited in the amount of attention they can give to public matters by a necessary preoccupation with minute balms to the egos of individual voters.[23] Every politician, to a greater or lesser extent, must furnish this personal attention. A large amount of this errand-boy work in many cases increases the independence later allowed on larger issues. Franklin D. Roosevelt's impregnable position among the poorer classes rested to a large extent upon a very personal relationship established through his various schemes of public welfare. This personal relationship allowed him considerable independence on large matters, little understood by his constituents, who, however, followed him faithfully.[24]

In discussing the scope and intensity of an act, it is worth while to point out the effects of the time of occurrence of the act upon the independence of the representative towards it. An unrepresentative act committed early in a term is not so costly in votes as one committed towards the end of the term. Consequently, Congresses are notoriously more independent at the beginning of their careers; they wax more anxious about home sentiment as the elections near. This is with reference to a static constituency. On the other hand the latter part of a term may be less representative because of shifts of sentiment in the electorate not paralleled by their representatives.

Types of Constituency

One of the chief targets of the attacks on democracy has been the "irrationality" of the masses. The defenders of democratic ideology

---

[23] J. T. Salter, *Boss Rule*, New York, 1935.
[24] J. T. Salter, "Letters from Men in Action II," *National Municipal Review*, Vol. 30 (August, 1941), p. 471.

turned to rationalizing the role of the untutored, the prejudiced, and the leveling mob. Some of the democratic writers in the recent past contended that though passions swayed many men, democratic government was still more reasonable than absolute government, and that a king was as capable of passion as a bootblack.

The much maligned emphasis on reason is apparent in the works of such defenders of representative government as John Stuart Mill. Thus, when speaking of the pledges of representatives and the absence of such, the famous political theorist said that "the result will depend less on the exact prescription or authoritative doctrine of political morality than on the general tone of mind of the electoral body, in respect to the important requisite of deference to mental superiority. Individuals, and peoples, who are acutely sensible to the value of superior wisdom, are likely to recognize it, when it exists, by other signs than thinking exactly as they do, and even in spite of considerable differences of opinion." [25]

More explicit in this respect, Lord Bryce wrote that government by public opinion was frequently government by one out of twenty men who activate and lead the other nineteen, resulting in a "system wherein the will of the people acts directly and constantly upon its executive and legislative agents." [26] He noticed the possibility of wide individual variations in opinion and the actual marked uniformity of opinion, and commented upon the detailed character of the demands among American as compared with English constituents. He implied a positive relationship between the class system and independence of representatives. The absence of definite domination-submission patterns in American life probably explains as much as any other factor the "direct democracy" movement and the often complete dependence of legislators on the direction of the political winds back home.

Where needs are immediate, personal, and primary, satisfaction of those needs will bring independence in other more distant, indirect, and impersonal spheres of legislation. Thus, in an American farming constituency whose principal crops were not protected by a

---

[25] *Considerations on Representative Government,* New York, E. P. Dutton & Company, Inc. (Everyman's Library), 1905, p. 319.
[26] *The American Commonwealth* (new edition), New York, 1927, Vol. 2, pp. 256, 267.

tariff, a representative who was "right" on questions affecting the farmers, or seeming to affect them, would have a wide choice in the international field, ranging from extreme isolationism to internationalism. Where the constituency is prosperous and without need for immediate protection, it is more likely to concern itself with broader questions of policy. Thus a British Conservative from a wealthy constituency would be free from some of the petty annoyances of nursing his constituency, but he would not dare defy the party leadership on major questions. Only when the poorer classes are fully awake to the final and ponderous effects of all legislation on their lives do they demand more dependence of their representatives. It often takes an educative (or propagandizing) movement as extensive as the British Labour Party's to arouse the lower income groups.

The very size of the constituency has far-reaching effects on the function of the representative. Small groups include face-to-face relationships impossible in a large group. Changes which alter the size of the electorate may involve new demands arising from the newly acquired right to vote. Adding a vast number of voters to a small, homogeneous group creates new problems in representation. The heterogeneity of the new constituency may demand altogether different qualities in its leaders.

To some extent, of course, new communication devices substitute for the old personal touch. The radio, press, and motion picture bring the candidate closer to his constituency, but these media are inadequate to restore a semblance of the old rapport. Many voters do not use the available methods of keeping in touch with their candidates. Minor representative offices receive little publicity, and most candidates cannot afford the time and money required for imitating the old techniques.

Writing about the Reform Bill of 1832, Disraeli observed in 1835 that "in a hasty and factious effort to get rid of representation without election, it will be as well if eventually we do not discover that we have only obtained election without representation." [27] By the multiplication of electors, the lines of each voter's control in the past century and a half in popular government have been immeasurably lengthened and entangled. Obviously, the smaller the electorate, the

---

[27] W. F. Monypenny, *The Life of Benjamin Disraeli,* New York, 1910, Vol. 1, p. 329.

easier it is to accomplish representation of those who are qualified voters, and consequently the more unrepresented are the great mass of disfranchised. On the other hand, the greater the size of the electorate, the less the political influence that any single group gets that has hitherto had the vote. Before suffrage became universal, the individual interest of electors in politics was more intense.[28] The demands for the personal attention of the representative were somewhat smaller, and the number of his acts fewer and more interesting to his constituency. All these matters facilitated tighter controls. With an unrestricted suffrage, appeals for election must be directed at huge groups which are tied together by the most general symbols. Any attempt to tie the group together on concrete issues is futile, and the amount of representation through deliberate and expressive acts becomes less.

Increased size frequently, but not always, introduces wide differences of opinion among constituents. A rural territory may sometimes be extended without introducing variant elements into the political system, but frequently differences in climate, soil, rainfall, and topography may bring changes in agricultural methods and ways of thinking. It has been demonstrated that the American farmers in the Middle Western corn belt behave politically in the same general fashion, with variations that are associated with fertility and rainfall.[29] An entirely different pattern of political behavior may be observed among the dairy farmers. On the other hand, small urban constituencies under universal suffrage will generally include diverse elements.

From earliest times cities have had their gold coasts and their slums, with many gradations in between. Groups having common and exclusive interests will draw together. Each will have its leaders, its slogans, and its programs of action. If strong enough, a homogeneous group will do all in its power to further its ends inside or outside of the governmental structure. "Extend the sphere," wrote Madison, "and you take in a greater variety of parties and interests; you make it less probable that a majority of the whole will have common motive to invade the rights of other citizens; or if such a common motive exists, it will be more difficult for all who

[28] See above, pp. 37-39.
[29] H. F. Gosnell, *Grass Roots Politics,* Washington, D. C., 1942.

feel it to discover their own strength, and to act in unison with each other." [30]

Homogeneity creates stricter control over representatives. It is easier to tell when the representative is or is not following the line pledged by him during a campaign and approved by his election. To get any sort of collective unity in a heterogeneous community, the appeal must be to general symbols. "Honor," "truth," and "democracy" are more effective than a vote for the bond issue or a stand on labor. There is no disagreement over their value. But, of course, once in office, a representative must solve problems not by the aid of symbols but by acts. With a very heterogeneous community he may use indefinite symbols to aid him, but, on the other hand, he must later alienate one or more groups by his acts. A frequent result is a high degree of verbalization but a low level of committal activity.

An interesting but rarely discussed aspect of this division of districts is the relation of the characteristics of the legislative member to the characteristics of his constituents. We discuss this partly under the heading "occupations" in the following chapter. It would be well if we had available more general materials on this subject, but it can safely be said that the voters of a given race or religion tend to choose representatives from their own group. In an American constituency where Negroes comprise a majority, and where they are permitted to vote, they tend to choose a Negro representative.[31] Similarly, where there are many religious sects, the members of a given sect tend to favor candidates who belong to that sect.[32] On the other hand, there might be a negative relationship between the nationality of a representative and the major nationality of his constituency, if it is composed of different nationalities, because of the impossibility of any member of any large group drawing a majority vote. In an American constituency where they were in a minority, Negroes would be likely to support white candidates, since candidates of their own would have no chance. An unpopular minority will sometimes support a candidate from outside its ranks in preference

[30] James Madison, Federalist No. 10, *Federalist,* with an introduction by Edward Mead Earle, New York, 1941, p. 61.
[31] H. F. Gosnell, *Negro Politicians,* Chicago, 1935; G. Myrdal, *The American Dilemma: The Negro Problem and Modern Democracy,* New York, 1944.
[32] Dewey Anderson and Percey E. Davidson, *Ballots and the Democratic Class Struggle,* Stanford University Press, 1943, pp. 74-76.

to one from within. It may not stand by its own leaders because they lack prestige in the larger community. There is no guarantee that a minority will be satisfied with electing its own members to the legislature. It may hold its representatives in contempt as being just like themselves; it may unreasonably accuse them of having sold out to the majority, and it may feel more isolated.[33]

In some cases a representative of superior wealth and prestige will have the difficulty of reconciling his own interests with those of his poorer constituents. Generally, a loose relationship between the representative and his constituents may be expected under such circumstances, unless the representative entered politics as a revolt against his class, as did Franklin D. Roosevelt. But, as happens often in England, when a person enters politics in accordance with a family tradition, his independence is stronger. If he is wealthy and does not look to politics for a livelihood, he will also be inclined to be more independent. The subservience of some American legislators to their constituents has been frequently traced to the fact that their bread and butter depends upon their staying in politics.

When the minority in a district is exceptionally large, the representative is usually more inactive, since he can afford to alienate few of his supporters. When issues rarely have a majority heartily in their favor but generally have a minority bitterly against them, a representative must use the utmost caution in proceeding with the majority program. It is frequently better to be unrepresentative of a majority than of a minority. This is because values vary in intensity, and a representative cannot afford merely to count noses. He must allow for the bitterness of the opposition whether it be small or large.

When the representative has a great majority behind him, he may be more independent in his acts by virtue of the measure of safety allowed him. Where there is a popular nominating system, he must have a huge personal as well as party majority. In those situations where the party controls the nomination, the representative must follow the party leadership, which may be local, as in the United States, or national, as in England.

---

[33] Everett Hughes, *Bulletin of the Society for Social Research* (August, 1940), p. 4; H. F. Gosnell, *op. cit.*

The feeling of being represented depends also upon the number and kind of alternatives presented to the voter. If only one candidate is presented, those voters who expected to contest will feel that they are not represented. If there is a choice between two candidates, it may happen that neither candidate is satisfactory to a large body of voters. If there are many candidates representing a wide variety of views, the voters may find their opinions represented, but they may be so split that they fail to see the basis of the unity which is necessary for democratic action.

A feeling of representation which exists during a campaign may persist afterwards if the winning candidate can unite divergent groups behind him. In the United States where party strife has not been too bitter, the voters who opposed the winning candidate will look to him as their representative after the election. If there are many bitterly partisan groups, the favorite candidates of a majority may be defeated, and the successful candidate may find it impossible to "represent" some groups. This was the situation in France under the Third Republic. Another type of situation where the feeling of representation may be dissipated is to be found when the winning candidate may make promises during the campaign which he finds he cannot fulfill afterwards. He may be saved by the short memories of the voters.

At all times, whether the majority be large or small and the constituency mixed or homogeneous, there will be pressure on the representative to conform to the views of this or that group. There is always the possibility that he may win over those who opposed him.

Even in matters brought to the attention of few of his constituents, the representative may be depended upon not to take action which will be offensive. For example, common law of contract has rarely been a matter of popular formulation and discussion. Yet the legislators, in amending and supplementing it, may be guided by what they think would be acceptable to their constituents if the matters were fully explained to them.

When voters are not obsessed by a single issue like the sales tax, the Townsend Plan, or proportional representation, they tend to vote on personalities rather than issues.[34] This is not because voters fail

---

[34] Robert Luce has stated: "Out of more than a million adult men and women in Massachusetts, it is safe to say that not one hundred thousand ever are informed

to realize the importance of issues in politics, but because they do recognize such importance and would rather trust another person than themselves. A statistical study of the senatorial primary elections of 1936 in Oklahoma shows that personality and speaking ability were apparently more important in getting votes than economic issues both in the original and run-off primaries.[35]

Voting for or against a person has many more psychological satisfactions than voting for or against an issue. The mere act of voting against a much criticized candidate may make the voter feel better. In the candidate he supports, the voter may find the qualities he admires, or he may find someone like himself. As T. V. Smith has poetically stated, we may abandon hope of personal glory and power and still "find secret fruition in the vicarious antics of those whom we may with impunity disdain. The politician is but the person who exhibits himself to us in the way we would have exhibited ourselves to him had he and the occasion made it our hour upon the stage."[36]

The final result of elections may not be representation at all. The successful candidate may not feel himself bound by his promises, or he may ignore the wishes of his constituents. Fairly complete representation of an individual or a group does not insure the support or the vote of the individual or group. Election depends upon the feeling of representation, and that feeling may be independent of the actuality of representation on the part of those persons whose sources of information are inadequate. Yet elections do have both a direct and indirect part in bringing about representation.

The election is a way of pledging faith in democracy. A procession of candidates marches before the voters, swearing fealty to democratic symbols, big or little, and cursing the devils of democracy. The whole process can be likened to a great expressive act of representation designed to develop a feeling of rapport between constituents and representatives, whereby the latter are bound to

about any single proposition coming before the legislature, or give any thought to it at all. If, indeed, the estimate were put at ten thousand, it would not be ludicrously far from the mark, save in the case of such exceptional questions as woman suffrage or prohibition." *Legislative Principles,* Boston, 1930, p. 497.

[35] Royden J. Dangerfield and Richard H. Flynn, "Voter Motivation in the 1936 Oklahoma Democratic Primary," *Southwestern Social Science Quarterly,* Vol. 17 (September, 1936), pp. 97-105.

[36] "Two Functions of the American State Legislator," *Annals of the American Academy of Political and Social Science,* Vol. 195 (January, 1938), p. 188.

reflect faithfully the proper kind of sentiments during their term of office. Towards the end of that time, the fire of enthusiasm begins to run low, and a renewal is required. New elections are held, and old troths are replighted. The system works well in this regard. Only great cynicism can break the spell of the acts.

Chapter 12

THE SIGNIFICANCE OF OCCUPATION
OF REPRESENTATIVES *

ONLY IN exceptional cases among representatives in parliamentary governments are there men born and bred to serve as statesmen. There has been no concerted, conscious effort to actualize the Platonic ideal of lifelong training in statesmanship. Nevertheless, if we were to assume a coincidence of success and merit, we could point to certain occupations as providing that training, because certain occupations have an incidence in legislatures far higher than their incidence in the whole population. To explain this high frequency and describe its effects is part of the task of discussing representation, and the ability of representatives becomes only one reason among many in accounting for their presence at the seat of government.

Two commonly found types of "overrepresentation" are frequently confused because of the ambiguity of the term *representation*. There may be first an "overrepresentation" on the basis of apportionment. In America this is typical of the State legislatures and the national Senate. The assumption underlying this complaint against "overrepresentation" is that an equal number of men should elect an equal number of representatives. Twenty-seven States allow the less populous areas to be favored over the more urban areas through constitutional provisions.[1]

But when Harold D. Lasswell writes, "Agriculturalists are almost universally underrepresented in proportion to numbers,"[2] he is

---

* Alfred DeGrazia assisted substantially in the preparation of this chapter.

[1] The constitutions of nineteen states guarantee at least one representative per county. In eight other state constitutions some other restriction prevents the representation of the more populous areas. Inequalities in the senatorial districts of twenty-six states are caused mostly by legislative inaction. The ninety-six metropolitan districts listed in the 1930 Census have on an average only three fourths of the representation due them in each house of the legislature. See D. O. Walter, "Reapportionment and Urban Representation," *Annals of the American Academy of Political and Social Science,* Vol. 195 (January, 1938), p. 11.

[2] *Politics: Who Gets What, When, and How,* New York, 1936, p. 130.

thinking in terms of the skills of the representative. The farmers are underrepresented because there is a greater proportion of farmers in the population than there is in the legislative halls. This, of course, defines representation as identity of occupation between constituent and legislator. With this as the sole criterion, it is plain that lawyers in America are highly overrepresented.[3]

Occupation may be considered to have some meaning in representation, if a survey of available information shows a tendency towards identity of occupation between representative and constituent. Occupation can be viewed both as a general external mark which is desirable in running for office, and as an activity which bears in its training and method the prerequisites for success in politics.

Offhand it will generally be conceded that electors are inclined to favor men of the same general occupational characteristics. This identity may be that of farmers with farmers, or negatively put, it may be that of white collar workers for anyone except a manual worker.[4] One must remember, though, that occupation is only one of a multitude of characteristics which may appeal or not appeal to the demand for a mirror of the constituent, even granting that occupation denotes a cluster of probable traits and is an unmistakable external mark of a man.

There is, however, a milder demand for superiority on the part of the elected men. This demand is more difficult to measure, and perhaps may work only within selected occupations rather than with reference to the whole hierarchy of occupations.[5] Thus a demand for superiority can be reconciled with a demand for identity by farmers' electing a superior and successful farmer. The frequency of negatively prestiged occupations (*e.g.,* saloonkeeping) in American

---

[3] Cf. Charles S. Hyneman, "Who Makes Our Laws?", *Political Science Quarterly,* Vol. 55 (December, 1940), pp. 575-578.

[4] The Economic Party of the German middle classes is a clear and concise case in point. Support was gained from innkeepers, grocers, shopkeepers, etc., and the party president was a master baker. One professor was allowed to be in a leading position because he was a house owner and could advocate their interests. F. A. Hermens, *Democracy or Anarchy,* Notre Dame, Indiana, 1941, pp. 224, 225.

[5] Grace Coyle's generalization applies here: "Even where the structure may allow for the flow of authority from membership to leadership, fixed habits of dominance and submission due to difference of age, sex, class, occupation, or income level are likely to keep the actual control in the hands of the socially dominant." *The Social Process in Organized Groups,* New York, 1930, p. 107.

legislative halls throws doubt upon the prevalence of desire for prestiged persons on the part of the public.[6] Dislike, more than low
prestige, seems in the United States to determine the absence of such
occupations as industrial worker or trade-union official.

A large measure of correspondence between members and constituents' occupations is to be found in the case of farming communities in America. But it is only among farmers in America that
this tendency is apparent. A study of all members of thirteen lower
chambers and twelve senates from 1925 to 1935 showed the number
of farmer members to be second only to the number of lawyer members.[7] Their totals amounted to 21.5 per cent and 28.0 per cent of
all memberships, respectively; merchants and other businessmen,
who came next, numbered only 10.0 per cent. For the rest of the
occupations, the proportion was almost insignificant, and any utiliza-
tion of their percentages would be meaningless. Although 2.8 per
cent of all memberships were held by bankers and brokers, and 3.0
per cent by real estate men, we cannot possibly say that they were
elected through identity of occupation; there is no ghetto of bankers
or realty men yet. On the other hand, the figure of 1.6 per cent of
laborers may be more meaningful, since laborers form a large proportion of the population and tend to live in more homogeneous
neighborhoods. The ratio is so low in comparison with the proportion of voters who are laborers that usually there is doubt, in their
case, that identity of occupation is demanded of their representatives.

Perhaps we have here a difference between farming constituencies
and laboring constituencies. The farm community arose under pio-
neering conditions. Specialists in anything except farming were
conspicuous by their absence. The farmers had to rule by themselves, and accomplishment builds self-respect. Since one of their
own number has generally ruled them, they see no reason for im-
porting specialists. Furthermore, on family farms, retirement at
fifty sometimes brings leisure and time for legislative activities. The
community is immobile. Knowledge of the secondary, contractual
arts is not so necessary.

---

[6] Even under P. R. a saloonkeeper may be chosen. See *National Municipal
Review,* February, 1946, p. 98.
[7] Hyneman, *op. cit.,* p. 557.

The laborers of a large American city are mobile, new to their environment, and ignorant of the secondary world in which they live. Originally, large numbers came into the city to find already there a professional machine with professional manipulators of men. It seemed perfectly natural that they should work and vote but not run for office. There was no tradition of working-class candidates. They did not get the vote as a result of a vigorous organization of trade-unions or Socialist working-class movement. They received the vote in many cases by being given certificates of naturalization through the aid of machine politicians.

But in some European countries, where the workers organized to get the vote, they maintain an organization to elect their own kind. About 14 per cent of the membership of the 1946 French National Assembly was composed of industrial workers. Of the membership of the British House of Commons, 14.2 per cent were trade-union officials. Industrial workers were third most frequent on the rolls of the Swedish popular chamber.

The profession which is most typical of the legislative assemblies of America is the law. In 1937, as many as 1800 of the 7500 State legislators, or 24 per cent, were lawyers.[8] A study of five successive United States Congresses showed that the percentage of lawyers in the Senate varied between sixty-one and seventy-six, with a tendency to increase. The percentage of lawyers in the House ranged from fifty-six to sixty-five, though giving no signs of increasing.[9]

The proportion of lawyers in the individual State legislatures does not seem to vary with the urban-rural character of the State,[10] but when there is no large body of farmers within the State, the

---

[8] M. Louise Rutherford, "Lawyers as Legislators," *Annals of the American Academy of Political and Social Science,* Vol. 195 (January, 1938), p. 53.

[9] John Brown Mason, "A Study of the Legal Education and Training of the Lawyers in the Seventy-third Congress," *The Bar Examiner,* September, 1934, pp. 254-259; "Lawyers in the Seventy-fourth Congress: Their Legal Education and Experience," *The Bar Examiner,* January, 1936, pp. 42-48; "Lawyers in the Seventy-first to Seventy-fifth Congress: Their Legal Education and Experience" (unpublished manuscript) ; Rutherford, *op. cit.,* pp. 53, 54.

[10] There is a complete lack of correlation between the per cent urban in each state and the per cent of lawyers in the legislatures. This would seem to contradict our following remarks unless each state were examined by itself with reference to its history. Thus, though a certain highly rural state might have a high proportion of lawyers when compared with a more urban state, inside itself there may be found a positive correlation between urbanization and the number of lawyers. The Southern States, where law and politics were long the perquisites of the governing aristocracy, show a high proportion of lawyers in the legislatures.

difference is made up by bankers, professional men, salesmen, and industrialists. This was to be found in New Jersey and Pennsylvania between the years 1925 and 1935, for example. Professor Hyneman divided eight States into urban and rural districts, and stated that "It is hard to find . . . any evidence of an established relationship between degree of urbanization and tendency to send lawyers to the legislature." Nevertheless, he goes on to say, "If the forty-seven figures (percentages of lawyer-representatives to all representatives) which are entered under the district-type headings are arranged in order from the smallest to the largest (*i.e.*, from 0 to 100), it will be found that seven of the ten smallest figures represent the strictly rural districts, and that only one of the ten largest figures represents the strictly rural. Fourteen of the seventeen figures which represent district-type II (strictly rural) fall below the median figure." [11] This seems to us to be adequate evidence for the generalization that the more rural the community, the less likely it will be to send a lawyer to the legislature as its representative.

Additional evidence is to be had for New York State and Pennsylvania. While New York State was becoming more and more urban, from 56.1 per cent in 1880 to 83.6 per cent in 1930, the proportion of lawyers in the legislature rose from 31.8 per cent in 1882 to 38.3 per cent in 1910, and to 47.2 per cent in 1935. The number of farmers dropped by about 10 per cent during the same period, and these were not replaced by occupations other than the law in a number equal to the drop.

A less marked rise in the percentage of lawyers is noticeable in the Pennsylvania legislature, the percentage increasing from 13.0 per cent in 1881 to 18.9 per cent in 1937, in the House, and remaining about the same in the Senate during the same period.

This last fact leads us to another generalization. The proportion of lawyers increases with the amount of urbanization of a community and with the respectability of the position, but also the proportion of lawyers is a function of the size of the constituency. Everywhere, lawyers constitute a higher proportion of the Senate than they do of the House. The number of people in a Senatorial constituency is generally larger than the number in a House of Rep-

---

[11] Hyneman, *op. cit.*, pp. 571, 572.

resentatives constituency, and a Senator must appeal to more people. A lawyer can do this, since his profession calls for the advocacy of other people's causes. This Senate, with its greater prestige, offers an attractive post for lawyers.

The greater shift from a perfect correspondence between occupations of constituents and representatives in the more urban areas is, for one thing, a result of greater heterogeneity. Compromise on occupations is necessary, since each group, under the single-member-district plan, cannot elect its own representative. The lawyer appears to have been most successful in satisfying the conditions of compromise in the American scene. It is probably true, too, that the political problems presented by a complex district are more legal, more secondary, and more delicate than those of a rural constituency. The multiple social contacts of an urbanite require greater specialization in ironing out social conflicts. The degree to which the law rather than the community enters into the solution of problems is greater.

The element of superiority enters here. Is the lawyer who becomes a legislator more fitted to rule than most of his constituents? There is moral fitness and a technical fitness. Both need to be considered in deciding how the constituents behave.

Certainly, moral fitness is hard to define. If it means merely good will, then good will towards whom? What is meant is good will towards the family, friends, and class of the lawyer, primarily, and then also good will towards his constituents. Insofar as there is no question about whether a representative should lead or follow his constituents, there is an absence of conflict in the definition of "good will" with reference to those acts of the representative which are known.

But whenever his conscience demands independent judgment, and when the constituents make explicit demands, accusations of "special interests," "self-interest," and "misrepresentation" are heard. Writers who have attacked the strong influence of lawyer-legislators have based most of their case on the "inevitable" results of legal training as it is conducted, the "conservative" influences playing upon the lawyer from childhood to his profession.[12] But no ready proof that the

---

[12] To this argument Hyneman retorts: "Might we not say, then, that lawyers make our most progressive legislators because they are practiced in studying how

study of law is the source of conservatism has been presented. To say that "It is not insignificant that every great period of social change in England has been accompanied by a temper of antagonism to lawyers," [13] is to give a rationality to political behavior which is not at all understandable.

The defenders of lawyer-legislators claim, in the first place, a lack of evidence for the opposite position, and second, that, on the contrary, legal training gives a person an impartial, objective frame of mind. Ingrained in the legal tradition is the idea that a lawyer is bound to act for others and not for himself. While the antilegal advocates base their claims on an implied premise that the representative is for the most part free and independent of his constituents, the pro-legal school base their arguments on the principle that lawyers are trained delegates to whom the interests of the principal are paramount, and whose principles operate, for the main part, only in the private sphere.

But, on the other hand, a good case can be made for the theory that lawyers in legislatures are conservative because they *are* delegates, and that, if they were allowed free rein, the laws they would enact would be far less conservative than they have been.

With evidence as scant as it is, no final answer to the question of the conservative effect of large numbers of lawyers is to be given. We are inclined to think that many other elements in the sociopolitical system account for social lag, and that if these other conditions were changed, liberal lawyers would be chosen. Certainly, it seems to us that the presence of many lawyers in legislatures is as much an effect of conservative public opinion as it is a cause of conservative legislation. Charles S. Hyneman thinks that any skill-group will have its private interest as well as the public interest in acting as a representative, and since legislation is the lawyer's stock in trade, his private interest may probably be wider in scope than those of other occupations in the legislature. We do not accept this, because we do not accept any distinction between private and public on a subjective level, *i.e.*, from the standpoint of the representative. To a legislator, every bill is private. A farmer-legislator may make

---

old rules might yield to new for the benefit of present and future generations." (*Op. cit.*, p. 580.)
[13] Harold J. Laski, *Grammar of Politics,* London, 1925, p. 573.

as many vicious intrusions on legislation for urban communities as may a lawyer on a legal code.[14]

If only identity and superiority were demanded of representatives, countries without elective systems of any significance might be expected to have less identity and more superiority. In a state based on the *Führerprinzip*, there might be more specialists in ruling men. In a revolutionary state, there might be fewer lawyers who uphold the status quo.

A study was made of the Italian agencies of government during the Fascist regime.[15] The authors divided the agencies into rising and declining, the former consisting in the novel institutions ushered in by the Fascist revolution, the latter consisting in the agencies of the old democratic government.[16] It was found that despite the diatribes frequently directed against attorneys, their number had not declined, and their role in the state appeared to be about what it was before.[17] Furthermore, a number of officials had become experts in a skill generally characteristic of lawyers. Among the less readily defined skills which were the basis of successful careers in the Fascist state, was skill in "fixing." The fixer was a negotiator who enhanced his private income by exercising, or seeming to exercise, governmental and party influence.[18] Thus the decline of an elective system did not seem to bring a decline in the position of legalists. Since western society is so complex in its interrelations, and since the knowledge of procedures becomes more necessary as the procedures become more exacting (another result of the growth of or-

[14] C. E. Merriam and A. Lepawsky, *The Government of the Metropolitan Region of Chicago*, Chicago, 1933, Chapter 27. A. Lepawsky, *Home Rule for Metropolitan Chicago*, Chicago, 1935, Chapter 9. S. Haxey, *op. cit.*, points out that 44 per cent of the conservative M.P.s are directors of companies, and that probably all of them are stockholders. Consequently, when they legislate on many corporate matters, they are violating a traditional taboo of English law by being judges in their own cause. (Pp. 37, 73, passim.)

[15] H. D. Lasswell and R. Sereno, "Governmental and Party Leaders in Fascist Italy," *American Political Science Review*, Vol. 31 (1937), pp. 914-929.

[16] "Among the pre-Fascist organs of government, two have risen; the cabinet and the prefects. The cabinet has attained more freedom from the control of Parliament, and widened its legislative scope. The prefects have more authority, including direct control over local government. The following organs of pre-Fascist Italy have fallen (or not risen): Senate, Chamber, ministers of state, and podestà. All of the new agencies introduced by the Fascists are obviously 'rising' (when compared with pre-Fascist institutions)."

[17] *Ibid.*, p. 922.
[18] *Ibid.*, p. 924.

ganization), one might say that the position of lawyers seems to be no mere vicious blight that might easily be done away with.[19]

The number of academicians in the Fascist régime showed a striking decline from that of the old democracy. Leaders who had proletarian origins were as few under Fascism as under Parliamentarism. The Fascist agencies had a much higher proportion of officials of lesser bourgeois origin, including half of the cabinet, Il Duce himself, three fourths of the provincial party secretaries, and an overwhelming proportion of all other Fascist party agencies.

In terms of skill, the Fascist agencies exhibited the relative predominance of those who were devoted to the arts of government and politics in the narrowest possible sense. Many owed their entire career to skill in violence, and had no antecedent skill before their entry into politics. Party organization and party propaganda, with no previous skill acquisition, was the foundation of other careers.[20]

A place had to be made in the government for the revolutionists, but lawyers still retained their importance. It is a striking fact that as the importance of the job and the intricacy of the work diminishes, the amount of correspondence between the occupations of the official and the general population increases. "The farther down one goes in the party and governmental hierarchy, the more completely does the personnel become representative of the nation as a whole. Indeed, many persons are advanced chiefly because they are identified with localities rather than for conspicuous party service. The most striking cases are from Sardinia or southern Italy in general. In such instances, special emphasis is put on the local attachment." [21]

In three American studies of party precinct committeemen, it is noticeable that the closeness of relationship between the composition of occupations in the general population and those of the committeemen was much greater than that generally found between the population and State or national representatives. In ten rural counties of Illinois, the number of professional people in the population was 3 per cent of the total population, of farmers 45 per cent. The number of professional workers who were precinct committeemen numbered

---

[19] Various studies have demonstrated that the lawyer-legislator is by no means in the most incompetent group of lawyers. Hyneman, *op. cit.*; Rutherford, *op. cit.*
[20] *Ibid.*, p. 928.
[21] *Ibid.*, p. 927.

6 per cent of the total committeemen, while the number of farmers totaled 48 per cent of the precinct committeemen. A study of appointed precinct committeemen in Chicago, and one regarding elected party committeemen in eighteen cities of New York State, corroborate this conclusion.[22] Among 3618 committeemen in the selected New York State cities, 60 per cent were clerks, laborers, salesmen, or members of other low socioeconomic groups, 19 per cent held governmental positions, 6 per cent were business executives, 6 per cent were merchants, 4 per cent were professional men and 5 per cent were attorneys. In Chicago, the appointive system brought some striking differences. In 1936 some 48.3 per cent of the precinct captains were government employees, 21.6 per cent were merchants, 6 per cent were attorneys, 12.6 per cent were clerks, salesmen, laborers, and the like, 5 per cent were professionals other than attorneys, and 6.5 per cent were business executives. Apparently, then, though there still is a greater correspondence between the occupations of constituents and their representative in the lower positions than in the higher posts, the election of precinct captains has a distinct tendency to diminish the number of public job holders.

The fact of greater identity between constituents and representatives (generally evidenced by a decline in the percentage of professional people) which is characteristic of small constituencies is a result of homogeneity of outlook. If this primary group outlook, with its unanimity of opinion, is introduced into a secondary, more complex sphere, action is impeded and consensus lost.[23] Proportional representation, as shown above, is one method of perpetuating the primary group in secondary spheres of heterogeneity and conflict situations. The presence, on the other hand, of a large proportion of lawyers and persons in politically neutral occupations who are skillful and objective in adapting means to ends conceals local differences and fosters compromise. Too flagrant an external mark sig-

---

[22] William E. Mosher, "Party and Government Control at the Grass Roots," *National Municipal Review*, Vol. 24 (January, 1935) ; p. 15. Harold F. Gosnell, *Machine Politics: Chicago Model,* Chicago, 1937, Chapter 3, "Character of Precinct Captains."

[23] Walter Bagehot made this point sharply: "Constituency government is the precise opposite of parliamentary government. It is the government of immoderate persons far from the scene of action ; it is the judgment of persons judging in the last resort and without a penalty, in lieu of persons judging in fear of a dissolution and ever conscious that they are subject to an appeal." *The English Constitution,* London, 1882, p. 214.

nifying emotional attachment is of negative value in becoming an elected official. It is a striking characteristic of some polyglot metropolitan constituencies in America that the elected official is of a nationality not at all numerous in the district. Similarly, where no occupation predominates, a theoretically neutral occupation has its opportunity.

A glance at some of the world's legislatures will reveal the situation. American legislatures are preponderantly composed of lawyers and farmers. These people are occupationally and socially middle-class. Professor Hyneman wrote:

> The *over-membership* of the "intermediate class," including lawyers, is our way of accomplishing the *overrepresentation* of the bourgeois classes, *grande* and *petite*.
>
> The task of devising a representative system for legislative assemblies, as practiced in the modern world, is not simply one of assuring spokesmen, directly or indirectly, for all classes of people or for all identities of interest. The task is, perhaps fully as much, one of making sure that the demands of certain groups will be submerged in the general public. I am not clear as to why the territorial or geographical constituency was originally established as our basic unit for representation. At least one of the reasons for our refusal to abandon territorial representation in favor of some form of economic or functional representation seems, on the other hand, to be pretty obvious— we are not willing to abandon our traditional symbol of equal representation for all; at the same time, we are not willing to permit a propertyless worker-unemployed group to have places, proportionate to their numbers, in our policy-making bodies. The use of territorial constituencies has at least up to now permitted us to maintain capitalist-middle-class control without avowedly violating the principle that, within the limits of enfranchisement, a man biologic is a man politic.[24]

This acute analysis suggests that the occupations of legislators are directly dependent upon the system or representation. A majority system is middle of the road. But we think more than "overrepresentation of the bourgeois classes" is involved. There is an actual occupational influence on legislation to mitigate primary group conflicts not necessarily accomplishing the dominance of anyone and inimical to the impulses of each.

The European parliaments which had few lawyers had proportional representation and powerful extremist parties which were split

---

[24] *Op. cit.*, p. 576.

against one another. Lawyers composed only 3.7 per cent of the German Reichstag in one year of the Weimar Republic. While they numbered 27.3 per cent of the French Chamber of Deputies in the twenties and thirties, in 1946 they came to only 13 per cent.[25] In the Swedish Parliament and the Irish Dail, the percentage of lawyers is small but other professional persons are present. In Great Britain [26] in 1936, and in Switzerland in 1928, about 20 per cent of the membership in the lower house were lawyers.

The demand for identity seems to coincide with extremism, both in the small constituency and in the national chamber. It is a sign of intolerance, a distrust of strangers, and a design for extracting strict allegiance from a representative. It will be characteristic, then, of lean and turbulent times for men to demand representatives in their own image.[27] We find the percentage of lawyers dropping in New York and Pennsylvania with the advent of depression. That there were not greater shifts shows how strong American governmental machinery is geared to prevent dislocation through class cleavages. We find claims by extremist groups exaggerated by the system of proportional representation used in Weimar Germany. We find in England a coincidence of the rise of the labor movement and a decline in the proportion of middle-class occupations, with a Conservative Party whose members engage in governing class occupations.[28] And, with more than a grain of truth, we can relate the Nazi "folk state" to the fact that there was a greater identity of occupation between representatives and constituents in a small community.

---

[25] K. Braunias, *Das Parlamentarische Wahlrecht*, Berlin, 1932, Vol. 2; Raoul Husson, *Élections et Referendums des 21 octobre, 1945, 5 mai et 2 juin, 1946*, Paris, 1946.

[26] J. F. S. Ross, *Parliamentary Representation*, London, 1943.

[27] Even theoretically extremist parties, in relatively stable times, have considerable numbers of intellectuals in their ranks. *E.g.*, the Socialists in the German Reichstag, 1903-1906, contained seventeen professional men, five bourgeois, twenty-four petty bourgeois, and thirty-five employees. Robert Michels, *Political Parties*, New York, 1915, p. 271.

[28] One hundred eighty-one conservative M.P.s are company directors, a majority are landowners; ninety-six were at one time in the army, apart from the first World War; seventy-eight are barristers; eleven of sixteen ex-civil servants were from the Diplomatic Service.

"These professions may be termed 'governing class professions,' both in the sense that their members play some part in governing the country, and that they are the chosen professions of the governing class of the country. The wealthy classes in Britain thus exercise a dual control over the Government, not only through their positions in Parliament, but also through their positions in the state services." Simon Haxey, *op. cit.*, pp. 184 ff.

Chapter 13

THE LEGISLATURE: PUBLIC INTEREST
AND PARTIES

Legislative Esprit de Corps

Representatives have been
discussed as leaders of their constituencies, with all the bounds and
restrictions which followers impose upon their leaders. But they
must also be thought of as members of another important group, the
legislature itself. It is not sufficient to describe the controls on a
legislator that are exercised by his electors, and his independence is
not to be judged solely by reference to his personality, his party
membership, or his dominant social characteristics. The assembly
of representatives is in many ways a unit, a group with morale,
conceptions of its role, restrictive devices on its members, and a prevailing way of thinking. The legislature is a cohesive and integrating force, molding men to its image and adding to the
representative's idea of himself as an agent of others, the idea of
himself as a functioning member of another organ with new obligations, benefits, and *esprit*.

Conflict exists between the two groups to which the legislator
belongs. He mingles with kindred souls, alike sharing the pleasures
of popular leadership, and the rebuffs and meanness of popular demands. Legislators draw together in their misery of exposure to
the populace. Alone among men do they know the humiliation of
serving as menials when they desire adulation. A philosopher and
legislator wrote that "The legislature itself is a problem-solving place
where men (and women) gather who owe little to one another, but
both duty and victory to constituents back home." [1] It is pleasurable
to be with one's own kind, who give something concrete in return

---

[1] T. V. Smith, *The Legislative Way of Life,* Chicago, 1940, pp. 3, 4.

for everything they receive. Smoke-filled cloakrooms and bars where one can rub elbows with his colleagues who have shared experiences with him and who know what he has been through to get there and stay there, are assimilating and conditioning grounds.

The new member can see and hear the great old statesmen. Traditions echo through the halls. Tales are told about the little incidents in the group life, of crafty coups, of great filibusters, of grim fights. Small amenities must be observed. Reference to the subject of a comment in the third person carries an air of military deference. Certain behavior patterns are expected of representatives, though such behavior has never been part of their lives before. The very traits which endeared a man to his masses are found to be shunned by parliamentary tradition. Ranting radicals were soothed and tamed by their membership in the British Parliament. An acute German commentator wrote the following words on British Parliamentary practice:

> To this day the House of Commons is predominantly an assembly of gentlemen. It has little in common with the parliaments of the Latin democracies, or with the American legislature. It much more closely resembles a club than a legislative chamber . . . the principal part of the labours of Parliament goes on not in the House but in the lobbies, the smoking-room, and the restaurants of this most influential, and in some respects, most exclusive club in the world. . . .
>
> The secret of the success of this Parliament — the only one in the whole world which has endured and has for centuries given its country efficient governments, and in doing so has kept free of all outward signs of corruption — lies, before all else, in the fact that it is an association with fixed rules which, in many respects, are of a social rather than a political nature. It is significant that the British parliamentarian is not called a Representative or Deputy, but a Member of the community of Parliament. . . . Such rules train even the social outsider into dignified membership of the club. Even such stiff-necked representatives of the proletariat as the men of the semi-Communist Independent Labour Party, who represent the only really radical enclave (radical in the Continental sense) in the British Isles, the industrial areas of the Clyde, have been unable in the long run to withstand this domesticating influence of the environment and the club rules of Westminster. The times when they made assaults on the dignity of the House, when they tried to get away with the Mace, seem to be gone for good. Even the one Communist who for several years has honoured

the House with his presence has lost much of his rawness, and as a rule observes the prescribed forms just as carefully as any Conservative die-hard on the other side of the gangway.[2]

As Abshagen implies, the failure of many assemblages has been due in part to the lack of a continuous community, a "club" spirit. Postwar European parliaments were notorious for their spirit of rebellion and factionalism rather than for their conviviality and *esprit de corps*. Factionalism is the product, too, of representation which is designed to promote opposition, and of rawness in the use of parliamentary etiquette. Bringing into a hall together opposing gangs from the streets does not in itself pacify those gangs. Proper mechanical devices of representation and procedure facilitate the compromise, but centuries of traditional behavior and a common ideology in leadership are crucial bonds.

The Senate of the United States, more than any other American legislature, has enduring ties on its members. Lord Bryce on this point wrote that "The Senate, like other assemblies, has a collective self-esteem,"[3] and the elder Henry Cabot Lodge said that "There may be no House of Representatives, but merely an unorganized body of members elect; there may be no President duly installed in office. But there is always the organized Senate of the United States."[4] The Senate has also "individual self-esteem," in each member's "insistence on the full enjoyment of executive prerogatives."[5]

In occupation, age, education, dress, and class, the legislators are far more like one another than like their constituents. A student who made a detailed study of the interpersonal relationships in the Illinois State Legislature wrote that, "In general, the *esprit de corps* displayed by legislative bodies, especially the smaller ones, is probably not rivaled by any other formally organized, self-governing body."[6]

---

[2] Karl Heinz Abshagen, *King, Lords, and Gentlemen,* London, 1939, pp. 99-101. Translated from the German edition of 1938 by E. W. Dickes.
[3] *The American Commonwealth,* New York, 1911, Vol. 1, p. 107.
[4] *The Senate of the United States and Other Essays,* 1921, p. 2, as quoted in Rogers, *op. cit.,* p. 21.
[5] *Ibid.*
[6] Garland C. Routt, "Interpersonal Relationships and the Legislative Process," *Annals of the American Academy of Political and Social Science,* Vol. 195 (January, 1938), p. 30.

This *esprit* smooths the clashing opinions of legislators, teaches them to bargain, to compromise, and to understand one another. The personal contacts of eleven Senators (six Democrats and five Republicans) were observed during the first fifteen minutes of each hour the Senate was in session from April 7, 1937, to adjournment, June 30, 1937. Of the three hundred and seventy-one contacts observed and recorded, two hundred and forty-two, or 65.2 per cent, were between members of the Democratic majority. Less than 10 per cent were between Republican members, and the remaining 25 per cent involved Senators of both parties.[7] Thus a mere enumeration of the contacts is sufficient to disclose a large amount of interpersonal contact, even between antagonistic partisans. A similar study of a foreign democratic legislature would give valuable material for analysis and comparison. The effect on group cohesion of tightly drawn party lines would perhaps then be evident in the amount of interpersonal contact between members of opposing factions. At present we can only point to, but not measure, the effects on the representative members of belonging to an exclusive social group.

Party Discipline and the General Interest

Another characteristic of representation in a democratic country is party membership. In order to get elected to a given office, the aspirant has to be presented to the voters by being nominated by a political party. Without parties the electorate in modern democracies would be helpless. How could fifty million American voters choose one man to be President of the United States unless the two major parties narrowed their choices to two men? Political parties have made modern representation possible by presenting the voters with alternatives which they can manage.

While there must be legislative *esprit de corps,* a characteristic of democracy is also that the lawmakers agree to disagree. In all democratic legislatures there are divisions along party and other lines. If these divisions do not exist, then the lawmaking body is not democratic. Mussolini's Chamber of Corporations and Hitler's Reichstag were not democratic institutions.

-----

[7] *Ibid.,* pp. 134, 135.

How serious may the divisions be in democratic legislatures? The experience of the Germans during the Weimar régime shows that if the intolerances are too great, democracy cannot survive. During the crucial years before 1933, party differences were so great in the Reichstag that no one could command a majority and form a stable government. The German Nationalists refused to co-operate with the Social Democrats, and the Communists refused to co-operate with any of the so-called "bourgeois" parties until the thirties, when it was too late. Hitler's National Socialist Party was rabidly antidemocratic and scornful of all other parties. Successful democratic legislatures cannot be made out of such materials. No firm majority could be formed. The Weimar Constitution failed because the parties were too well disciplined and too little concerned with the general interest.[8]

The situation in France in 1940 was somewhat similar. The differences between the parties in the French Parliament were so sharp that it was impossible to form a strong government to defend the country. It has been commonly said that one of the defects of the French Parliamentary system is the multiplicity of parties and the looseness of their discipline. Regarding the multiplicity, there was no question but French parties of the Third Republic were not poorly disciplined.[9] As a matter of fact, they were too highly disciplined. They opposed one another with such bitterness that they failed to get together when the country itself was in danger. Lulled to security behind the Maginot line, the different party groups thought that they could indulge their special interests. They lost sight of the common interest of defense against a powerful and ruthless foe. The French Conservatives were so afraid of the Popular Front composed of the Communists, the Socialists, and the Radical Socialists, that they looked for protection against their countrymen in the delusive promises of the enemy.[10] The French Communists were non-co-operative in the twenties, part of the thirties, and then again in 1939-1941 when the truce between Soviet Russia and Hitler's

[8] Karl Lowenstein, "Government and Politics in Germany," in *Governments of Continental Europe,* edited by James T. Shotwell, New York, 1940.
[9] Ralph Burton, "The French Chamber of Deputies: A Study of Party Allegiance, Attitudes, and Cohesion," *American Political Science Review,* Vol. 30 (June, 1936), pp. 549-556.
[10] W. Root, *The Secret History of the War,* New York, 1945.

Reich was in operation. The French Communists were lukewarm about the defense of the Republic in the crucial years.

The British Parliament since Cromwell's time has been characterized by divisions which were not too great to form a workable government. It has been the shining example of tolerant party differences. In the nineteenth century, Conservative and Liberal governments could be interchanged without great upheavals. When the Liberal Party declined in the twentieth century, and the Labour Party became the largest group opposed to the Conservative Party, the party lines in the House of Commons were more sharply drawn, but the unity of the House as a whole was not broken. In two world wars the Labour Party members of Parliament joined in the formation of war cabinets.

An examination of the divisions in the House of Commons during the past hundred years shows that the amount of strictly party voting has been increasing.[11] The members of the major parties have more and more tended to stick together on opposing sides of controversial questions. The votes have to an increasing degree been in accordance with the instructions of the party whips. In spite of this increasing sharpness of party divisions, the common interest has not been forgotten. Loyalty to Great Britain has come before loyalty to a party. This meant that while the Conservatives were more vigorously opposed to the Labour Party measures than they were to the Liberal Party measures, and while the Labour Party fought the Conservative Party policies more vigorously than the Liberal Party had, both the Conservative and Labour parties were willing to give up some of their avowed party aims in order to live with each other. Thus the Conservative Party was actually becoming less conservative, and the Labour Party less of an exclusive trade-union party. The leaders of the Conservative Party modified their views in order to accommodate themselves to the demands of the time for expanding government functions. The Labour Party leaders were constantly trying to increase the size of their base by appealing to non-labor elements. This could only be done by aban-

---

[11] A. L. Lowell, "The Influence of Party upon Legislation in England and America," *Annual Report of the American Historical Association*, Vol. 1 (1901), p. 323; Russel Jones, "Party Voting in the English House of Commons," unpublished Master of Arts thesis, University of Chicago, 1933.

doning some of the egocentric aims of the trade-unions. This tendency in British politics was one of the secrets of the vitality of British democracy.

During the last century the Americans were less fortunate than the British in developing a party system which would solve difficulties by compromise rather than by force. The differences between the Southern and Northern States were presented by the opposing factions in Congress as irreconcilable. Party leaders got to the point where they could no longer work out a peaceful solution of the slavery question, and the result was the bloodiest civil war in history.

Having learned this bitter lesson, the parties since that day have been more tolerant of each other. American party representatives in Congress tend to vote along sectional and group lines rather than on a party basis. The discipline of these parties in the two Houses of Congress is loose, and party lines are shattered on many issues.[12] The cleavages between the Republican and Democratic parties are not sharp, and the electorate has shown relatively little interest in such intolerant movements as the Communist Party from the time of the Russian Revolution, and the antidemocratic party movements that sprang up between the two world wars. Neither of the two major parties is able to enforce strict discipline upon its members in Congress.

The two-party tradition in England and the United States is in part the secret of democratic tolerances in these countries. Though American and British political institutions are quite different in form, they are alike in that they are operated by means of the two-party system under which the great mass of the voters have the fixed idea that voting for a minor party is wasted effort.

The two-party system does not mean that there are never more than two parties. It has rather signified that in these countries most of the voters, over a period of time, have cast their choices for the candidates of one of the two major parties rather than for candidates of minor parties which are not serious contenders for power. Except under extraordinary conditions candidates of the minor parties have no chance of being elected or, if elected, of influencing the formation of a government.

[12] A. L. Lowell, *op. cit.*, and P. Odegard and E. A. Helms, *American Politics*, New York, 1938.

The two-party system might be defined as the party system under which ordinarily there are only two parties that have a chance of controlling the government. There may be periods of transition when there are three or more parties, and when a coalition or agreement between the parties is necessary to form a government. This was the situation in Great Britain during the twenties and thirties, but the election of 1945 so reduced the third party (the Liberal Party) that once more the British voters were presented with two major parties, the Conservative and the Labour Parties, both of which have demonstrated their ability to win a majority of the seats in the House of Commons. Before 1945 the Labour Party had not done this, and the first two Labour Governments had an uncertain tenure which was dependent upon the tolerance of the Liberal members in Parliament. With the success of the Labour Party in 1945, the normal two-party system was again in operation in Great Britain.

In the United States a candidate of a third party has practically no chance of winning the Presidency — the key position in the American political system. At least this did not happen during the first one hundred and sixty years of the Republic. Immediately prior to the Civil War there was a period when the parties were in a state of flux, and it was not clear in advance of the elections how the party alignments would crystallize. The fact is, however, that following the Presidential election of 1852 the Whig Party disappeared as a major party, and in the election of 1856 the Republican Party appeared as the second largest party.

Two parties come to the top in English-speaking countries for a variety of reasons, among which is the fact that the constitutions of these countries favor this dichotomy and discourage minor parties. In Great Britain, the self-governing dominions, and the United States, the use of the single-member-district system for electing representatives has brought great pressure upon the voters to abandon hope in minor parties. The candidates of such parties, except in time of great political changes, have no chance of winning the greatest political prize, namely, control of the government. In Great Britain the election of 1922 inaugurated such a period. The Labour Party had been a third party since it first presented candidates in 1896. In 1922, however, it became the second largest party, and from that time on Liberal Party candidates had harder and harder sledding. Whereas the Liberal Party elected one candidate for every 25,000 votes cast in 1923, it only elected one candidate for every 207,000 votes cast in 1945. For these two elections the Labour Party marshalled, respectively, for each candidate elected, 22,300 votes in 1922, and 30,700 votes in 1945. Supporters of the Liberal candidates found it increasingly difficult to obtain representation. Although the party had money and candidates of great political talent, it continued to lose out against increasing odds.

In the United States, the single-member-district plurality plan is not only used for electing members of the two houses of Congress, but also for electing one of the most powerful representative officials in the world, the President of the United States. The peculiar system of the electoral college has resulted in making the Presidential election a choice of the aggregate of State pluralities. According to the United States Constitution, the President is elected by a majority of the electoral college, a body whose selection is left to the States, which in practice have provided that the members are elected at large by popular vote and are pledged to support their party candidates. Electoral-college elections in the United States accentuate reliance upon the two-party system, since shifts in the electoral college are far more violent than those in the total popular vote for the entire country.

A third party must not only win success in a sufficient number of States in order to win a majority in the electoral college, but it must also win pluralities in a majority of the Congressional districts in order to win control of the House of Representatives. Thus Theodore Roosevelt in the election of 1912 won more popular and electoral votes as the Progressive candidate than President Taft, his Republican opponent, but the Progressive candidates for seats in the House of Representatives came out third. After the election, the Progressives had little to show for their efforts (eighteen seats), but the Republicans still controlled one hundred and twenty-seven seats in the House, two governorships, and a body of other State and local officeholders that kept the organization together until the tide turned in 1920 and the party was swept into national office again. Theodore Roosevelt presented a grave challenge to the Republican

Party in 1912, but he failed to win a vantage point in Congress and was unwilling or unable to capitalize on what he won in the nation-at-large.

In Great Britain the two-party system is also perpetuated by the type of parliamentary government which the British have evolved. The Prime Minister can dissolve Parliament and declare new elections. This gives the party in power a firm grip over its members in the House of Commons, and discourages their trying any insurrections or new ventures, since re-election is a troublesome and uncertain matter. In doubtful British constituencies, winning an election is difficult, and the support of a major party is almost a necessity. The party in power keeps its members in the House from straying, and the opposition party is well disciplined because this is the only way that it can hope to come to power.

While institutional arrangements have been important in producing the two-party system in English-speaking democracies, the social composition and political attitudes of the electorate have also been important. An irreconcilable minority may prevent operation of the forces that tend to amalgamate voters into two large groups.

Prior to the establishment of the Irish Free State, the Irish Nationalist Party presented an unassimilated element in the British House of Commons. If the British population had been less homogeneous, and if it had contained more of such minorities, it might not have worked out its two-party system. The essence of the two-party system is the willingness of the defeated party and candidates, and their supporters, to accept the rule of the opposing party. The British elections of 1945 brought a supreme test to the Conservative Party, which it met in accordance with British parliamentary traditions. A Labour majority did not precipitate civil war or the sabotage of representative institutions.

The two-party system in the United States is also based upon the homogeneity of the political views of the population. While there are many nationalistic minorities (groups of foreign origin), these have been so scattered and so rapidly absorbed into American life that they have not furnished the basis for minority party representation. The largest racial minority, the Negro group, has not been absorbed as have the foreign-born, but it has not been in position to exercise much political power in the Southern States, and it is so distributed in the Northern States that it can control only two Congressional districts. Negro voters do not furnish the basis for a minor party and, recognizing this, they have aligned themselves with one or the other of the major parties.

The relative merits of the two-party system, as opposed to the multiple-party system found on the continent of Europe, are hard to determine. In English-speaking countries high praise has been bestowed upon the two-party system, and condemnation has been heaped upon the instability of coalition governments based upon many parties. The two-party system is said to provide a stable government, to foster national unity, and to provide a kind of representation which is easily understandable and manageable by the electorate. Each of the major parties adopts a set of principles, and the election of its candidates means that the government will be in the hands of officials pledged to carry out policies which a majority of the voters have endorsed.

The weaknesses of the two-party system have also been the subject of much comment. To divide the voters into two main camps in a country as large as the United States is regarded as an impossible task. It can easily be demonstrated that almost any voter can find much that is wrong with both parties. Neither party represents his views on many issues. Party platforms tend to be alike, and the parties are two groups of hungry office seekers who appeal to this and that prejudice or local pride in order to win votes. Political campaigns under such a party system tend to confuse the voters, since the party leaders try to dodge as many issues as they can.

Multiple-Party System

On the continent of Europe, the multiple-party system has been the rule in representative democracies. Governments have been formed on the basis of coalitions between party groups. The number of parties presenting candidates to the voters has varied from three or four groups, in Belgium, to seven or more groups, in France.

The multiple-party system has been the product of political institutions and social conditions. Proportional representation, in its various forms, encourages multiplicity of parties. No country having a list system of proportional representation has developed a two-party system. The adoption of proportional representation has usually increased the number of political parties, since under it minority groups are not penalized. The system has facilitated the representation of many different viewpoints, but it cannot be said that it is crucial in producing the multiple-party system, since the Germans and Swiss had multiple-party systems prior to 1919 in spite of the fact that they used the single-member-district plan or the majority-block plan.

Opposing religious groups, class-conscious upper-, middle-, or lower-income groups, conflicting nationalistic loyalties, and clashing political philosophies have from time to time encouraged the multiplication of political parties in different countries.

The division between the clerical and the anticlerical groups might be said to be a product of the French Revolution, which led to the disestablishment of the Catholic Church in many European countries in the nineteenth and twentieth centuries. While Catholic political parties were frowned upon by the Vatican for many years, such parties were gradually recognized in country after country as one of the means of protecting religious freedom. This was particularly true after the antireligious tendencies of Communism and Fascism became apparent. National elections held in 1946 found the purely anticlerical parties such as the French Radical Socialist Party in decline. The French Popular Republican Movement, however, showed considerable strength. Catholic parties have persisted in Switzerland, Belgium, and Italy. Protestant political parties are found in Holland.

Class parties are the product of the Industrial Revolution and the Marxian ideology. On the continent of Europe, since the publication of the Communist Manifesto in 1848, there have been Socialist and Communist parties which have brought forward varying programs for economic and social change, frequently revolutionary in character. The interpreters of Karl Marx have not always agreed upon political tactics and objectives. As a matter of fact, Socialists and Communists have bitterly fought each other from time to time. Communism was given its great impetus by the Russian Revolution of 1917, which left a permanent impress upon world party systems. Why should these doctrines and movements find fuller expression in continental Europe than in English-speaking countries? Among the theories advanced to explain this situation have been the class stratification explanation, the clerical analogy, and the abstract philosophical thought pattern. These theories will be examined in turn. According to the class stratification theory, the income groups on the continent of Europe are more highly conscious of caste differences than are the British and the Americans. Landlord and peasant status are more marked on the Continent than in England, and there is also a greater gulf between employer and employee. It has been harder for a lower-income-group member to raise his income status, and therefore lower-income groups are more likely to accept their status and look to political methods for improving their lot. A man who joins a Socialist or a Communist party is admitting that he is a working-class member. He is giving up hope of becoming a member of the middle class — the bourgeoisie. A refusal on Hitler's part to join the Socialist Party indicated how this worked.

In the United States high social mobility has made Marxian doctrines relatively unpopular. The fact that the British Labour Party has grown so strong, whereas no American labor party has developed, may be attributed to greater social mobility in the United States than in Great Britain. The Labour Party is not Marxian, but it is closer to being this than any American major party has ever been.

The church analogy may be explained as follows. Marxian parties have developed in countries where there have been strong Roman Catholic, Greek Orthodox, or Lutheran churches. Marxian parties may have been influenced by ecclesiastical patterns. Marxian Socialists and Communists try to substitute their dogma for church dogma, party expulsion for the Inquisition, the party leader (trade-union secretary) for the priest, party membership dues for church tithes, the various internationals for the Universal Church, and *Das Kapital* for the Bible. Marxian parties have been strongest in Roman Catholic countries such as France, Italy, Belgium, Poland, Austria, Bavaria, and Spain, in Greek Orthdox countries such as Russia, and in Lutheran countries such as Prussia, Norway, and Sweden. The Protestant churches of Great Britain and the United States do not seem to have furnished such an analogy. Episcopalianism, Presbyterianism, Methodism, Baptism, and other Anglo-American Protestant sects have been loosely organized, and highly individualistic.

It has been possible for British Labour Party leaders to reconcile strong religious convictions with their Labour Party platforms and aims. This was a characteristic of the British Labour movement which seemed incomprehensible to Lenin and Trotsky.[13]

The abstract political thought pattern of Continental countries has been different from the Anglo-American and has furnished a more fertile soil for Marxian idealism. Karl Marx was a follower of Hegel. British political thought has been more pragmatic and utilitarian. Adam Smith, Bentham, the Mills, the Webbs, Thomas Jefferson, William James, John Dewey, and other Anglo-American theorists have not been Hegelian idealists. Marxian dogmas have not appealed to Anglo-American thinkers. Anglo-American civilization has called for a more practical, empirical, experimental approach to life and to politics.

Conflicting nationalistic loyalties have also caused the proliferation of political movements on the continent of Europe. Prior to 1914 there were nationalistic political parties in Germany and the Austro-Hungarian Empire. In the period between World Wars I and II, there were nationalistic parties in Czechoslovakia and Belgium. These parties have had linguistic, geographical, and sentimental foundations. Czechoslovakian parties before 1938 included Czech, Slovak, German, and Hungarian wings.

A combination of factors has produced the multiple-party system on the continent of Europe. How representative have the governments been that have been formed on this basis? From one point of view, multiplicity is desirable. In modern complex society there are many interests, and they do not fall into a dichotomy but into many complex patterns. Where there is a multiple-party system, the voter is more likely to find some candidates or party groups that do not do too much violence to his ideas. If the assembly is to be a "mirror" of the electorate, then the multiple-party system fits the specifications.

The multiple-party system has been attacked from the standpoint that coalition governments are hard to form and are weak and unstable when formed. In France under the Third Republic, governments were notoriously short-lived. The average ministry stayed in

[13] Leon Trotsky, *Whither England?*, New York, 1925.

power less than a year. The weakness of the German governments under the Weimar Constitution were ascribed by some to proportional representation and the multiple-party system.[14] It was charged that the splintering of the electorate into many parties made Hitler possible. He seized power at a time when the Reichstag was a scene of bickering, inconclusiveness, and indecision. Hitler promised to bring order out of chaos, to substitute discipline for license, and to bring prosperity instead of unemployment. Could the multiple-party system bring these things? To a large portion of the German population it was obvious that the Weimar system of representation could not accomplish this. Hitler's rash promises looked more plausible.

The terrible holocaust of World War II has again convinced the populations of European countries not under the shadow of the Russian Soviet colossus that the multiple-party system furnishes a form of representative government which may be operated. The French, Belgians, Dutch, Italians, and Greeks have returned to the many-party system of the pre-Nazi occupation period. It also appears that Czechoslovakia may preserve its prewar system even under the watchful eyes of the Russians.

The essential conditions for the operation of representative democratic government are tolerance, acceptance of the substitution of peaceful means of persuasion for force, and a system of government which develops leadership. The multiple-party system should survive when these conditions are fulfilled.

Nominating Systems

One of the primary functions of political parties is the selection of candidates to run for elective offices. The methods employed for winning the consent of party members to the candidates nominated vary widely. That consent must be obtained is a *sine qua non* of party existence. If the party members bolt the party ticket, then the party has failed to make its selections stick.

It is especially clear under the two-party system of the American Presidential form of government that the essence of party existence is the making of nominations which will be accepted by the rank

---

[14] Hermens, see above, pp. 194, 195.

and file of the party. The Republican Party in the United States failed to do this in 1912, and the party went down to disastrous defeat in that year.

Nominations in Great Britain have been and are controlled by the party organizations. In order to run for the House of Commons as a Conservative, the aspirant has to be adopted by a Conservative constituency association, and he has to be acceptable to the national leaders of the party. Centralized control over nominations in the Labour Party is even greater.

On the Continent the control of nominating machinery varies from party to party. The Marxian parties have had the most elaborate organization, with regular dues required of party members and strict discipline enforced on representatives. Candidates for elective office have to be acceptable to the party hierarchy. In Germany, under the Weimar Constitution, the Social Democratic Party organization had complete control over the choice of representatives, since voters in the final election had no choice as between individual candidates. The Belgian Labour Party is more democratic, since the district federations made up of representatives of the local political unions, the trade-unions, and the co-operatives select candidates. The local organizations submit nominations, and a poll of all dues-paying members of the federation determines the selection.[15]

It is in the United States that the most elaborate nominating systems have been devised. Here there have been worked out caucuses, delegate primaries, direct primaries, preference primaries, run-off primaries, alternative vote primaries, mixed direct primaries and conventions, single-transferable-vote plans with multi-membered districts, State and local conventions, and that monster of all democratic institutions, the national nominating convention toward which the major parties direct all their energies every four years, when, no matter what national crisis the country may be facing, it must go through with the ritual of choosing candidates for the election of Presidential electors in accordance with the provision of the Constitution drafted over one hundred and fifty years ago by a group of well-meaning but politically naïve men who thought that such electors could actually exercise free choices and would not become the most

---

[15] T. H. Reed, *Government and Politics of Belgium*, Yonkers, 1924.

abject of all elected representatives in their subserviency to the persons they were representing. Such is the course of history. The Constitution, having become sacrosanct, and being difficult to amend, has embalmed these political institutions so that it is extremely difficult to alter them.

It is not necessary here to go into all the details of the American nominating systems. The literature is voluminous, and the end of the output is not in sight.[16] These nominating systems are necessary because of the country's having a Presidential system of government and not a parliamentary one. The chief characteristics of the Presidential system are the independence of the executive from the legislature, and the system of checks and balances. The chief earmarks of the parliamentary system are the dependence of the executive upon the legislature. In Great Britain the House of Commons can turn a Prime Minister out who fails to control a majority of the members. The Prime Minister must be a member of Parliament. This system makes possible the exercise of central controls over the party system. In the United States the combination of the Presidential and the Federal plans makes it difficult for the central party organization to exercise much control over the constituent parts of the party. Nominating systems are therefore varied and complicated. Each of the forty-eight States must have its own nominating system, and the existence of municipal home rule in some States means that each city or town can have its own nominating methods.

American nominating systems are a part of the American theory of democratic government, which assumes a great competence on the part of the voter, a lack of competence on the part of the elected representative, and the efficacy of elaborate electoral machinery. These assumptions are not sound, but somehow the system works, not perfectly, of course, but with a sufficient degree of efficiency to furnish the basis for one of the world's toughest political units.

Democracy could not operate in a large representative state without two or more political parties. On the other hand, when one or

---

[16] C. E. Merriam and L. Overacker, *Primary Elections*, Chicago, 1928; C. E. Merriam and H. F. Gosnell, *The American Party System*, 3rd ed., New York, 1940; V. O. Key, *Politics, Parties, and Pressure Groups*, New York, 1942; J. K. Pollock, *The Direct Primary in Michigan*, Ann Arbor, 1943; L. Overacker, *The Presidential Primary*, New York, 1926; L. Overacker, *Money in Elections*, New York, 1932; E. M. Sait, *American Parties and Elections*, rev. ed., New York, 1939; E. E. Schattschneider, *Party Government*, New York, 1942.

more of these parties becomes intolerant and unwilling to use and abide by democratic methods, then democracy is in danger in that country. Party loyalty must yield to national patriotism and the spirit of democratic compromise, or the representative system will not operate. The legislature is the reflection of the party system. When the members of the lawmaking body are so divided and enraged against each other that they cannot talk out their differences, this is a danger signal for lovers of freedom and liberty.

Chapter 14

ORGANIZED INSTITUTIONAL CONTROL
OVER REPRESENTATION

THE FORMS of representation
influence a society just as the society's behavior influences the forms
of representation. People will demand a certain minimum of these
forms in order to feel represented. Their primary demand is for participation in the selection of representatives. It was of little avail that
Hobbes and Burke declared that the government of England represented the whole people, whether or not the whole selected the leaders.
Walter Bagehot wrote regretfully:

> There is a saying of the Eighteenth Century, that in politics "gross
> appearances are great realities." It is vain to demonstrate that the
> working classes have no grievances; that the middle classes have done
> all that is possible for them, and so on with a crowd of arguments
> which I need not repeat, for the newspapers keep them in type, and
> we can say them by heart. But so long as the "gross appearance" is
> that there are no evident, incessant representatives to speak the wants
> of artizans, the "great reality" will be diffused dissatisfaction.[1]

We must look at the representative from the eyes of the people
whom he supposedly represents. People who have had no voice in
the selection of their representative may not feel that they have any
influence in his acts, although to an outsider or neutral observer it
might appear that the representative is acting completely to their
interests.

Yet even the participation in the selection is no guarantee of feeling adequately represented. Any representative who does not reflect
the dominant opinion of his constituency may have a disturbing influence out of all proportion to his actual power. He may stimulate
vast bodies of people to discontent. His symbols are not theirs, and
he may therefore provoke them into feeling unrepresented. If there
are more than a few such men in the legislature, and if their acts

---

[1] *The English Constitution,* London, 1882, p. 242.

seem socially or personally destructive, the larger body of people may be inclined to feel more represented by one man, though his grasp on power be illegal and not achieved through elections.

If a man represents the people over whom he exercises power, they will be inclined to undervalue the mode of selection of leaders, for the public is essentially pragmatic in matters politic. Of course, given an unbiased and full account of the acts and characteristics of the leader, the people might well consider themselves unrepresented. Or, to put it otherwise, there may be basic negative association between the amount of propaganda used in the accomplishing of the feeling of representation and the use of elections.

It may appear at times that a monarch represents a number of individuals better than a representative assembly does. When conflict groups within the representative body are bitterly engaged, the dominant popular forces may feel that they are the dupes of these groups who apparently rule without representing them. Each faction fights for its extremist views, and the person who belongs to any one interest group with only part of his personality feels battered by the clashing of many groups, no one of which reflects his ideas adequately.

Feelings of misrepresentation also become prevalent when, in order to represent a number of individuals, the representative is highly unrepresentative of some of the individuals in the group. The amount of agreement a representative's actions find in individuals 1, 2, 3, 4, 5, 6, 7, and 8, is the amount of *individual* representation present. But taking 1 to 8 as a group, representation for the majority may consist in using coercive measures on the minority.

Thus there may be popular participation in the selection of representatives, and yet a widespread feeling of being unrepresented. If this occurs in a society that has great faith in the basic principles of democracy, the result may be agitation for reforms which will "bring government back to the people." In America the traditional devices to achieve such reforms have been the initiative, referendum, and recall.

The Initiative and Referendum

Deciding where the devices of the initiative, referendum, and recall should be treated in a general work on democracies is a discomfiting task. Conceivably, these devices of "direct democracy" might be attached to a treatment of the origins of the democratic forms as a sort of atavism. The Athenian assembly, the Swiss cantons, and the New England town meetings have been cited to show how democracy originates through the organization of a crowd to determine policies.

On the other hand, we have chosen to include this subject under the discussion of representation, taking its main premise to locate its position. In America these devices, excepting the constitutional referendum, arose in the late nineteenth century as part of a general protest against corruption and conservatism in the legislatures. The advocates of direct lawmaking felt that the government should be brought back to the arms of the "uncorruptible" people. They felt that representative democracy was failing to "represent" the whole people, and was becoming, rather, a representative of special interests. They considered that elections were not sufficient to insure representativeness, and that elected men could not be entrusted with power without great danger of corruption. "Direct Democracy" came with Populism, Progressivism, and muckraking.

With considerable popular support, the movement surged through the United States gathering momentum. It finally subsided, however, leaving a number of States with laws allowing the use of the three devices. As indicated by the number of articles on the initiative and referendum listed in the *Reader's Guide to Periodical Literature,* popular attention was considerable in 1900, rose with fair constancy to a peak of forty articles in 1911, and dropped thereafter until at the beginning of 1920 little attention was given these measures in the press. The number of States adopting the measures followed approximately the same pattern, maximum legislation for the devices occurring in 1912.[2]

Measures involving direct popular participation are of eight kinds: (1) a constitutional amendment originating in the legislature and requiring the approval of the electorate; (2) a constitutional amendment initiated by a petition signed by a specified proportion of the electorate and requiring popular approval; (3) a law initiated in a similar manner and requiring popular approval; (4) a law required by constitutional provision to be submitted to popular vote; (5) a

---

[2] The President's Research Committee on Social Trends, *Recent Social Trends,* New York, 1933, p. 428.

law referred by the legislature under a constitutional authorization to a popular vote; (6) a law referred to popular vote after a petition has been signed by a specified number of voters; (7) a public policy measure which is only advisory to and not mandatory upon the legislature; and (8) a special election to determine whether an official should be superseded before his term is completed. In our discussion of these devices we shall take the first seven as a whole and treat the recall separately.

The initiative and referendum had been used since 1874 in Switzerland, many years before they became part of the "direct democracy" movement in the United States.. Between 1878 and 1928, thirty-five ordinary constitutional amendments, twenty initiated constitutional amendments, and thirty ordinary laws had been submitted to the voters of Switzerland.[3] Voting participation was on a high level in most cases. Ordinary amendments passed by both houses showed the least electoral interest; initiated constitutional amendments were next in extent of interest; and ordinary laws drew greatest popular attention at the polls. During the ten-year period from 1918-1927, only twenty-nine federal proposals were submitted to the people. The burden of direct popular legislation was not so great as the voters in some American States have experienced. The subjects for referendums varied from unimportant to very significant matters, including a law on motor traffic and the question of joining the League of Nations. In the former vote, the participation was 35.6 per cent, in the latter 76.5 per cent. Generally, the questions were not of the detailed type found in America, but, rather, for the most part of a kind whose significance could be readily grasped by the electorate. There were no issues that brought the French-speaking and German-speaking groups into direct conflict with each other. The two thirds of the population who speak German did not use the initiative and referendum to deprive the French-speaking and Italian-speaking peoples of any privileges. On the other hand, the structure of the government and the substance of its laws were not changed to a marked extent through the use of these measures. It has been stated by Professor Brooks that they were used in several cases to "destroy hopeful projects for centralization, the people showing

---

[3] Robert C. Brooks, *Civic Training in Switzerland*, Chicago, 1930, pp. 112-118.

themselves much less willing to take steps in this direction than their chosen representatives at Bern." Most of the feelings of the people on these matters would probably have been expressed through their representatives at a later time. No great tyranny of the majority is at all evident. As a symbolic gesture of attachment to democracy, in Switzerland the initiative and referendum have been called a most potent institution.[4]

America has had a quite similar experience, with unique additions of "bigness" and bestness." The direct lawmaking movement achieved its first success in South Dakota in 1898, and in 1936 twenty States had the initiative and referendum. Some form of direct participation in lawmaking is found in every State except Delaware. There has been little activity in extending these measures since World War I, though there has been an extensive use of them up to the present.

Between 1924 and 1935, a total of 1299 measures were submitted to a popular vote in the States of the American union. Of these, eight hundred and eighty-one were referred constitutional amendments, one hundred and twenty-eight were initiated laws, and eighty-four were initiated constitutional amendments. Referendums on laws required by constitutional provisions numbered seventy-four, on laws by petition seventy, on laws by the legislatures fifty-seven, and on public policy measures five. Most of the measures (974) were on the level of State government; one hundred and twenty-eight affected counties; ninety-one referred to city government, twenty-seven to school districts, twenty-nine to special districts, and fifty to combinations of levels.[5]

During the same period the largest number of propositions voted upon at any one time was in South Carolina, where there were fifty-two in 1924. On eleven occasions twenty or more measures were proposed at the same time, and on nineteen occasions from ten to nineteen measures were proposed. In California, where one hundred and seventy-three measures were submitted to the electorate in twelve years, the highest votes were cast on measures relating to Bible

---

[4] *Ibid.*, p. 118.
[5] H. F. Gosnell and M. J. Schmidt, "Popular Law Making in the United States," in New York State Constitutional Convention Committee, *Problems Relating to Legislative Organization and Powers*, New York, 1938, Vol. 7.

reading, sale of oleomargarine, gasoline tax, repeal of prohibition, repeal of law legalizing boxing, anti-cruelty to animals, daylight saving, Sunday closing laws, and unemployment relief. The least interest was shown on technical questions concerning private corporations, methods of voting on local referenda, a judicial council, election of judges, a governor's council, municipal and county charter amendments, and intergovernmental arrangements.

The difference of interest shows the striking features of the devices of direct democracy. Technical subjects are slighted, while morals are emphasized. In order of participation, the highest votes of the 1299 measures were on matters dealing with public morals (82.1 per cent vote), and the next highest on education (76.6 per cent), the limitation of revenue (70.8 per cent), highways (69.7 per cent), increasing revenue (69.4 per cent), and public welfare (69.0 per cent). The vote was much lower on questions of public debt (45.7 per cent), minor constitutional questions (49.3 per cent), and bond issues (52.8 per cent). A study of 429 of the 1299 measures showed that on the average less than half of the registered voters took the trouble to express their opinions on measures before them.[6]

There was no general tendency for voters to take negative attitudes toward legislation before them, except in measures imposing new taxes or regulating government expenditures. They have been most willing to support bond issues and measures to regulate the public debts. Because of the influence of small interest-groups in initiating legislation, the general body of voters has been adverse to such measures. Moreover, the referendum by petition has defeated acts passed by the legislature in most cases.

The recent experience of particular States (California and Michigan) corroborates the findings with regard to all States. Students of the California experience have written that "The initiators of propositions have usually been pressure organizations representing interests — commercial, industrial, financial, reform, religious, political — which have been unable to persuade the legislature to follow a particular line of action. The history of direct legislation shows a marked change in the character of the groups utilizing the initiative. It appears that now well-financed interest-groups initiate measures

---

[6] *Ibid.*

ORGANIZED CONTROL OVER REPRESENTATION 257

more frequently than do spontaneously created reform-groups. This
has resulted from two trends. The increase in the number of signatures required to qualify a measure for the ballot has made it
difficult for any but the well-financed organizations to circulate petitions. Along with this tendency there appears to have been a decline
in the reform spirit, which was running strong in the heyday of the
Progressive Movement."[7]
Paralleling the same conclusion, the Michigan study reports: "It
was thought by many of the sponsors of direct government that 'the
people' would circulate petitions and place proposals on the ballot.
. . . It has not been difficult for organized groups to secure sufficient petitions to present measures to the people, but it has been
almost impossible for citizen groups interested in good government
to initiate and carry through a successful program."[8]
Though the fondest hopes of the advocates of direct democracy
have not materialized in the matter of participation, neither have
the nightmares of the conservatives been realized in the types of
legislation brought about. Rather, in the United States the prophecy
of Dicey that the voters are conservative has been realized. In 1914,
Oregon voters rejected an eight-hour law for women. Oregon and
California rejected the single tax during the World War I period.
Action on public ownership of public utilities was neither far ahead
nor far behind that of the legislatures in other States.[9]
Only a handful of measures have involved religious questions, and
these were with reference to compulsory school attendance, none of
which survived the American checks against violations of constitutional rights. There has been little abuse of minorities otherwise.[10]
In addition to the questions as to who initiates the measures,
how great an interest the propositions arouse, and how radical are
the measures voted upon, there are the matters concerning how
carefully drawn the measures are, how well known they are, and
what are the chief values of the initiative and referendum.
In some cases it is impossible to know who drew up the measures

[7] V. O. Key, Jr. and Winston W. Crouch, *The Initiative and Referendum in
California*, Berkeley, 1939, pp. 565-568.
[8] James W. Pollock, *The Initiative and Referendum in Michigan*, Ann Arbor,
1940, p. 69.
[9] A. N. Holcombe, *State Government in the United States*, New York, 1929,
"The Popular Initiative," pp. 505 ff.
[10] *Ibid.*

to be initiated. The more important measures in Oregon were carefully prepared and criticized by a number of groups.[11] In the case
of measures drawn up by the State legislature, of course, the measures were generally no better or no worse drawn than ordinary bills.
The fact remains that the body of voters is not at all equipped to
understand even ordinary bills, and one of the chief failings of the
referendum has been the inability of the voters to use it intelligently.
Part of the difficulty is traceable to the nature of the measures proposed, part to the inadequate precautions in presenting them to the
public. In Oregon, during a thirty-year period, it was found that
the simpler the question submitted, the larger the vote. There were
high votes on prohibition, woman suffrage, compulsory education,
and the anti-cigarette amendment. There was a low vote on additional counties, limitation of indebtedness, and filling legislative
vacancies.[12]

The simpler the measure submitted, the better it is known. It
can be related to other persons and made part of an understandable
conversation.[13] Still there was a lack of preponderant opinion (50
per cent or more of those appearing at the polls voting for one side)
on initiative and referendum measures in Oregon in 68 per cent of
the cases during the first thirty years of its use. In several elections
where logically similar propositions were submitted separately, a
small number of persons voted "blindly," i.e., in a logically inconsistent manner.[14]

In some elections a voter finds it almost impossible to be con-
versant with the many measures he must face. In 1940, Louisiana
citizens had to render a verdict on thirty-two proposals.[15] Citizens
of Shreveport had an additional seven measures.[16] These were added

---

[11] J. D. Barnett, *The Operation of the Initiative, Referendum, and Recall in
Oregon*, New York, 1915.
[12] W. Schumacher, "Thirty Years of People's Rule in Oregon: An Analysis,"
Political Science Quarterly, Vol. 47 (June, 1932), p. 242.
[13] Simplicity and suitability for direct legislation need not always coincide.
One community voted on the length of the lunch hour in the fire department. W.
B. Munro, "Initiative and Referendum," *Encyclopaedia of the Social Sciences*,
New York, 1932, Vol. 8, pp. 50, 52.
[14] *Ibid.*, Table 8.
[15] United States Department of Commerce, Bureau of the Census, Division of
State and Local Government, *State Proposals Voted Upon: 1940*, Special Study
No. 11, January 6, 1941.
[16] *Ibid.*, *City Proposals Voted Upon: 1940*, Special Study No. 12, January 28,
1941.

to the burden of elections of representatives. This is an extreme case, but the same situation has faced the voters of other States in other years. Few people think of direct democracy in a case like Louisiana, where the real trouble is a constitution so detailed that amendments are recurrently necessary. The resulting lack of interest shows how little known are the proposals. It also creates other problems. In Chicago, fraud and error have distorted the count; obscure, confusing titles and an overloaded ballot have added to the great indifference on many occasions.[17]

In Tennessee, in 1932, a measure was to be submitted to the electorate according to the Session Laws. The Secretary of State several years later had no record of the amendment, and investigation showed that it had been omitted from the ballot in many counties and that no results were tabulated.[18] Knowing the demerits of indifference does not efface some presumed advantages of the direct democratic devices. Nor does admitting the grievance that resulted in Progressivism admit the success of the attempted cure.

First of all, it has been claimed that the initiative and referendum have been educative devices, stimulating a greater interest in democracy and acquainting citizens with the work of their government and representatives.[19] It is doubtful, *a priori,* whether educational experience of a general sort can emerge from the proposals which are given every year. The citizen probably does not learn any more about choosing worth-while representatives, which remains his chief responsibility.

More credence can be given the claim that popular voting on issues creates a feeling of national unity.[20] In Switzerland popular law-making is on a national basis, but in the United States it is State and local. National unity might be aided if the issues were moral and consensus regarding them could be established. But issues are frequently trivial or technical, and little emotion is aroused over them; certainly, no mass spirit is evident. Furthermore, there are differences of opinion in the end result, so consensus is lacking. As

---

[17] H. F. Gosnell, *Machine Politics: Chicago Model,* Chicago, 1937, p. 135.

[18] Correspondence with the Secretary of State.

[19] William B. Munro, *The Initiative, Referendum, and Recall,* New York, 1912, Chapter 8; Ellis P. Oberholtzer, *The Referendum in America,* New York, 1912, Chapters 1 and 19.

[20] Munro, *op. cit.,* and Oberholtzer, *op. cit.*

Lowell suggested, consensus may be retarded by popular voting.[21] Since a minority most frequently initiates laws, questions of a moral and sectarian nature may be raised, the discussion of which leaves scars. And also, the frequent indifference to referendum issues suggests that a great part of the public does not participate in the unity of action.

A third claim, the chief one of the American Progressives, is the most plausible. Direct democracy can accomplish things impossible of actualization under government that is merely representative in nature. A study of the laws enacted by the people shows hardly any striking examples of legislative backwardness. Retrospective prophecy is impossible under the circumstances, though a careful study might be made of two similar States, one that has used initiative and referendum extensively and another that has not. It might be surmised from the lack of outstanding acts of repression or socialization that popular legislation has brought no great changes. The conclusions of most writers from the beginning agree with this thesis.[22]

In several ways some healthy effects are derived. A large number of people may receive a heightened contentment with the government, knowing their power over it; though, again, these people may be matched in number by members of a minority who fear popular repression. This minority would feel safer in the hands of representatives who need 2 per cent or 3 per cent more of the electorate on their side. As a great act of dedication, a sacred symbol of the fount of power, a new constitution or constitutional amendments may well be approved by popular vote.[23] Out of all the types of legislation subject to referenda, this is most proper.

As a solution to the problem of apportionment, the initiative and referendum may be useful devices. In Illinois, for example, the people are frustrated in arriving at a just apportionment by the legislature's refusal to act, though it is commanded to do so by the Constitution of the State. If the State had had a constitutional initiative,

---

[21] A. Lawrence Lowell, *Public Opinion and Popular Government*, New York, 1913, Chapter 15.

[22] Lowell, *op. cit.*; A. B. Hall, *Popular Government*, New York, 1921, Chapter 6.

[23] Clauses in a constitution vary greatly in their technicality and import. A constitution might well provide two procedures for amendment, a popular procedure for the broadest, most important sections, and a simple legislative procedure for the detailed, transient, and less important sections.

the question of reapportionment would undoubtedly have been voted upon.[24] Still, one cannot be too sure. Professor Aiken wrote about the constitutional initiative in California:

> It has given the people the feeling that, however poor the Constitution, they themselves are responsible and the power of change rests with them. The present system of reapportionment, for example, defies most rules of representative government, but as it was adopted by the people, much less resentment is shown than one finds among the citizens of Illinois in regard to their state system. I feel that the great advantage of the initiative lies in the fact that the people can themselves alter any situation that proves to be decidedly unsatisfactory.[25]

The importance of a measure is in itself no criterion for the use of the initiative and the referendum. Many of the most important problems (if not all of them) are incapable of being decided in the most beneficial manner by the whole people.[26] Direct legislation is a most meager substitute for representative government.

In emergencies, of course, the initiative and referendum involve risks. They may by an excess of "democracy" destroy the democratic state entirely. It is a sad commentary on the nature of direct government in the world crisis of today that the groups most clamorous for a referendum on matters of foreign policy are at the same time the groups who would profit most from the obstruction of the policies of the representative bodies. It follows that the law of South Dakota is worth while in theory when it declares the referendum not applicable to "such laws as may be necessary for the immediate preservation of the public peace, health, or safety, support of the State government and its existing public institutions."[27] The difficulty which ensues is the tendency of the legislature to define "emergency" in a manner pleasing to itself.

---

[24] A legislature might thwart such a move, nullifying thereby the effects of the machinery of the popular control. In Vaud, Switzerland, in 1878, an initiated measure involved the reduction of members in the assembly. The assembly, however, reluctant to submit to a reduction, submitted a companion measure, involving the same feature though differing in detail. The majority of voters were for reduction, but split over the better plan, and so the *status quo* was maintained. E. V. Raynolds, "The Referendum and Other Forms of Direct Democracy in Switzerland," *Yale Review*, Vol. 4 (November, 1895), pp. 297, 298.

[25] Letter published in *Problems Relating to Legislative Organization and Powers*, New York State Constitutional Convention Committee, 1938, p. 392.

[26] See Hall, *op. cit.*, pp. 124 ff.

[27] The Oregon law allows abrogation of the referendum provisions when "necessary for the immediate preservation of the public peace, health, or safety."

Since the initiative and referendum were proposed initially to push through legislation against the vested interests of the legislators, it might be expected that large majorities for the initiated legislation and against legislative referendums would be found in many cases. This is not the true situation. The most important measures had close fights, whereas huge majorities were found in connection with measures to which most people were indifferent and for which the legislature was not reprimanded for inactivity.[28] The evidence points strongly to the theory that representative government has rarely gone *contra mores*.

The effects of direct democratic devices on the legislature are incalculable, but should nevertheless be considered. They probably cause legislators to feel less responsible for new ideas and more dependent upon the electorate. An initiated measure is an accusation of "irresponsibility." A referendum is a "demonstration" of "irresponsibility." Both are branding irons labeled "popular omniscience" and "legislative incompetence." It is a question whether the devices on a few matters make the legislature generally more responsible or more irresponsible. Certainly, the greater an assembly's prestige, the greater its power. The greater both are, the more attention is given the assembly; and the more public attention the general conduct of a body receives, the greater its feeling of responsibility, and the more decorous and proper its conduct of affairs in general.

The Recall

The recall of particular officers to stand for re-election to their office achieved its greatest scope in America, beginning with its adoption in the Los Angeles City Charter in 1903. Within the next few years other States adopted it, in some cases for State officers, in others for municipal officials. Oregon was the pioneer in allowing the recall of any elective public officer of the State in 1908. By

---

[28] Three examples may be given here.
Vote on Income Tax in Oregon (1912): In favor, 38.75 per cent. Against, 38.92 per cent. Not Voting, 22.00 per cent.
Vote on Civil Service System in Colorado (1912): In favor, 14.61 per cent. Against, 13.42 per cent. Not voting, 72.00 per cent.
(Hall, *op. cit.*, p. 140.)
Vote on Civil Service System in Michigan (1940): In favor, 38.3 per cent. Against 35.3 per cent. Not voting, 27.26 per cent.
(Pollock, *op. cit.*, p. 86.)

1920 the recall movement had reached its peak of legal acceptance and popular and party approval.[29] Then, like the initiative and referendum, its appeal waned among the Americans who were obsessed with the "return to normalcy." Today, though still the law in many places, it is comparable to old-fashioned Socialism, Bryanism, Progressivism, and anti-trust sentiment — a catchword that may ring out, but one that produces nostalgia rather than action.

The Los Angeles experience was not the first with devices like the recall, even in America. The Canton of Schaffhausen in Switzerland has a general recall which stretches back to the remote past, with many revisions and probably an ultimate basis in custom rather than enactment. Written petitions, signed by at least one thousand qualified voters of the canton, must present the demand for recall to the Executive Council. If the petitions are legally acceptable, the Executive Council is required to order the election for removal within thirty days after the close of the period for completing the petition.[30] For the election, the whole assembly, or council, is dissolved, and the re-elected or newly elected members fill out the rest of the unexpired terms. Eight other cantons besides Schaffhausen have this procedure. It is similar to the British Parliament's going to the country after a dissolution. The difference which is most striking is between the fixed term for Swiss elected officials and the undetermined term for British members of Parliament.

The recall was found in the program of the German Socialist Party as early as the sixties of the nineteenth century. It and the initiative and referendum were used in some municipalities before World War I. Following that war, all three devices were included in the laws of all the states of Germany, but were seldom used. Only one large city, Munich, held a recall election, but the measure was

---

[29] Eleven states had the recall with reference to state officers: Oregon, California, Arizona, Colorado, Idaho, Nevada, Washington, Michigan, Kansas, Louisiana, North Dakota—all between 1908 and 1920. W. Brooke Graves, *American State Government,* New York, 1936, p. 139. Today the following fifteen states have the recall for all cities: Arizona, California, Colorado, Idaho, Illinois, Kansas, Louisiana, Michigan, Mississippi, Missouri, Nevada, North Dakota, Oregon, Washington, and Wisconsin. Twenty-three states have provided for its partial use, generally where the commission and city-manager types of government are concerned. F. L. Bird and F. M. Ryan, *The Recall of Public Officers,* New York, 1930, p. 5.

[30] M. A. Schaffner, "The Recall," *Yale Review,* Vol. 18 (August, 1909), pp. 207, 208.

defeated. Other towns had a similar record of failure to recall officials.

Like Switzerland, the recall in Germany was used mostly for whole councils rather than for individuals, though provisions were made in some cases for recalling the latter. The infrequent use of the recall, Professor R. H. Wells ascribes to the difficulty of getting signatures, and the expenses and trouble a party must undergo for an uncertain cause.[31]

In America the recall was found under the Articles of Confederation. It could hardly be called an unexpected device in a country where States were sovereign and Congress was an assembly of ambassadors.[32] The recall of Senators was also discussed with reference to the Constitution in the Federal and New York conventions.[33] In these cases the recall was an expected practice because of the small constituencies (the State legislatures).[34] Doubtless if the American States had had very limited electorates, some form of recall would have prospered much more than the present form has. But, of course, such an argument presumes that there would have been a demand for a recall under conditions of a restricted suffrage, a not very likely possibility.

The five different varieties of recall advocated in America have been these: (1) the recall of elected officials, (2) the advisory recall of Federal elected officials, (3) the recall of judges, (4) the recall of judicial decisions involving the constitutionality of laws, and (5) the recall of administrative officials. The recall of elected officials deserves most attention as the most used form of the device. All others have been used sparingly and have been severely criticized.[35]

An estimate made in 1930 put the number of cases where the recall has been employed at one hundred and fifty, an average of six per year during the first quarter century.[36] In two cases, only,

---

[31] "The Initiative, Referendum, and Recall in German Cities," *National Municipal Review*, Vol. 18 (January, 1929), pp. 29-36.

[32] Article V.

[33] H. S. Swan, "The Recall," in W. B. Munro, *The Initiative, Referendum, and Recall*, New York, 1916, Chapter 12.

[34] The next part of this section will treat the doctrine of instructions wherein the frequency of resignation of Senators suggests very strongly the power of recall.

[35] For a discussion of them, see Bird and Ryan, *op. cit.*, pp. 11-17.

[36] *Ibid.*, p. 20.

were officials of the whole State subjected to recall. But this estimate was far below the actual number, as the study of Bird and Ryan in California shows. There, ten officials a year retired from office between 1920 and 1930. A total of one hundred and thirty public officials were recalled since the beginning. Considering the large number of officials who held office during this period, the use of the recall has been remarkably sparing. Those threatened with recall usually "came back alive." "Sixteen per cent of all recall petitions have been declared insufficient, ten per cent of all recall movements have terminated in litigation, and in only forty-six per cent of the movements which have come to an election have the officials been removed from office." [37] A few cases of excess were noted in small towns, and the resulting improvement was not of a startling nature. Like the initiative and referendum, the recall has been neither an *enfant terrible* nor a *deus ex machina*.

Most reproaches against the initiative and referendum are valid against the recall. Participation is much higher, however, if the experience of California can be considered typical.[38] And individual issues may even mean more. Officials must be careful to avoid identification with a point which, by its emotional significance, may result not only in repudiation of the point but also in their own removal. Two members of the Public Utilities Commission in the State of Oregon were recalled because of popular dissatisfaction with their authorization of certain rate increases.[39] This has not been a common occurrence because of the general neglect of recall provisions and the large amount of trouble involved in utilizing the recall machinery. These reasons undoubtedly have also worked against the use of the recall where it was most desperately needed. If it were easy to use, it might be more than a "gun behind the door" as Wilson described it; it might, in fact, be a "pistol at one's head."

Public Opinion Polls

The direct lawmaking devices and the recall must necessarily be used sparingly. Even in the most extreme cases, the electorate is called upon to pass judgment on only a small fraction of what a

---

[37] *Ibid.,* p. 343.
[38] *Ibid.,* pp. 182, 183.
[39] *Ibid.,* p. 19.

legislature must pass upon in each session. These devices are expensive and cumbersome.

But in recent times a new device has been invented which is a much more flexible instrument than the initiative and referendum. The modern public opinion poll can be used to sample public opinion on any subject within a relatively short time and at a nominal expense as compared with a proposition vote. A comparison of the results of the polls with the final election returns shows that a small sample which is carefully chosen can be remarkably accurate.[40] While a poll can never take the place of an election, since it fails to give all the eligible voters a chance to register their choices, it nevertheless furnished a reliable index of the trends of public thought. It is not necessary to poll every voter to discover a trend. Such improvements have been made in the framing of questions that it is possible to get a poll on almost any subject.[41]

The public opinion survey could be used by a legislative body to ascertain the unexpressed wishes of the voters. Actually legislators have been less sympathetic toward this device than have executives and administrators.[42] With the public opinion survey available, there is no excuse for a legislator not to know something about the wishes of the voters on many subjects. If he relied upon the published returns of existing private polling organizations, he would, of course, obtain a sample only of national or state opinion and not a sample of opinion in his district. This raises the question whether law makers should represent a small locality where they happen to live or the country as a whole. But it would be possible for a legislator to poll his own constituents without too much trouble and this has been done in some isolated cases.[43] Some legislators have taken advantage of the nationwide polls. Where the polls and the thinking of the legislator tend to coincide, the legislator has an effective

[40] Daniel Katz, "The Polls and the 1944 Election," *Public Opinion Quarterly,* Vol. 8 (1944-1945), pp. 468-487, and titles given in Bruce L. Smith, Harold D. Lasswell, and Ralph D. Casey, *Propaganda, Communication, and Public Opinion,* Princeton, Princeton University Press, 1946, pp. 352-357.

[41] Hadley Cantril, *Gauging Public Opinion,* Princeton, Princeton University Press, 1944, and George Gallup, *A Guide to Public Opinion Polls,* Princeton, Princeton University Press, 1944.

[42] Martin Kriesberg, "What Congressmen and Administrators Think of the Polls," *Public Opinion Quarterly,* Vol. 9 (1945), p. 333.

[43] Chester Bowles in his Connecticut campaign used one of the polling organizations. Congressmen Corbett of Pa. and McGregor of Ohio have used public opinion surveys.

weapon with which to combat the one-sided propaganda of minority pressure groups. When the poll and the legislator disagree, then the lawmaker knows what kind of educational work he must do to gain popular acceptance of his views. In either case, the poll is a useful tool of democracy. The consent element in the democratic process has been given a great impetus. The characteristics of conformance may also be subjected to closer scrutiny by means of this device.

If representatives should take the view that the voice of the people is infallible as expressed in a poll, then the democratic process is in danger since the polls indicate clearly that on many subjects the voters are uninformed. Accurate and honestly conducted polls may be a part of the democratic process but they should not be regarded as ends in themselves. The polls have indicated that public opinion is variable with a turn of events. Opinions may be changed as a result of a carefully planned educational program.

Instructions

At the beginning of the American republic, the election of United States Senators to Congress by the State legislatures made inevitable the use of instructions. It was easy for the State legislators to vote on instructions to the representatives whom they elected. The use of instructions is also common in economic and social pressure groups, and, to a noticeable extent, in countries with restricted suffrages. Prior to the Reform Act of 1832, when members of the British Parliament were elected by a few landowners or burgesses, instructions were universally given and accepted. Once the suffrage was extended to large sections of the population, however, instructions came from the party organizations rather than from constituency citizens' associations.

On instructions, Clay asked in the Senate, "And what is the doctrine of instructions, as it is held by all? Is it not that we are to act, not in our own, but in a delegated character? . . . Is it not the doctrine, that we are nothing more than the mirror to reflect the will of those who called us to our dignified office?" [44] The question

---

[44] January 14, 1838. Quoted in D. Mallory, *Life and Speeches of Henry Clay,* New York, 1843.

persisted, as Clay stated it, from the first Senate to the latter part of the nineteenth century.

"In September, 1793, was reached the formula that became customary, the vote being to the effect that Senators 'hereby are instructed, and the Representatives requested' to adopt the most speedy and effective measures in their power to obtain certain amendments to the Constitution. The discrimination was, of course, no accident. It followed the theory that the Legislatures were the constituents of the Senators, but that the Legislatures had no control over the members of the Lower House." [45] Evasions occurred, and sometimes the Senator ruled the State legislature which was supposed to instruct him.

Both the initiative and public-opinion polls are making clearer the will of the electorate on any particular matter.[46] Perhaps it may be expected that some of the numerous clauses of State constitutions which declare that a representative must be instructed by his constituents will be reinvigorated. At present there is no foolproof method of instructing American representatives.

British and European representative governments had the same difficulties in regulating the relationship between representative and constituency. Generally, the nation is supposed to be represented, not any piece of it. Benito Mussolini once stated that it was impossible in practice for an elected man to represent only the nation. Yet, when he represents his constituency, local disputes and logrolling result. Mussolini followed with the proposal for representation on the basis of group interests. He should have realized, and in fact Fascism did realize, that groups could logroll as well as any geographical district.

Herman Finer wrote that constitutional clauses about mandates "might be removed and no harm at all would follow; they cover up a potent fact. The party gives a mandate to the member: he has

---

[45] Luce, *op. cit.*, p. 461.

[46] The word "clearer" is better used than "clear," because, like most political inventions, the initiative and public opinion polls are easily corrupted for private purposes by politicians. At best, both instruments render only a limited, temporary, and forced verdict by the electorate. It might be said that a straw poll lives in a world of its own, unrestrained and undirected by the urgent need for conference, co-operation, and compromise inherent in the legislative process. See H. F. Gosnell, *Grass Roots Politics,* New York, 1942, Chapter 1; Lindsay Rogers, "Do the Gallup Polls Measure Opinion?", *Harpers Magazine,* Vol. 183 (November, 1941), pp. 623-632.

his instructions from them; more, he carries them out." But "So do men play hide-and-seek with their consciences; for to admit the existence of a thing which does exist, may, they believe, cause its pathological growth." [47]

It is clear that the mechanisms of rigidity are many, and that the representative must in most cases conform through institutional, if not conscientious, pressure when the constituents know of a proposed law and have felt desires on the subject.

---

[47] *The Theory and Practice of Modern Government,* New York, 1934, p. 377.

Chapter 15

THE COMPETENCE OF THE VOTER

W<small>HAT</small> <small>ARE</small> the tasks of the voters in the different democratic countries, and how competent are the voters to perform them? It is obvious that if impossible burdens are imposed upon the voters, the democratic process will not operate as successfully or smoothly as it should.

The Task of the Voter

To state the problem of the voter in certain parts of the United States is sufficient to show why some parts of the American democratic machinery are creaking. In recent Presidential elections, American voters have been called upon to exercise anywhere from a single choice, that of Presidential electors, to over sixty choices.[1] To expect a voter to go into an uncomfortable polling booth and exercise some sixty choices in an intelligent manner in the few minutes allowed to him is unreasonable. The sources of information available to the voters are inadequate for the task; it is not possible for the ordinary voter to devote the necessary time to mastering the details, even if the information were available; and the diffusion of responsibility among a large number of elective officials makes efficient and honest administration difficult. The long ballot has little to commend it, and experts have condemned it for over half a century.[2] Experience has shown that it is a device which is easy to adopt and almost impossible to abolish.

The jungle ballot in the United States is a product of the utilitarian theory which emphasizes the rational character of human behavior; of the frontier conditions where the view was taken that all were equally qualified to hold government positions; of the

---

[1] Council of State Governments, *The Book of the States: 1941-1942,* Chicago, 1943.

[2] Richard S. Childs, *Short Ballot Principles,* Boston, 1911.

rapid growth of cities and the failure of the State constitutions to keep up with the pace; of the development of vested local interests at the expense of the interests of the larger public; and of the excessive rigidity of American political institutions. A few examples will suffice to show how this process operates. A hundred and fifty years ago, the founders of the United States Government were very sensitive about the power over taxation. The Revolutionary War had in part been fought over this issue. There grew up a demand for the popular election of tax assessors. At the time, the country was largely rural; and while tax assessment was a technical problem, even then it was not so technical as it became when the great urban centers sprang up. Farms and improvements made upon them were visible, and the grossest errors could be easily checked. In the twentieth century, however, the situation was entirely different. Large amounts of personal property were intangible in the form of stocks and bonds. The elected assessor might or might not be technically qualified to appraise real estate and personal property in a highly complex community. Usually he was not. He was nominated by a political party, sometimes a political machine, which saw in the assessment power a weapon which could be used to extract campaign funds, to punish political opponents, and to award political friends. The average voter was helpless, since the two major parties might get together in a bipartisan deal to perpetuate the practice of political assessments. When a demand was made for a change from the elective to the appointive system, demagogues could appeal to all the old slogans about taxation without representation and government by the people.[3]

Not only were tax officials elective, but so, too, were many other administrative officials, as well as prosecuting attorneys, clerks, sheriffs, surveyors, superintendents of schools, recorders, auditors, highway commissioners, constables, treasurers, coroners, engineers, comptrollers, marshalls, jailers, police jurors, inspectors of hides and animals, weighers, and others too numerous to mention.[4] In the United States the elective principle has been carried to an absurd

---

[3] The proposal in Cook County, Illinois, to make the county assessor appointive rather than elective was attacked on these grounds in 1934.

[4] Materials gathered by William Anderson in connection with the preparation of his *The Units of Government in the United States,* Chicago, 1934.

extreme. Psychologists and publicists have pointed out for many years that the voters are capable of exercising only the most general choices. The smaller the number of elective positions to be filled, the more important those positions are, and the fewer and more dramatic the elections, the more discriminating will be the selections. The British have carried these simple rules to a logical conclusion; they choose only members of the House of Commons, members of their county councils, and members of their borough, urban-district or rural-district councils. No administrative officials are chosen by the voters. In the United States, the council-manager plan of government is a step in this direction. Under this plan the council is elected by the voters, and it in turn chooses the manager who serves as the chief administrator.

In the United States, the choosing of administrative officials by popular election has been made more objectionable because of the small size of some of the election districts. In a rapidly growing urban community, the multiplication of incorporated places and special districts has meant that the government of the entire region is greatly handicapped. The immediate interests of a small sub-urban area may run counter to the interests of the larger community; the smaller area may be unwilling to assume obligations which properly belong to it as a part of the larger community, and the constitutional arrangements are such that the smaller community is well protected against any attempts to remedy the situation. In other words, the thesis is that if the units of local self-government are not carefully chosen and easily adjustable, local self-government for hundreds of tiny areas will mean the defeat of self-government for the larger community which is based upon the identity of economic and social values.

A corollary of this proposition would be that the larger the electoral unit, the greater are the chances of serving the interests of the largest possible number. In trying to apply this principle, one runs into another series of problems, namely, that the larger the electoral unit, the greater are the technical problems in running an election. This is most clearly illustrated when the largest unit possible is taken, i.e., the world. The problems of representation, voting procedure, nomination and election in a world organization have baffled statesmen throughout the ages. It is not possible then, to apply with rigid logic the proposition that the area should be as large as possible. The application of this thesis depends upon the character of the community concerned, the homogeneity of the population, the acceptability of democratic techniques, the development of leadership, and the mastery of differences created by physical and social distances.

Returning to the glorification of the tiny, non-self-sufficient, egocentric electoral units, we have not far to go to find examples of how disastrous this theory has been to the attainment of desired social and economic ends. Educational units have been of this character in some democracies, with the result that the educational opportunities in the more backward areas, whether rural or urban, have suffered. The one-room country schoolhouse serving a handful of pupils may have been acceptable in pioneer days, but in the modern industrial world such facilities are inadequate. Educational administrators have agreed upon this for many years, but consolidation of these hundreds of thousands of tiny school electoral areas has proceeded very slowly and painfully.[5] The tax base is insufficient in the bulk of these districts to support an adequate educational system. Elected school trustees oppose their own liquidation, however, although such action would improve the educational opportunities of their children.

The election of judicial and protective officers from minute electoral areas is also accompanied by most unfortunate results. Local values with reference to safety and justice are sometimes badly distorted, and the election of local peace officers and local judges results in gross miscarriages of justice. In spite of this, the election of constables, sheriffs, coroners, justices of the peace, and local judges is widespread in the American States—embalmed as it is in antiquated constitutions which reflect the thinking of by-gone days. It is worth while to quote a foreign observer from a friendly democratic country on this travesty of the democratic principle. Gunnar Myrdal in his *American Dilemma* describes how the quaint American custom of electing these local officials results in the administration of justice in accordance with local prejudices rather than in accordance with law. He says:

---

[5] Anderson, *op. cit.*

The immediate dependence of court and police officials upon popular election—that is, upon local public opinion and political machines—instead of upon appointment strictly according to merit, and the uncertainty of tenure implied in this system naturally decreases the attractiveness of these important positions to many of the best persons who would otherwise be available. Professional standards are thus kept lower than those which could be attained under another system. The courts do not get the cream of the legal profession. The social prestige of judges in local courts is not as supreme as could be wished. Corruption and undue political influences are not absent even from the courtrooms. The facts themselves have the circular effect of keeping the best men from judicial positions.

But, apart from such general effects, the fact that the administration of justice is dependent upon the local voters is likely to imply discrimination against an unpopular minority group, particularly when this group is disfranchised as Negroes are in the South. The elected judge knows that sooner or later he must come back to the polls, and that a decision running counter to local opinion may cost him his position. He may be conscious of it or not, but this control of his future career must tend to increase his difficulties in keeping aloof from local prejudices and emotions. Of course, the judge's attitudes are also formed by conditions prevalent in his local community, but he has a degree of acquaintance with the law, and with public and legal opinion outside his community. This would tend to emancipate him from local opinion were it not for his direct dependence on it.

The dependence of the judge on local prejudices strikes at the very root of orderly government. It results in the danger of breaking down the law in its primary function of protecting the minority against the majority, the individual against society, indeed, of democracy itself against the danger of its nullifying, in practice, the settled principles of law and impartiality of justice. This danger is higher in the problem regions where there is acute race friction and in rural areas where the population is small and provincial, and where personal contacts are direct. . . .

The extreme democracy in the American system turns out, thus, to be the greatest menace to legal democracy when it is based on restricted political participation and an ingrained tradition of caste suppression.[6]

Mr. Myrdal goes on to indicate that a shift from election to appointment of court and police officials would also be expected to increase efficiency, reduce corruption, and raise the level of the persons appointed. He suggests appointments of police officials

---

[6] New York, Harper & Brothers, 1944, Vol. 1, pp. 523, 524.

under the civil service system and the appointments of higher judicial officers directly by the governor of the State.[7]

The short-ballot movement in the United States was founded in 1911 with Woodrow Wilson, then Governor of New Jersey, as president. It was based on the principles, first, that only those offices should be elective which are important enough to attract (and deserve) public examination; and second, that very few offices should be filled by election at one time, so as to permit adequate and unconfused public examination of the candidates.[8]

These are simple principles which any intelligent person can understand, and every bit of evidence available shows that they are substantiated in practice. Take, for instance, what might be called the fatigue curve of the voters' interest. This may be stated in proposition form as follows: The longer the ballot, the greater will be the difference in the size of the vote as between the most and the least important candidate or issue voted upon. A corollary of this proposition would be that the position of the candidate (or issue) on the ballot has more to do with the size of the vote than should be expected on purely rational grounds. This is shown by the spread between the number of votes for the top-position candidates and for the bottom-position candidates. The indifference of many voters to the tail of the ticket may be overcome by extraordinary efforts, but if the voters are left to their own devices the fatigue principle invariably begins to operate when there is more than one choice to make.

A few illustrations will show how these principles operate in practice. In California, Titus found that in 1926 some 30.1 per cent fewer voters marked their ballots for superintendent of public instruction than for governor, and in Kansas he found a one-fifth divergence between the vote for governor and state printer.[9] Martin's study of Chicago elections showed a variation of 23 per cent between the vote for President and the vote for associate justice of the Municipal Court of Chicago to be the rule in Presidential elections. When he compared the proportion of the eligible voters who came out to vote for President with those participating in

[7] *Ibid.,* p. 544.
[8] Richard S. Childs, *Short-Ballot Principles,* Boston, 1911, p. 7.
[9] Charles H. Titus, *Voting Behavior in the United States,* Berkeley, 1935, p. 48.

special elections, he found that the difference was 70 per cent. Whereas 93 per cent of the registered voters voted for President, only 23 per cent took part in superior court elections. He summarized the disastrous results of the long ballot as follows:

> Instead of an electorate free in spirit and action, intelligently choosing between candidates of known merit, we find, due largely to the long ballot, an electorate indifferent, disillusioned, and frustrated, who have a restricted choice of candidates, for lawyers of optimum qualifications are reluctant to forego private practice for the "agonies of the Bench." [10]

The voters' oversight of positions farther down on the ballot may be overcome only by extraordinary publicity efforts. In primary elections in Illinois, ward committeemen are popularly elected. This position appears at the bottom of the ballot. To the politicians, however, it is the most important position of all, and consequently they bend every effort to advertise it. As a rule, of those participating in the primary, 90 per cent vote for ward committeeman, a relatively high ratio. [11]

The task of the voter is an impossible one in some parts of the United States because of difficulty in getting impartial objective information regarding the multitude of candidates. Thus, where the voter has fifty or sixty choices to make, he will have the problem of finding out something about more than a hundred candidates. In this he has to rely upon newspapers, political parties, civic organizations, local improvement associations, business associations or trade-unions, friends, and personal impressions obtained through such media as the radio, the newsreel, the platform, and the face-to-face meeting. These sources of information will be considered in turn.

Newspapers

Democracy on a large scale was made possible by the invention of the printing press and the development of mass education. The ancient Greeks assumed that a community of self-governing citizens could not be larger than one voice could reach, and thus the city-

---

[10] Edward M. Martin, *The Role of the Bar in Electing the Bench in Chicago,* Chicago, University of Chicago Press, 1936, p. 221.
[11] H. F. Gosnell, *Machine Politics: Chicago Model,* Chicago, 1937, p. 35.

state was the ideal state. With the invention of the telegraph, wireless communications, the camera, and telephotography, the newspapers have become even more indispensable to large-scale democracies.

One of the tenets of democratic theory has been that the press should be free. Democracy is a safe form of government because the mistakes of officials can be criticized and the way paved for a change. Opposition candidates may have their day in the press.

The rise of dictatorships has raised in a sharp form the question, "How free can the press be?" The military governments occupying Germany frown upon complete freedom of the press because that would mean that the Nazis would be free to start their bid for world power all over again.

In democratic countries, the press wants to be free, irresponsible, and profitable. These aims frequently bring a given newspaper into conflict with the elected officials, and also with the democratic ideal of truth. In time of war there is a greater recognition of the responsibility of the press. Then newspapers refrain from making unwarranted attacks on the officials and policies that might help the enemy. If a newspaper should overstep the bounds, there are usually wartime sedition laws which could be invoked. In peacetime, however, parts of the press in a democracy may be highly irresponsible. Some papers may distort the truth, unfairly suppress one side of the case, and thus keep their readers in ignorance.

Since newspapers in large-scale democracies are commercial enterprises, they try to cater to the opinions of their readers and advertisers. The newspaper or magazine without advertisers is rare but not unknown.[12] If advertisers take a strong dislike to a given party or candidate, they may in some cases influence the treatment of that party in the news.

Regarding the major party candidates in this country for such important positions as President, Governor, Congressman, or Mayor, the newspapers print a considerable amount of information. Some of this information may be colored by the views of the proprietor, but if the voter is sophisticated and buys enough newspapers he may get a fairly well-balanced picture regarding the

---

[12] New York City's *P.M.* (until 1945) and *The Reader's Digest.*

major candidates. Even the most partisan American newspaper will print something about an opposition candidate for President. The information may be incomplete, only the unfavorable aspects may be presented, the pictures printed may be uncomplimentary, and the cartoons may be devastating, but the candidate is not ignored. If a newspaper is too obviously biased in its views regarding a given candidate, it may defeat its purpose, since many of its readers will discount the views expressed.

If all the American States had short ballots as do Maryland, Connecticut, Maine, and Vermont in Presidential years, then the problem of keeping the voters informed as to the qualifications of the candidates would not be a serious one. This is not the case, however, since in fifteen States there were forty or more choices to be made in Presidential years.[13] On a recent Indiana ballot there were over three hundred names and the voter had to exercise fifty-six choices. The newspapers can print something about the leading candidates, but they do not have the space to devote much to each of the candidates for the minor offices. Even if they did have the space, the ordinary reader would not take the time to read and ponder over such material. The result is that the minor candidates are neglected in the press. Time and time again it can be shown that the voters will vote one way on the major choices where the press has made the issues clear, but they will vote on the opposite side on some of the minor choices. This inconsistent behavior, which is due largely to ignorance and indifference, is particularly prevalent in primary elections where there are no labels to distinguish between the candidates of rival factions.[14]

In American elections since the Civil War the partisanship of the press has not been evenly balanced between the two major parties, since the newspapers with the largest circulation have strongly favored the Republican Party. In the thirties and forties this bias of the press was, if anything, more pronounced than in the earlier decades. This meant that the voters could not rely on the press for impartial information regarding candidates. The wide variation between the strength of the parties, as shown by the

---

[13] Spencer O. Albright, "How Does Your Ballot Grow?", *The American Legislators' Association.*
[14] H. F. Gosnell, *Machine Politics,* Chicago, 1937, p. 36.

popular vote and the partisan affiliations of the press, was clear evidence that the voters did not look to the newspapers for political guidance on the major candidates.[15] This is not to say that the press was without influence, but it was heavily discounted in national elections. In local and primary elections the press was more effective since the candidates had less chance to make direct appeals to the voters through such other media as the radio, the platform, and the newsreel.[16]

Political Parties and Organized Groups

A great deal of electoral information is brought to the individual voters by means of political parties and organized groups. A political party advertises its candidates by means of holding mass meetings, radio broadcasting, distributing literature, and making telephone or house-to-house calls. The meetings may be mammoth gatherings which attract a hundred thousand voters or so, or they may be small block meetings in a party worker's home. Party literature takes the form of brief biographies, platforms, reprints of speeches, sample marked ballots, posters, appeals to special groups, and various types of leaflet. The information furnished by the political parties is one-sided in character, and a careful weighing of the claims of all the parties would be necessary for anyone who sought guidance from this source. Party activities are more usually designed to inspire the faithful than to inform the doubtful and wavering. Considerable use is made, however, of arguments presented by independents who command the respect of large masses of voters. Thus, the parties will distribute reprints of editorials of well-known commentators who have furnished reasons for their preferences.

A political party which does not have the support of a substantial number of newspapers must use advertising or pamphlets to bring printed material about its candidates before the voters. Campaign publications vary from a single-page leaflet to an elaborate book. While the distribution of campaign literature is usually wasteful, skillfully designed printed material may help bring voters to the

---

[15] In the 1944 Presidential election, 86 per cent of the newspapers circulated were unfriendly to President Roosevelt, but in spite of this he received 53 per cent of the popular vote. See *The New York Times,* November 10, 1944.

[16] *Machine Politics,* p. 180.

polls. In a democracy of great geographical area and large population, the circularization of the voters is a very expensive process and can only be undertaken by a major political party.

The arguments presented by the party workers in going from house to house are not always highly rational. Some party workers appeal for votes, not on the basis of the merits of their party candidates, but on the basis of sympathy for themselves or the potential services which their party may render locally. The so-called "bread and butter" argument is common in American cities.[17] Precinct captains appeal for votes on the ground that their livelihood depends on getting those votes. The indifferent citizen who does not have strong political connections may be influenced by such an argument. These votes furnish one of the foundation stones of the political machines.

While the voters who are able to see and hear party candidates are sometimes influenced by nonrational factors, in the long run they show powers of discrimination. In the United States some examples can be found of candidates who won votes by clowning, by singing, by leading a hillbilly band, and by various other demagogic devices. Voters have been misled by good showmen. The campaigns of the late William Hale Thompson, Mayor of Chicago, show how the voters may be bamboozled. He would campaign with a halter, a donkey, a burro, a horse, and a cage of rats, and win votes by these bizarre methods. On the other hand, when his administration faced the serious problems of relief and unemployment in the depression which started in 1929, the voters turned to a more serious candidate.[18] In Great Britain, also, the voters may be influenced by personal appeals which have little bearing on the major issues at stake, but such appeals are likely to be controlling in only a few constituencies. Frank Gray, the Liberal candidate for Oxford, could win elections by the canvassing techniques of a door-to-door salesman, but in the country at large the Liberal Party declined.[19]

With the coming of the radio, the political parties had a new and wonderfully effective means of advertising their wares. The radio

---

[17] J. T. Salter, *Boss Rule*, New York, 1935.
[18] H. F. Gosnell, *Machine Politics: Chicago Model*, Chicago, 1937.
[19] Frank Gray, *Confessions of a Candidate*, London, 1925.

has been much fairer than the press.[20] The candidate who has a good radio personality is an enormous asset to his party. The grip that Franklin D. Roosevelt and Winston Churchill gained on the hearts and minds of their constituents by their stirring radio appeals was one of the bases of their popularity. In the United States, where the radio has been commercialized, it is impossible for a candidate to have access to it without the backing of a huge party fund. On the other hand, the greater fairness of the radio has tended to offset the bias of the press. The voters have come to place more reliance upon the radio than upon the press.[21]

Political parties may also use the motion picture to bring their candidate before the voters. When campaigning for the governorship of New York State in 1928, Franklin D. Roosevelt made a sound-motion-picture short to send around to all parts of the State. In this way he helped overcome the handicap of his physical immobility. Candidates for city elections have used this device from time to time with varying success. Important officeholders such as the President of the United States or the governor of a large American State have the advantage of appearance from time to time in the newsreels. The major party conventions in the United States are always well covered by the newsreel companies.

In democratic jurisdictions where the parties are unbalanced or corrupt, where the press and radio are unfair, where the organized pressure groups are unduly powerful, it is still possible for citizens who have the common interest at heart to organize nonpartisan civic groups to obtain and disseminate the truth about the candidates and their policies. In the United States an outstanding organization of this type is the League of Women Voters which has twenty-five years of constructive political effort behind it. The League may have its faults, but as a democratic device for keeping the voters informed it stands as a monument of civic accomplishment that has withstood the storms of selfish partisan endeavors. Its chief weakness is the selected character of its membership. If all women were to join, the United States would be the smoothest-

---

[20] D. Waples and B. Berelson, "Public Communications and Public Opinion," Chicago, 1941.
[21] Paul Lazarsfeld, B. Berelson, and H. Gaudet, *The People's Choice*, New York, 1945.

running democracy in the world. Its strength is least where it is most needed, in the poorer residential areas. American men have no organization which corresponds to the League, although there are civic clubs, city voters leagues, city clubs, citizens' associations, and other organizations which make reports on candidates from time to time.

The voter in a modern democracy which has universal free education, well-developed and responsible press and radio industries, well-balanced political parties, fully formed nonpartisan civic groups, and a tolerance of opposing opinions can count on sufficient information to make an intelligent choice.

Chapter 16

DEMOCRACY AND VALUES

I

W<small>HAT</small> IS the balance sheet of
modern democracy? It would be fairer to ask, "What is the balance
sheet of those countries that call themselves democracies?" These
countries all fall far short of the democratic ideal. They fail to
apply the principles of equality, majority rule, and the brotherhood
of man in a logical fashion. Persons are still disfranchised because
of such accidental characteristics as color of skin, place of birth, or
residence. Some democracies still disfranchise women, others persons under twenty-five years of age, and still others retain vestiges
of a property system of voting.

Suffrage as a right has always been a disappointment to those
who have just won it. This is because its advocates were too sweeping
in their claims as to what it might accomplish. Suffrage is but the
threshold of democracy, not the throne. There are many doors, long
halls, and blind passageways between the threshold and the throne.
The defenders of the disfranchised poor, the disfranchised women,
the disfranchised minority races, and the disfranchised youth fail
to see that the right to vote is but a small beginning. Once past the
threshold, the newly enfranchised citizen must be organized before
he even goes to the polls to exercise a choice; then he must be educated as to how to exercise his choice; a trusted few in his group
must be trained to run for elective office; and another trusted few
must be trained to watch the representatives. At this stage the new
voters are nearest to the throne. To get this far takes money or self-
sacrifice, skill, courage, determination, and a toughness that can
stand disappointments. Elections may no longer be bloody, but they
take plenty of sweat and tears.

There is no short cut to power in a democracy. The Belgian
workers who thought that universal suffrage would solve their

problems had their hopes dashed. Their party has never come close to a majority. The women suffragists who thought that equality of the sexes would follow the winning of the ballot are still fighting for that equality. The Negroes who fought for the vote in local elections discovered that they had the battle of the party primary to win. The young men of eighteen, nineteen, and twenty who voted in Georgia, Albania, and the Swiss Canton of Schwyz found that there were still problems of youth to solve.

Yet it must be remembered that suffrage *is* a threshold. The lower-income groups that vote are better off than those having no vote. Any new group of voters has a weapon in its hands. They might be organized so as to use the ballot. Women are nearer to equality where they vote than where they do not vote. Negroes with the ballot protect themselves better than those who do not have the ballot.

Ignorance, selfishness, greed, apathy, timidity, and lack of training keep the new voters from making their influence fully felt. These are all defects which can be cured by time and effort. Education, moral and intellectual, experience, small triumphs and great disappointments, weld the new voters into effective political organizations.

Consent is not always obtained by approved democratic techniques. Majorities may be bought and sold. Outright bribery is still found in some alleged democracies. The fact that Switzerland, Sweden, and England are free from direct vote buying shows, however, that this form of perversion is preventable. In these countries electoral bribery has been eliminated by civic education and strict corrupt practices legislation. In the United States the use of flagrant bribery has become rare.

The indirect influences of wealth upon the democratic process have been much harder to control. By means of party campaign fund contributions, financial control of mass media, and highly paid lobbyists and public relations experts the upper-income groups have been able to exercise political power out of all proportion to their numbers. The British Corrupt Practices Act operates more effectively than any American law on the subject, but it does not touch the problem of campaign contributions to the central party funds involving the subtle relationship between the creation of peerages and party fund donations. The control of mass media in English-speaking democracies has come more and more into the hands of big capitalists. Even the British Labour Party could not by itself operate its principal newspaper, the London *Daily Herald;* it sold the newspaper to a syndicate, retaining control only over editorial policy.

Votes may be bought, they may also be stolen. The achievement of democracy depends upon the elimination, or virtual elimination, of election frauds. Ballot-box stuffing, alteration of ballots, and falsification of returns are among the practices used for stealing popular votes. Procedures have been designed which make it very difficult to employ these methods successfully, but basic is an alert electorate that is intolerant of such abuses. In England, Sweden, Switzerland, and most American jurisdictions, such methods are unheard of. But in a few places such methods, though declining, are still found.[1]

The electoral process may also be perverted by intimidation and the actual use of force. In some areas, where fraud is still found, strong-arm methods are also employed from time to time. Leaders of the underworld loan their gangsters to the politicians who are determined to win at any cost. Opposition watchers are intimidated, and opposition voters are scared away from the polls.[2]

As far as methods used to obtain conformance are concerned, the differences between democracy and dictatorship are relative. Under existing democracies the citizen is never free from ideological, sentimental, and bodily restraints, and under modern dictatorships the citizen is never completely regimented in these respects. There are degrees of freedom. In general, the degree of freedom in a democracy is much higher than in a dictatorship, but there are mixed régimes where the degree of freedom is intermediate; it would be hard to classify such régimes as either democratic or dictatorial.

A common complaint in modern democracies is that people are losing their freedom. It is claimed that the executive encroachments in the legislature, the growth of a huge bureaucracy, the expansion of government subsidies and regulations, the undermining of traditional

---

[1] J. P. Harris, *Election Administration in the United States,* Washington, D. C., 1934.

[2] H. F. Gosnell, *Machine Politics,* Chicago, 1937; *Negro Politicians,* Chicago, 1935.

legal restraints on the executive branch of the government, and the suspension in times of crisis of the normal electoral procedures are bringing democracies closer to the dictatorships.

Let us examine some of these claims in accordance with the classification suggested above. How free are citizens in modern democracies from ideological restraints? The mass media are for the most part in private hands. The British government controls radio broadcasting, but the British press is under the control of private enterprise. In the United States, the Federal Communications Commission regulates the radio industry, but the press is virtually unregulated. Even in time of war only a voluntary system of censorship of press and radio is employed. During World War II the Office of War Information leased the short-wave stations used in overseas information work, but the domestic stations were left under private ownership and operation.

In modern democracies there are some group loyalties which are frowned upon. In the United States, membership in a Communist or Fascist front organization has been condemned by law and by public opinion. The waving of the red flag in an American patriotic gathering would at once bring a violent reaction. If the police did not handle the situation, the citizens would take the matter into their own hands. On such subjects a crowd of Americans would be intolerant.

The sentimental restraints in the dictatorial régimes have never been complete. The Soviet and Nazi systems both failed to uproot religious loyalties. German Catholics and German Lutherans defied the Nazi pressures to make statism the supreme faith.

Any government which is to survive must protect itself against civil strife by imposing bodily restraints upon those who insist upon upsetting the public order. The dictatorial régimes include a much wider range of acts as antigovernmental, and bodily restraints are imposed with comparatively little protection for the individual citizen. In time of crisis, a democracy is also compelled to reduce the protection given to the individual. The American trial of the Nazi saboteurs was a secret, military trial, not a civil trial, and the usual safeguards were absent. It is safe to say, however, that no democratic régime could survive an action such as the famous blood purge which Hitler perpetrated on June 30, 1934. Der Fuehrer was witness, jury, prosecutor, judge, and executioner, all rolled into one. It would hardly be possible to imagine an American President or a British Prime Minister in such a role.

II

By what means may the relative efficiency of democracies and dictatorships be measured? The late Lord Bryce set up as a rough standard for making comparisons the following items: Safety against external attack, order within the community, justice, efficient administration, and assistance to citizens.

In the discussion that follows, these and other value patterns will be considered. Money income, safety, and deference will be taken up first.

The value patterns of human societies have varied in time and space. Pecuniary income may have a high value in one society and a low one in another. In the United States money income has a high value in most places, but in the Amana Society of Iowa, a religious community, it was not given a high priority.[3] The individual members of this society received no money income. They received their share in goods and services. There are similar variations in prestige, power, safety, and deference as social values. Some persons are not interested in acquiring power, and these would rather follow than lead. Some prize security, while others glory in danger.

While great wealth is not one of the supreme values of all societies, it may be said that freedom from want is a universal objective. Have democracies given more adequate safeguards than dictatorships against freedom from want? If a German had been asked this question before 1942, he might very well have answered in the negative. During the twenties the democratic régime in Germany failed to solve the problem of unemployment. The solution of this problem furnished by the Nazi régime, however, was a temporary one, and the price will not be paid for many years to come. The Nazi economy was one which produced more guns than butter. The average German citizen may for a while have enjoyed freedom from fear of loss of work, but he was soon faced with economic ruin following military disaster. The Nazi system produced booty for a

---

[3] B. M. Shambaugh, *Amana, the Community of True Inspiration,* Iowa City, 1908. This society has been disbanded.

time, but it failed to produce friends, and it resulted in the destruction of much of the wealth of Europe, including that of Germany. The Fascist régime in Italy was an economic failure long before the fall of Mussolini.

Freedom from want must be relative. It concerns the equitable distribution of existing goods at a given time in a given country rather than any absolute standards. If a given country is poor in natural resources, the definition of want must be different from what it would be in a country which is rich in resources, both human and natural. An American would regard as low a standard of living which a Chinese would regard as high.

Freedom from want has not been achieved by many in the United States and Great Britain. The provisions for shelter, clothing, and food that are available to some Anglo-Americans are inadequate to support what is regarded as a decent standard of living. The Beveridge Report, in England, and the report of the National Resources Planning Board, in the United States, are typical of efforts designed to remedy this situation.[4] It is yet to be demonstrated whether these two democracies can put such systems into operation. The English-speaking democracies, however, have expressed the hope that some of these things may be achieved, not at the expense of others, but in such a way that the total world economy is advanced. Modern technology has provided the means for an era of relative plenty. Will these means be used for exploitive and destructive purposes, or for building a better world order? Democracy, with its doctrines of the brotherhood of man, furnishes a much better chance for the achievement of these aims than Fascism, with its doctrine of the superior and inferior races.

A minimum of safety is also a human value that is almost universally prized. Human beings like to feel that their persons and their property, especially their personal belongings, are relatively secure. A government which cannot guarantee a minimum of safety is not regarded as a satisfactory one. This safety should include safety from foreign attack and safety from domestic turmoil.

---

[4] Sir William Beveridge, *Social Insurance and Allied Services* (American edition), New York, 1942, and U. S. National Resources Planning Board, *After the War Toward Security*, Washington, D. C., 1942.

It might be argued that democracies tend to neglect their defenses until disaster is upon them. The history of the thirties would seem to substantiate this thesis. The British, French, Belgians, Dutch, Norwegians, and Americans were not prepared psychologically and materially to meet the 1939-1942 aggressions of the Axis powers. Freedom of speech means that the pacifists and isolationists can talk against defense budgets. Self-determination makes it difficult for democratic régimes to get together for mutual protection. The Dutch and Belgians refused to co-operate with the British and French until the last minute, and then it was too late. The democracies had a clear superiority over the Germans in the early thirties, and they permitted this advantage to slip to the other side.

Not all the European democracies were unprepared to defend themselves. The Swiss and the Swedes were well enough prepared to cause the Axis powers to hesitate to attack them. If the Germans had concentrated on these countries, they could have overwhelmed them but the cost would have been high. The German High Command was unwilling to pay the price. The Swiss have for many years had compulsory military training and a well-worked-out system of defenses which includes the demolition of bridges and tunnels.

It might be argued that the French were well enough prepared for what they thought was coming. The French High Command drew the wrong lessons from World War I, and it was too inflexible to appreciate the changed conditions of warfare. The Maginot-line psychology was based on the history of Verdun in 1914-1918, and the French felt that they were safe behind their defenses. Mistaken judgment was certainly one of the causes of the inadequacy of the French military preparation. No government can guarantee wisdom on the part of its rulers at any given time. A democratic system guarantees that there is an opportunity to replace those who show a lack of wisdom. If the French had been given time, they might have worked out a democratic solution. France fell because a state of irreconcilable disunity paralyzed her defenses. Many wealthy people and powerful militarists preferred to collaborate with the Nazis rather than face what they thought were the dangers of Communism. The power of the resistance movements, and the remarkable revival of the French state, have shown that it was not the majority of the

French people that lacked the will to defend the nation, but rather the few who seized power in the fateful days of June, 1940.

The British were not prepared in 1939-1942 for the kind of land warfare waged by the Germans and Japanese. Again it was a case of miscalculation. They counted on the French lines' holding in Europe until they had time to equip and train a modern army, and they counted on their defenses in the Pacific. On the sea, the British were better prepared to meet the onslaught, at least in Europe, and the British Isles were not invaded. The small but efficient Royal Air Force also made its contribution. In other words, though the margin was slight, the British were prepared for a last-line defense. On the verge of national disaster, the British made the sacrifices necessary to defend their country on land and in the air as well as on the sea.

Shortsightedness in defense matters is not a monopoly of modern democracies. The Polish government was dictatorial in form, and its diplomatic and military defenses were as inadequate as those of the French. The war test also showed that Fascist Italy's defenses were weak. Mussolini's armies were poorly equipped and poorly led, and his alliance with Hitler brought Italy nothing but grief. Mussolini failed not only to protect the Italian Empire, but also to protect the territory of Italy itself.

It is thus apparent that neither democracy nor dictatorship will guarantee national defenses. The theory of dictatorship involves the justification of the use of violence in international affairs. For a dictatorship to be poorly prepared to use that violence is worse than for a democracy to be unprepared. The democratic ideal is one of peace, the brotherhood of man. Modern democracies have been far from realizing this ideal. The leading democracies have been aggressive in dealing with peoples with primitive cultures. Imperialistic aims have been mingled with democratic.

When the deference patterns of society are considered, democracy rates high. The foundation stone of a democracy is respect for the individual human being. In democratic theory, all men are equal in the sense that there should be equal opportunities for all. It is essentially a humanitarian doctrine which protects the weak on the assumption that every human being, no matter how sick or how helpless, has a respected place in society. The Nazi philosophy challenged this with its doctrines of race superiority, its sterilization practices, its so-called "mercy" killings, and its ruthless murder by starvation and torture of so-called inferior peoples.

In practice, there are deference hierarchies in democracies. At the bottom of the social ladder are unpopular groups whose status sometimes takes on the characteristics of a caste. The Negroes in the Southern American States and South Africa lack deference status. Democracy, however, offers them hope. The dominant white groups must violate democratic credos to maintain these discriminations. Prevailing ideological doctrines can be used to secure greater social recognition.

III

Until recently there were many who contended that dictatorship was a more efficient form of government than democracy. Though the Italian Fascist régime gave little proof of this thesis, the German experience presented some strong arguments. Efficiency in government is hard to define. An economical government might not be the most efficient. It might be so parsimonious that it failed to accomplish the ends desired. An efficient government would be one which did well and as economically as possible the tasks which the regularly constituted policy-determining agency decided to undertake.

Democracies tend to be inefficient because of the conflict between the abstract and the concrete, the inevitable time lag, the disruptions of political conflict, the poor administrative talents of the average successful political leader, and an institutional conservatism which blocks the adoption of rational reorganization. Each of these defects will be considered in turn.

Only the most general questions can be decided by the electorate. Political issues in a campaign must necessarily be couched in vague language. The program which is too concrete makes an easy target for the opposition. In those cases where the voters are expected to pass upon the merits of propositions, the propositions must be general or the process breaks down. Technical and involved questions are not for the masses to decide. Yet government must be concrete. A law which will work must be administratively sound. The translation of an abstract mandate into concrete terms is a difficult task, and in a democracy it is all too easy to attack the specific as not being in accordance with the general. Under a dictatorship, the government can shout that the particulars fit into the general scheme, whether they actually do or not.

The time lag between decision and action is likely to be greater under a democracy than under a dictatorship. Elections are infrequent, legislative bodies are slow in acting unless they abdicate their powers, and there is always a lag between a legislative act and administrative action. A democratic government is usually slow in recognizing the need for action. A dictator does not have to wait for a popular mandate or a legislative deliberation before acting. Actually, a dictator may hesitate and be slow in making up his mind, but if so, this is a personal fault, not a fault of the system. American democracy, with its system of checks and balances, is even slower than need be. It is built, as Bryce put it, for safety not for speed.

There are occasions when the time lag may be fatal. "Too little" and "too late" aptly described the democracies in 1939-1940. The British, French, Dutch, Belgians, and Norwegians had the means and skills to obtain airplanes before 1940, but they did not wake up to the need for them until it was too late to prevent German aggressions.

Political conflicts of at least a verbal order are invited by the democratic process. These conflicts are disrupting to public business. In the middle of the biggest war in history, Prime Minister Churchill and President Roosevelt had to take time off to answer unfair criticism. Secretary of the Interior Harold L. Ickes took great pride in the fact that just as carping criticisms were permitted in the United States as were tolerated in Great Britain. If the criticisms had all been directed toward winning the war, the situation would not have been serious; but such was not the case. Secretary Ickes asked how it could possibly have aided the war effort for a newspaper to devote space "to an interview with a half-baked crackpot described as 'an ex-D.C. raid warden' who predicted 'bloody revolt' among us, the shooting of 'gentiles,' a 'war-guilt trial and punishment for the President' and 'a dictatorship occupying the White House within three years.' And that's what some editors call news." [5] Public discussion is sometimes a disintegrating influence. In a measure, it can

---

[5] *The Autobiography of a Curmudgeon,* New York, Reynal & Hitchcock, 1943, pp. 69-71.

be said that in Italy and Germany democratic freedom of speech in the years immediately following 1918 helped to disrupt national unity and paved the way for the coming of dictatorship. Instead of clarifying the issue, public discussion may confuse the issue. As Lasswell has put it:

> The time has come to abandon the assumption that the problem of politics is the problem of promoting discussion among all the interests concerned in a given problem. Discussion frequently complicates social difficulties, for the discussion by far-flung interests arouses a psychology of conflict which produces obstructive, fictitious, and irrelevant values. The problem of politics is less to solve conflicts than to prevent them; less to serve as a safety valve for social protest than to apply social energy to the abolition of recurrent source of strain in society.[6]

One does not have to look far in democracies to find examples of successful vote getters who are poor administrators. The qualities that are needed for winning votes are not the same as those we look for in good administrators. The late William Hale Thompson, Mayor of Chicago, was a classic example. He was a master showman and a firm believer in the idea that bad publicity was better than none. He could win votes by bizarre campaign methods, but when it came to administration he was lazy, inefficient, incompetent, and a spoilsman. Democratic leaders get things done, but not always in the most efficient way. A country which is rich can afford the luxury of poor administration.

Democracies are also inefficient because of institutional lags. The British House of Lords, the American bicameral system, the American checks and balances, "rotten boroughs," and constitutional straitjackets on local government are examples of political institutions which greatly lower efficiency. Yet it is almost impossible to change these institutions. The reform of the British House of Lords has been before every British Parliament since 1910, but nothing has yet been done about it. Only one American State has a unicameral legislature. A fair reapportionment of the House of Commons and the American Congress was retarded by those who would lose thereby.

The rational reorganization of metropolitan and rural government in the United States has been thwarted by local interests.

---

[6] Harold D. Lasswell, *Psychopathology and Politics,* Chicago, University of Chicago Press, 1930, pp. 196, 197.

Since reorganizations have political repercussions, they are avoided in democracies. A dictatorship can put administrative reforms into effect without worrying about the petty interests of local politicians. Thus the Nazi régime instituted many reforms in local government which had been held up for one reason or another under the Weimar régime.

Finally, democracies are inefficient because responsibility is diffused. An A B C of sound administration is the fixing of responsibility. Modern democracies have great difficulty in doing this. Some come much nearer to achieving this end than others. The British have done much better in this regard than have the Americans. The parliamentary system concentrates power and responsibility in the Prime Minister and his cabinet. But there are still some undefined areas such as the responsibility of the King, the House of Lords, the House of Commons, and the electorate. Any one of these may be a stumbling block to a Prime Minister. In the United States, responsibility is shared by the President, the Senate, the House of Representatives, the Supreme Court, the governors, the State legislatures, the State courts, and the State electorates. It is extremely difficult to get concerted action out of this confusion of powers and responsibilities.

From the administrative standpoint, there is no question about responsibility under a dictatorship. In fact, the garrison state or the bureaucratic state is another name for dictatorship. The hierarchical principle is logically and fully applied. During wartime the democratic state approaches the garrison state. More responsibility is concentrated in the executive which is organized along hierarchical lines.

In what respects, then, can we say democracy is more efficient than dictatorship? In the long run, modern democracies have shown that they have greater continuity of leadership. A change in leadership may be brought about with relatively little disruption. Churchill replaced Chamberlain in Great Britain in the middle of the country's greatest military crisis. It proved impossible for the Germans to get rid of Hitler by themselves. When Mussolini was ousted he left confusion.

Democracy thus provides a more orderly method for bringing about changes in the highest positions. Mussolini and Hitler were themselves products of parliamentarism in the sense that without freedom of speech they would never have built up the followings with which to seize power. The dictators did away with the methods by which they came to power. Mussolini and Hitler came to power by exercising democratic rights. Since the rise of modern dictatorship there has been a change in Turkey, and if we classify Soviet Russia as a dictatorship, there also. The transition from Lenin to Stalin in the Soviet Union was marked by uncertainty, confusion, bloodshed, banishment. If Trotsky had been in more robust health, there might well have been a civil war. In Turkey, the transition from Kemal Atatürk to General Ismet Inonu in 1938 was brought about very quietly, and no disturbance took place in internal or external affairs. This was the result of the distinguished career of General Ismet as a soldier, diplomat, and administrator. If there had been no one so outstanding, the result might have been different. While in many respects the South American dictatorships differ from the European, the experience of these countries in changing dictators shows how precarious is the process. Bloodshed and considerable property damage usually accompany South American revolutions. And so it has been through the ages.

The British for nearly three hundred years have changed Prime Ministers without violence or disruption. For seventy years the French did the same. The American record dates back to the Civil War, 1861-1865, since when there has been no violent upheaval following a Presidential election. In Switzerland there has been no violent political revolution since the Civil War of 1848. As human political institutions go, these are records of which the democracies may justly be proud.

Tyranny is a much older form of government than democracy. Where has it such a record of peaceful change and adjustments?

Finally and perhaps the most important, democracy produces better *esprit de corps* over a period of time. Efficiency depends upon the will to work. Slavery, oppression, tyranny, have never developed the will to work that is found in a régime where the workers think they are fairly treated and that they will be rewarded in accordance with their endeavors. As the temporary conquerors of Europe, the Germans were most unpopular. Their régime had little appeal as a new world order. As for Italian morale, adversity found it to be very brittle. Oppression is like a dirty stick. The more you use it, the dirtier it gets. Goebbels with his lies and Hitler with his assassination squads could not build morale that compared with the British, American, and yes, the French morale which was maintained during the darkest days of German occupation. Freedom of speech, assembly, and action develops individual initiative, adaptability, and responsibility.

It was a German student, a wounded veteran of Stalingrad, who rose in the classroom to defy the Nazi official, to defy the state monopoly of force and of the means of communication, to express that human desire for freedom which is stronger than the desire for security or grandeur. He may be the real hero of a new Germany. He will be the type to replace such degenerates as Horst Wessel. He may furnish the spirit of martyrdom against which no dictator or tyrant can stand.

On the wider front, it is clear that democracy may furnish the foundation stones for a new world order. In the Philippines, where a measure of democracy was practiced, the best resistance was put up against the Japanese. British, French, or Dutch imperialism has been more humanitarian than German or Japanese imperialism. The Japanese built an empire on oppression which tumbled about their heads. After years, the Japanese were never able to build up any good will in Korea. A lasting empire cannot be built on such a shaky foundation.

By a peculiar combination of circumstances, democracy and militant nationalism have grown up together. The theories of democracy, however, are more compatible with internationalism. A world order based on peace, on orderly methods for deciding disputes, upon the brotherhood of man regardless of color, history, physical characteristics, or early conditioning, is the kind of order envisaged by the tenets of democracy.

APPENDICES

Appendix A

TABLE I

Per Cent Women of the Total Number of Registered Voters: 1920-1940*

Date	Selected States							Cities		
	Arizona	Indiana	Louisiana †	Oregon	Pennsyl-vania	Rhode Island	Vermont	Chicago	Los Angeles	Milwaukee
1920		45.5	18.2	38.5		38.9	41.0	37.8		44.0
1922	40.5		19.9			40.2	41.1	36.5		
1924			28.5		41.8	44.1	44.2	38.5		38.9
1926		44.4	29.1		43.9	42.8	44.8	36.4		
1928	43.0		30.5		46.0	45.2	47.3	43.2	49.0	41.3
1930	43.0		32.1		44.5	45.4	46.9	41.7	49.0	41.0
1932			34.3		45.2		47.2	43.3		41.5
1934	40.0				45.2		47.2	43.3		41.2
1936							47.6	46.3		43.8
1940							48.3	48.3		

* Information was obtained from the following sources: *Arizona Blue Book, Indiana Year Book, Report of the Secretary of State to his Excellency the Governor of Louisiana, Oregon Blue Book, Pennsylvania State Manual*, Records of the Secretary of State of Rhode Island, Records of the Secretary of State of Vermont, Records of the Board of Election Commissioners of the City of Chicago, Records of the Registrar of Elections of Los Angeles, Board of Election Commissioners of the City of Milwaukee *Annual Report.*

† Louisiana has a large Catholic population.

APPENDIX A

TABLE II

PARTY REGISTRATION BY SEX: 1924-1935 *

Per Cent   Distribution

	1917	1921	1924	1926	1928	1930	1932	1934	1935
Pennsylvania									
Republican									
Men			71.6	72.8	73.2	76.5	74.6	62.2	57.6
Women			65.4	68.0	70.7	74.3	74.2	64.1	59.8
Democratic									
Men			21.7	20.7	22.0	19.4	21.9	35.2	39.2
Women			21.2	20.0	21.6	18.9	20.6	31.8	35.7
Other Parties									
Men			1.4	1.1	0.8	0.6	0.8		0.7
Women			1.9	1.6	1.0	0.7	0.8		0.6
No Party Named.									
Men			5.3	5.4	4.0	3.5	2.8	2.6	2.4
Women			11.5	10.5	6.7	6.1	4.4	4.1	3.8
Arizona									
Republican									
Men			30.6		31.3	30.3		11.6	
Women			33.1		34.4	33.5		13.2	
Democratic									
Men			66.4		66.7	67.6		87.4	
Women			64.2		63.8	64.8		86.3	
Nonpartisan									
Men			2.9		2.0	2.1		0.6	
Women			2.7		1.8	1.7		0.4	
Oregon									
Republican									
Men	65.2	68.2	68.3						
Women	62.4	67.5	68.4						
Democratic									
Men	27.0	26.2	26.9						
Women	27.9	26.5	26.7						
Socialist									
Men	2.8	1.6	0.7						
Women	1.9	1.1	0.5						
Prohibition									
Men	1.3	0.8	0.3						
Women	3.9	2.1	0.8						
Miscellaneous									
Men	3.8	3.2	3.7						
Women	3.8	2.8	3.6						

* Information was obtained from the following sources: *Pennsylvania State Manual* (1924-1935), *Arizona Blue Book* (1924-1934), and the *Oregon Blue Book* (1917-1924).

TABLE III

OCCUPATION OF THE MEMBERS OF THE GERMAN REICHSTAGS AND THE
PRUSSIAN LANDTAGS *

	Germany		Prussia	
	1912	1919	1913	1919
Large landed proprietors	10.3%	0.9%	21.9%	0.7%
Middle landed proprietors	9.4	2.1	9.5	2.5
Small landed proprietors	3.5	4.9	1.5	1.2
Subtotal agricultural proprietors	23.2	8.0	32.9	4.4
Merchants	6.8	3.5	3.6	4.0
Industrialists	1.0	2.6	3.4	1.2
Tradesmen	1.0	0.9	1.3	1.5
Subtotal commerce and industry	8.8	7.0	8.3	6.7
Teachers	5.0	7.5	5.4	15.5
Clergymen	5.3	2.6	4.9	3.7
Lawyers, notaries	10.1	7.3	6.5	6.2
Physicians	1.7	0.5	0.9	1.2
Authors	14.4	15.2	2.0	7.9
Subtotal professional	36.5	33.1	19.7	34.5
Private officials	3.5	4.5	4.7	6.7
Party officials	3.0	6.1	0.7	6.0
Secretaries of trade-unions	5.6	20.5	0.6	14.4
Total private secretaries	12.1	31.1	6.0	27.1
Artisans	2.5	1.9	1.4	2.7
Workers	0.5	2.4	0.2	4.0
Employees	1.8	2.1	—	4.0
Total artisans	4.8	6.4	1.6	10.7
Government officials	11.6	11.4	25.2	13.5
Independent gentlemen	2.0	0.9	5.4	0.7
Others	0.2	0.9	0.4	2.1
Total others	13.8	13.2	31.0	16.3

* Source: Dr. Karl Braunias, *Das parlamentarische Wahlrecht*, Band 2, Heft 18a, Berlin und Leipzig, 1932, p. 104.

Appendix B

VOTING SYSTEMS

Alternative Vote

An example of the alternative vote follows. Below are the ballots of voters a, b, c, etc., through j. They are voting for candidates A, B, and C.

Candidates	Voters $a\ b\ c\ d\ e\ f\ g\ h\ i\ j$	First Choices
A	1 2 1 2 2 1 1 3 3 1	5
B	3 1 3 1 3 2 3 1 2 3	3
C	2 3 2 3 1 3 2 2 1 2	2
		10

In this example, candidate A receives five first choices, but this is not a majority (majority $=\dfrac{\text{total plus 1}}{2}=\dfrac{11}{2}=5\frac{1}{2}=6$). Therefore it is necessary to continue the process. Candidate C is the low man. His two first ballots are counted in turn. The first one, that of voter e, indicates that candidate A is e's second choice. This is the one vote that candidate A needed to be elected. He is therefore declared elected and the count ceases. Suppose, however, that there had been four candidates instead of three, and that the votes for the four candidates had been divided as follows:

Candidates	Voters $a\,b\,c\,d\,e\,f\,g\,h\,i\,j$	First Choices	Second Count Elimination of C	Result	Third Count Elimination of B	Result
A	1231112423	4		4	2	6
B	3142341334	2		2	-2	
C	2323224241	1	-1			
D	4414433112	3	1	4		4
		10	0	10	0	10

Since no candidate received a majority of the first-choice ballots, the count continues. Candidate C is eliminated, and his ballot (cast by j) is marked second choice for D, so it gives D a total of four votes.

Proportional Representation Count (Three to be Elected)

Candidates	Voters a	b	c	d	e	f	g	h	i	j	k	l	m	n	o	p	q	r	s	t	u	First Choices	Transfer of A's Surplus	Transfer of F's Ballots	Transfer of D's Ballots	Transfer of E's Ballots	Transfer of G's Ballots
A	1	1	3	3	2	1	4	1	2	3	4	1	7	1	2	1	2	1	6	3	2	8	-2 6	6	6	6	6
B	2	3	2	6	5	3	5	4	5	5	3	2	6	3	3	2	1	4	7	1	1	3	1 4	4	1 5	1 6	6
C	5	2	1	7	3	2	7	7	3	4	5	3	5	5	5	3	3	3	4	2	3	1	1 2	1 3	1 4	1 5	1 6
D	4	5	4	2	1	7	2	6	4	7	2	4	4	2	1	4	5	5	2	4	4	2	2	2	-2 0	0	0
E	6	4	7	1	7	5	6	5	7	6	1	5	3	6	4	7	4	2	1	7	6	3	3	3	3	-3 0	0
F	7	7	6	5	4	4	3	2	1	2	6	6	2	7	6	6	7	7	3	6	7	1	1	-1 0	0	0	0
G	3	6	5	4	6	6	1	3	6	1	7	7	1	4	7	5	6	6	5	5	5	3	3	3	3	1 4	-4

$$\text{Quota} = \frac{21}{3+1} = \frac{21}{4} = 5+ = 6$$

The next count calls for the elimination of B, and both of his ballots (those cast by *b* and *g*) go to candidate A, who is thereby elected.

Hare System

An example of the Hare system comes next. Let us assume that three seats are to be filled, that there are seven candidates running, and (for purposes of convenience) that there are twenty-one voters, who marked their ballots as shown on page 303:

The quota in the example given is six, which is the smallest number which will elect three but not four. If the simple quota had been used ($\frac{21}{3} = 7$), a larger number would have been obtained. Candidate A, who received eight first-choice ballots, is the only one elected on the first count. He has two more ballots than he needs. The selection of the surplus ballots is sometimes done by chance and sometimes by a rigid formula. Where party or group lines are clearly drawn, the chance system gives good results. In the example given, if all the second choices of A's first-choice ballots are distributed, the result would be three for B, two for C, and one each for D, E, and F, which would mean that the two surplus ballots should be divided between B and C. Taking the ballots of *a* and *b* would give the same result.

INDEX